Community
A TRINITY OF MODELS

FRANK G. KIRKPATRICK

GEORGETOWN UNIVERSITY PRESS
WASHINGTON, D.C.

To Amy, Liz, Amy, Daniel, and the Covenant Group,
without whom community would have remained
only an abstraction.

Copyright © 1986 by Frank G. Kirkpatrick

Library of Congress Cataloging-in-Publication Data

Kirkpatrick, Frank G.
  Community: a trinity of models.

  Bibliography: p.
  1. Community—Philosophy—History. 2. Christian communities. I. Title.
  B105.C46K57   1986   307.1   85-24913
  ISBN 0-87840-431-7
  ISBN 0-87840-424-4 (pbk.)

Printed in the United States of America
All Rights Reserved

Cover art from *The Last Judgment* by Giovanni di Paolo (active 1420, d. 1482), Pinacoteca Nazionale, Siena.

CONTENTS

Preface   vii

Acknowledgments   xi

1. Introduction   1
    THE THREE BASIC MODELS   2

2. The Atomistic/Contractarian Model of Community   13
    GESELLSCHAFT AND THE SOCIAL CONTRACT   13
    THOMAS HOBBES   17
    JOHN LOCKE   23
    ATOMISM IN AMERICAN THOUGHT   34
    ATOMISM TODAY   37
    INDIVIDUALISM, THE FREE MARKET, AND COMMUNITY   51

3. The Organic/Functional Model of Community: Part One—Social Visions from Hegel to Marx and Some Sociologists   62
    ORGANISM AND THE SOCIAL WHOLE   62
    G.W.F. HEGEL   67
    THE ORGANIC MODEL AND SOME SOCIOLOGISTS   70
    KARL MARX'S VISION OF COMMUNITY   79

4. The Organic/Functional Model of Community: Part Two—The Metaphysics of the Organic Community from Whitehead to Systems Philosophy   99
    ALFRED NORTH WHITEHEAD   99
    SYSTEMS THEORY AND THE PHILOSOPHY OF HIERARCHY   116
    EDWARD POLS AND A HIERARCHICAL MODEL OF THE PERSON AS AGENT   126

5. **The Mutual/Personal Model of Community: Metaphysical Foundations** — 137
   - COMMUNITY IN THE RELIGIOUS CONTEXT — 137
   - BUBER'S I-THOU AND VISION OF INTERRELATIONSHIP — 140
   - THE METAPHYSICAL FOUNDATIONS OF THE MODEL: JOHN MACMURRAY — 146
   - THE PERSONAL UNITY-PATTERN — 158
   - THE CHARACTERISTICS OF PERSONS — 166
   - PERSONS IN RELATION — 173

6. **Religion and the Nature of the Loving Community** — 186
   - THE COMMUNAL MODE OF RELATIONSHIP — 186
   - TOWARD AN INCLUSIVE COMMUNITY: RECONCILING THE MODELS — 204

7. **Conclusion: Koinonia as a Community among Communities** — 221
   - THE NATURE OF AGAPE — 221
   - THE CHURCH AS A COMMUNITY AMONG COMMUNITIES — 227

Preface

This book grew out of my enduring interest in the thought of the long-neglected Scottish moral philosopher and metaphysician, John Macmurray. The interest was sparked over 25 years ago by my former teacher and later colleague in the Department of Religion at Trinity College, Edmund LaB. Cherbonnier. I continued my study of Macmurray through graduate school, eventually completing a doctoral thesis on his idea of God. I subsequently explored some of the implications of Macmurray's work for understanding divine action and religious knowledge, especially in relation to process theology.

Over the past seven years, I have found my interests moving much more in the direction of social philosophy. This interest is directly related to a belief that the theologies of liberation and feminism point us back toward a more authentic, more liberating, and more human vision of community which is more faithful to the Christian vision of koinonia than it is to the rhetoric of community associated with individualism and late twentieth century American capitalism. My earlier reading of Macmurray had led me to believe that his metaphysical principles, summarized as the philosophy of the personal, could provide a substantial grounding for a Christian vision of community congruent with liberationist and feminist concerns.

During a previous sabbatical in England, I had the opportunity to explore the political and economic views of Macmurray, especially those of the 1930s when he published a great deal on the theoretical and political links between Christianity and Marxian thought. I became convinced that while his thought was perhaps more stimulating and correct in its broad outlines than it was in its details, it contained the principles for a vision of community which was both faithful to the Christian tradition (though technically unorthodox in many respects) and a viable alternative to other models of community which presently either pervade our society or attract the attention of groups who feel excluded or oppressed by that society.

It has seemed to me that American society is dominated by an implicit model of association built upon the principles of individualism and contract. I have called this model the atomistic/contractarian. In reaction to what many regard as the alienation, oppression, and injustice of this kind of social order, as well as its apparent lack of congruence with the Christian vision of koinonia, an alternative model of community built upon the principles of organic interdependence and social cooperation has become attractive. The organic metaphor in Karl Marx, combined with his attack upon the injustice and alienation of the capitalist system which relies upon an atomistic model of association, has led many contemporary liberation and feminist theologians to explore the resources of Marxian thought for building an alternative form of community. This interest in Marx has been complemented, among those who are more metaphysically inclined, by an interest in the systematically developed organic model of Alfred North Whitehead.

Both liberation theology and feminist theology seem attracted to a model of organic association precisely because it stresses interdependence and thus a repudiation of male, capitalistic domination in the social world and of patriarchal, divine domination in the theological realm. Nevertheless, my interest in Macmurray has led me to believe that there are inadequacies in an exclusively organic model of community, such as the potential for totalitarianism, a denial of unique individuality (as distinct from individual*ism*), the reduction of persons to their functionality, and a neglect of both agape and the intrinsic delights of mutuality per se. I am convinced that these inadequacies are remedied, at least in principle, in the basic metaphysical scheme of mutual/personal community found in John Macmurray.

In this book, I attempt to sketch the basic principles of the three models of community and to suggest a way of reconciling their strengths. In addition, I try to indicate what I think are the links between the model of mutual/personal community and the Christian vision of koinonia. But this laying out of the metaphysical or conceptual differences in the three basic models of community is not ultimately sufficient. As Macmurray himself would have said, I have only provided the theory: the practice through which the theory has to be proven can only come when the conceptual models are used to interpret and critique the actual communities in which we live. That task, given the extraordinary complexity of these communities and their interweaving and overlapping, has not been attempted in this study. Such a task is essential but it must be guided, I believe, by a clear understanding of the basic principles and assumptions which undergird the ideology and rhetoric of the models of community which presently dominate our lives and inform our visions of what life together should be like.

If the model of the mutual/personal community is sound, as I believe it is, then it should provide an alternative foundation for notions of community for liberationist and feminist theologies which seek to move beyond the limitations of the atomistic or individualistic ideologies of association. Unless that foundation is well laid in theory, the community which is built upon it in fact cannot be maintained for long. There is a great deal of wisdom in process and feminist theologies, as well as in some Marxian thought. But this wisdom needs the deepening and extension which a vision of mutuality, found in the Bible and developed metaphysically by John Macmurray, can provide it. It is to that task that this work is dedicated.

Acknowledgments

This book would not have been written except for the following: a sabbatical seven years ago in England, during which I explored the social thought of John Macmurray, especially with the kind assistance of Irene and Donald Grant and extensive correspondence with Macmurray's widow, Betty; the extensive and generous wisdom of Lewis Ford who helped me to understand Whitehead (though he may well not believe that I have grasped it fully even now); a more recent sabbatical during which I was able, with the help of a word processor which I skeptically purchased with my wife's encouragement and my college's financial assistance, to write the text; the unhurried and flexible attitude of my college regarding publication; the continuing support and encouragement of my mentor and former colleague, Edmund LaB. Cherbonnier; the public school system of my town, which by law saw to it that my children Amy and Daniel were otherwise occupied each school day of my sabbatical from 8:30 a.m. to 3:30 p.m.; those same children's respect and growing love for the task of writing; and, above all, for my wife Liz's quiet, patient nurturing and continual acts of agape throughout our twenty-two years together, without which neither this book nor much of anything else would have been done half as well, if done at all.

1. Introduction

> "[T]he human race is given, by creation, the task of becoming a community and . . . according to the promise, the achievement of this goal of creation is eschatologically true."[1] (Martin Buber, *Philosophical Interrogations*)

> "The primary aspiration of all history is a genuine community of human beings . . ."[2] (Martin Buber, *Paths in Utopia*)

> "Persons are constituted by their mutual relation to one another . . . . The inherent ideal of the personal is a universal community of persons in which each cares for all the others and no one for himself."[3] (John Macmurray, *Persons in Relation*)

These sentiments, taken from the foremost Jewish philosopher of our time and from one of its most neglected Christian philosophers, underline the religious and philosophical importance of "community," perhaps the most overused word and least consistently employed concept in the disciplines of theology, sociology, and social philosophy today.

A recent sociological study discovered that in that field alone there are over ninety definitions of community and that the only element common to all of them was "man."[4] Numerous studies have been done on "the concept of community," the "quest for community," the "search for community," the nature of community, Christian basic communities, community and life, religion and the community, the community of faith, etc. It is virtually impossible to read contemporary Christian writings, in particular, without finding references to, and more often, implicit assumptions about, "community."

This persistent and ubiquitous appeal to "community" hardly needs extended explanation. Since "community" means essentially a group of some kind living together, we all live in a multitude of communities. We use the word "community" in everyday discourse to refer to any social grouping. "The" community refers to social structures of the area in which we reside or work: colleges call themselves communities, as do churches, neighborhoods, towns, cities, nations, and even confederations of nations. People doing similar work, even when scattered around the world, form a community, such as the medical, legal, and academic communities. Because of its extraordinarily broad application, "community" covers a number of groups, to some of which each of us probably belongs. We live in a community, perhaps work in another community, belong to a professional community, worship in still another community, and support a whole host of still more communities by virtue of our taxes, citizenship, and voluntary membership. Because of this enormous flexibility in the word "community," we often become either confused by its use or, more likely, so inured to hearing it used in a multitude of ways that it eventually collapses into a meaningless term evoked more for rhetorical or emotional reasons than for illumination or explanation.

THE THREE BASIC MODELS

I believe that in the welter of usages for "community," three basic models of human association can be discerned. These three ways of understanding persons in relation have been implicitly appealed to historically by much social philosophy and religion, and still continue to control our thinking about the kind of community we believe persons do (or should) live in and through which they find (or can find) meaning and fulfillment.

The first model is what I shall call the atomistic/contractarian. Its controlling metaphor is that of independent atoms rationally contracting with each other for the terms of their enforced relationship. The second model I shall call the organic/functional. Its metaphor is that of organs, interdependent and functionally related to each other within a larger organism. The third model I shall call the mutual/personal. It understands community as a mutuality in which distinct persons find fulfillment in and through living for each other in loving fellowship.

These models are abstractions drawn from the actual communities in which persons live or in which philosophers and religious visionaries would have them live. Except on the very smallest of levels, there is no living community which is a perfect embodiment of any of them. But as models, they can help us to understand the kinds of relationships we do have with others, and the kinds we would like to have. Models of community enable us to gain clarity about our present forms of association and to suggest alternative ways of relating to others. They both describe and prescribe. As David Minar has put it, "the importance of the concept of community lies in its very ambiguity. Like the concept of the human, it embodies both the descriptive and the ideal; it recalls to us our power to make as well as to accept, to act as well as to behave. Community refers to whatever groups exist; it also refers to our aspirations for such groups."[5]

In actual discourse, these models are often confused with each other. Or, more accurately, their metaphors are often used interchangeably. A community in which persons are assumed to be essentially independent and isolated is sometimes described in imagery drawn from the organic world. An essentially functional relation between entities within a community is sometimes expressed as if it were the relation between two distinct persons who freely intend the relationship. This is often the case simply because we do live in such a multitude of overlapping communities. I do not want to suggest that the solution to the confusion of language is to try to live in only one kind of community. But I do think we need to be clear about what kind of community we take to be the dominant or controlling one in any particular context. For that will determine the place and meaning of language appropriate to other, subsidiary forms of association.

For example, if the dominant form of association is one based on contract (as when I legally agree with a group of individuals to remodel my basement), then language based on the kind of self-giving, altruistic love which characterizes a mutual/personal relationship simply would not be appropriate to describe the community I have entered into. In the context of the work to be done, the dominant form of association will be that of contract, not mutuality. On the other hand, if the context is one in which I have willingly entered a fellowship based on shared love, then to describe that as an agreement subject to legal sanctions intended to secure my self-interest by rational means would be misleading. Such a fellowship could contract with someone else to perform a specific task for it and in that limited context the atomistic/contract model would be appropriate; but the dominant or controlling model for the community as a whole would still be determined by the mutual/personal one.

Each model represents in theory a coherent, self-consistent whole in which the bases of association and their implications for living together are drawn out. When this is done, the model provides a kind of blueprint which a community can hold up to itself in order to see whether it is building or sustaining the kind of relationship it intends.

There is a virtue, therefore, in delineating the "logic" of each model of community. In addition to helping each model understand itself more consistently and coherently, such an exploration of the logic of the models can assist them in dialogue with each other. If they are not entirely mutually exclusive (despite the very real differences between them), then the "fit" they have to each other can be made more coherent by understanding how the logic of each is related to the logic of the others.

This means that each form of community is valid for a particular context or for particular purposes. No one model is "ultimately" right for all possible forms of human association. As persons we relate to each other in a variety of ways for a variety of reasons, and each of these models represents one or more of these ways. Nevertheless, the models do represent different ways of relating. They contain different expectations for relationship with others and they lay down different conditions for meeting those expectations. There are some kinds of expectations which cannot be satisfactorily met by some of the models. For example, in a contract association, such as a large profit-making insurance company, one would not expect to find unlimited institutional support for self-sacrificial acts of benevolent altruism either on the part of the institution itself or among its employees. Nor would we expect a religious community to treat its members simply as interchangeable functional units serving a greater whole.

But the fact that a particular model does not understand its dominant forms of relationship in the same way as the other models does not mean that it is a "false" or "erroneous" form of relationship. Nevertheless, there may be some forms of relationship which go further in developing the fullness of our human nature than other forms. Each form does believe that it represents the essentials of human nature. In fact, the fundamental difference between the models of community is the difference in the way they understand human nature and its fulfillment. Once the notion of fulfillment is identified, the other forms of human association become subsidiary to or infrastructures for its achievement. For example, if, as I will try to show, the mutual/personal model goes further than the others in developing an adequate notion of personal fulfillment, then it will incorporate as secondary and instrumental parts of itself models of association employing contract and organic functionality. A community of mutuality will have an economic structure but its essential design and evaluation will be controlled by the dominant model of mutuality. A community built primarily around economic production will, conversely, determine what limits must be put on relationships of love and mutuality.

These models in practice determine a large number of the actual associations in which we live most of our lives. They inform and guide, justify and criticize the structures, groups, expectations, and purposes in the real social, political, economic, and religious worlds in which we live. A great deal of what is called capitalistic individualism is lived under the implicit dominance of the atomistic/contractarian model of community. Much of the socialistic, Marxian rejection of capitalism appeals implicitly to an organic/functional model of community. And much Christian and Jewish thinking about the Kingdom of God is informed by a vision of agape (or love) most at home in the mutual/personal model.

Each model's view of human nature has practical significance for the way in which it structures economic, political, social, and more intimate forms of relationship. As Ellen Wood has put it, "a conscious or unconscious conception of human nature underlies every choice of social or political views;... Moreover, social and political systems tend to institutionalize certain conceptions of man by favoring, rewarding, or placing a premium on certain exemplary human types. Indeed, images of man can be self-fulfilling prophecies."[6] And these self-fulfilling prophecies will involve the practical task of organizing social and political structures so as to enable human nature to realize itself in the most effective way. As Erich Fromm has said, "Man's solution to his own needs is exceedingly complex and it depends... not least on the way society is organised and how this organisation determines the relations within it."[7]

The Mutual Model, Christianity, and Metaphysics. One of the images of the person which has been part of the Western tradition is that found within the Christian understanding of community. It will be my thesis that the mutual/personal model captures more satisfactorily than the other models those elements in human relationship, including a relationship with God, which Christianity has regarded as essential to the meaning of being human and to the intention of God for His creation. This Christian vision of community has traditionally been regarded by most social philosophers and hard-headed "realists" as naive and utopian, because it fails to accommodate the truths of *realpolitik*. However, I believe that if Wood's reference to self-fulfilling prophecies is taken seriously, the Christian model of community might well prove to be a self-fulfilling prophecy for those persons who find their whole nature and possibilities less than fully realized in exclusively atomistic or organic associations.

The charge of utopianism can be countered by religious believers, at least in part, by their claim that not only is reality supportive of their vision (since it was created by God), but also that God has taken an active hand in working toward its implementation. To be sure, these claims require the evidence of faith not always visible to the naked eye. But they are claims that can acquire some measure of metaphysical and even empirical corroboration. As Martin Buber has said, in speaking of the differences between an "eschatological" hope for community (which looks to a divine act to make the hope real) and a "utopian" hope (which looks for the unfolding of potentialities already present in nature), "neither of them [are] mere cloud castles: if they seek to stimulate or intensify in the reader or listener his critical relationship to the present, they also seek to show him perfection—in the light of the Absolute, but at the same time as something towards which an active path leads from the present. And what may seem impossible as a concept arouses, as an image, the whole might of faith, ordains purpose and place. It does this because it is in league with powers latent in the depths of reality. Eschatology, in so far as it is prophetic, Utopia, in so far as it is philosophical, both have the character of realism."[8] It is the realistic character of the religious vision of community which must be preserved and it can be preserved if the metaphysical support for that vision has a place for the activity of God and human persons in the building of community.

Precisely because it does have a place for the divine intention, I believe the mutual/personal model expresses a more complete "metaphysical" understanding of persons than do the other models. I will argue that one of the virtues of the mutual/personal model is that it includes within it both atomistic and organic forms of relationship, but only as subsets or infrastructures which exist as necessary but not sufficient conditions for mutual love.

Reference to a "metaphysical" understanding of persons should not be misinterpreted. Sometimes the words "metaphysical" or "ontological" have blocked the path to a deeper understanding of human nature as it is experienced in everyday life. These words have been seen as leading only into lifeless abstraction and away from the immediacy of experience. But that is not how I intend to employ "metaphysical" reflection. Metaphysics is essentially a reflection on the nature of reality as it is (or as we can best understand it to be). A model of community must be based on the best understanding it can secure of what persons are "really" like and what kind of relationship with others is most fulfilling to them. I am not convinced we can prove ultimate metaphysical claims about persons, but a model of community which is fundamentally at odds with the reality of persons is ultimately incapable of informing a fulfilling kind of relationship. On the other hand, if a model of community does capture the metaphysical essence of persons, and if, as a matter of fact, it turns out that that essence is really related to a divine Person who created human persons such that they could ultimately be fulfilled only by living in mutuality, then understanding and acting upon that model will be a necessary precondition for the experience of fulfillment. In that sense, a metaphysical understanding is an indispensable ingredient in working toward the kind of community which is most true to our real nature as persons.

A metaphysical understanding of persons does not necessarily render them static or sterile, as some recent critics of metaphysics have argued on behalf of the liberation of persons. In her otherwise very persuasive study of mutuality and relation as a basis for understanding God, feminist theologian Carter Heyward protests against what she calls losing "the relational quality of what I experience by stuffing pieces of reality into conceptual boxes and concocting a stasis of differentiation by labels and definitions."[9] Her rejection of metaphysics is based on the incorrect assumption that metaphysics means breaking up reality into static boxes and rigid definitions. But such a "static" definition of metaphysics overlooks its very purpose: to find a language and set of concepts which capture reality as it is. If reality is not, in fact, static, rigid, or fixed; if it is instead dynamic, fluid, and relational (as Heyward herself claims), then an adequate metaphysics will necessarily reflect that claim. Metaphysics as a method does not prescribe but describes reality. Just as Whitehead's organic philosophy of process does the very opposite of what Heyward believes (it expresses in radically new terminology a philosophy of change and fluidity), so the metaphysical scheme of John Macmurray (the mutual/personal model of community) tries to capture the essence of relationality and mutuality, and in so doing to provide an alternative both to the atomistic model of the individualistic tradition and to the organic model of Whitehead.

The Historical Context of the Models. Historically, the atomistic/contractarian model of community has had the most decisive influence on the understanding of political association during the past 200 years in European and American cultures. This view was given theoretical formulation for the modern age by Thomas Hobbes and practical influence by John Locke, especially on the American understanding of association and its commitment to individualism. It has played a major role in the formation of what is known as liberal philosophy, without which most of English and American social thinking would be unintelligible. It continues to influence American notions of community through its implicit acceptance by major contemporary religious and philosophical thinkers. It can be found in the works of such diverse, but influential, persons as George Gilder (whose views on economics have influenced recent presidential administrations), Michael Novak (who has written the most detailed theological defense of capitalism in recent memory), and the two moral philosophers, John Rawls and Robert Nozick, who have not only been extensively commented upon in philosophical circles but who are now known to the general public as well because of their extensive analyses of society.

The organic/functional model of community was developed in large part to overcome the deficiencies believed to be inherent in the atomistic/contractarian model. Its first modern expositor, whose work haunts most of his successors, was G.W.F. Hegel. One of those most influenced by Hegel's relational view (a metaphysics of interdependence intended to refute the independence of the atomistic model) was Karl Marx. Marx was, according to one interpreter, the first philosopher of the modern age to introduce "social relatedness into the very heart of consciousness."[10] Prior to Marx, all social philosophy had "simply added the social dimension to an already constituted individual subject," as a result of which social thought "had mostly been devoted to the impossible project of showing how essentially self-sufficient subjects can nevertheless build an authentic society."[11] In addition, Marx's thought, for better or for worse, has influenced a multitude of attempts to establish forms of political and economic association as alternatives to those of capitalism. While many of these are rightly regarded as repressive, corrupt systems which have destroyed the last shred of meaning in human relationships, Marx's thought is still appealed to by many of those who would reject both the corruptions of his thought and the structures of capitalism. The claim is made that Marx himself would reject many of the social systems erected in his name. It is, therefore, important in any study of community to examine in some detail the nature of community in the thought of Marx, especially the degree to which he accepts the organic/functional model and the degree to which he implicitly tries to go beyond it.

In addition to the work of Marx and Hegel, there are two other forms of the organic/functional model presently being discussed by philosophers. Both forms are influenced by the work of one of the greatest metaphysicians of our time, Alfred North Whitehead. Those who follow Whitehead in the area of philosophy and religion are called process thinkers. But there are also scientists, especially biologists and "systems" thinkers, who are trying to apply Whitehead's work to the study of human nature in relation to the natural order as a whole. While dependent in part upon Whitehead's metaphysical development of the organic model (the most detailed and comprehensive development yet achieved), some of these scientists and philosophers have suggested a way in which an expanded organic model can incorporate in the concept of human persons both elements drawn from the material and organic levels of nature, and those elements unique to persons which are the hallmark of the mutual model. The concept which can link the broader interpretation of the organic model with the mutual/personal model is that of "systems" or "hierarchy." This concept holds that persons are unitary wholes (systems), presided over by a level of reality (characterized by intentionality and agency) which incorporates under its control a hierarchical series of lower levels (characterized by materiality and organic functionality). This "systems" or "hierarchical" notion avoids reducing persons to lower levels of nature but also avoids creating an incoherent dualism between persons and the rest of the natural order. The success of the mutual/personal model in reconciling the atomistic and organic models to itself will depend upon the adequacy of this systems or hierarchical concept.

The contrast between the atomistic and organic models of community has often been drawn by sociologists and social philosophers, beginning in the recent past with the monumental work of the sociologist Ferdinand Tönnies. In fact, in the attempt to find an alternative to the individualistic, fear-based understanding of association of the atomistic and liberal philosophers, most thinkers have rushed to embrace what they have regarded as the only logical alternative: an organic community. Because the common image of the organism conveys such a strong sense of interdependence, relationality, and interconnectedness, the organic model of community has seemed a genuine and even exclusive alternative to an association based on separation and self-interest. In theological circles the influence of the organic image has been reinforced by St. Paul's frequent appeal to an organic metaphor in his famous description of community in First and Second Corinthians: a metaphor of the organs of the body in relation to the whole in which each plays an indispensable functional part.

What I will argue is that while this appeal to the organic interrelatedness of parts within a whole goes a very long way toward providing a satisfactory alternative to the atomistic understanding of community, it does not go far enough. The mutual/personal model captures in a more adequate way the fact that persons have more than functional worth for others or for a greater whole which they ostensibly serve; that persons are in some sense different from and cannot be reduced to the organic functioning appropriate to the level of plants and animals; and, most importantly, that mutuality is more than the cooperation of interdependent individuals, each seeking self-realization. Mutuality involves an intention to live *for* others and not for oneself. It is this sense of love which the Christian term "agape" has tried to convey and which I believe can be conveyed best within a mutual/personal model of community. The mutual/personal understanding does enable us to say some things about persons in relation which the organic model, strictly speaking, cannot say if it remains consistent with its own internal logic and the implications of its dominant metaphor.

A major step toward the development of the mutual/personal model occurs in the thought of Martin Buber, the famous Jewish philosopher. Buber, however, often expresses it in imagery drawn from the organic tradition. The purest and most comprehensive metaphysical exposition of the mutual/personal model (paralleling the kind of treatment given by Whitehead to the organic/functional model) is that of the Christian philosopher John Macmurray, whose thought will be given more extended treatment here than it has received elsewhere to date.

Macmurray was one of the most prolific philosophers in Great Britain from the early 1930s until the mid-1960s. His best known works include the prestigious Gifford Lectures in 1953-54 (published as *The Self as Agent* and *Persons in Relation*), and *Reason and Emotion, Freedom in the Modern World, Conditions of Freedom,* and *Creative Society*. He is the only major philosopher of our time to place the category of "persons in community" at the very center of his metaphysical scheme. Many philosophers and theologians *deal* with persons but Macmurray is the only one who has developed a comprehensive metaphysical scheme in which persons in community is the fundamental category.

It is Macmurray, in fact, who has suggested that in addition to the atomistic and organic models of community, there is a third model which he called the form of the personal. He even restricted (confusingly, I believe) the word "community" to this third model. His essential claim was that only the "personal" model of community is fully adequate to the "ontological" nature of persons, that this nature was created by God, and that alternative views of human nature and community are derived or abstracted from and are therefore actually included within the personal view. He believed his view was faithful to the Christian understanding of community and expressed that understanding in metaphysically persuasive categories. I will examine the nature of Macmurray's claims especially in relation to the claims of the other two models of community.

In the following chapters, we will examine each of the three models of community by tracing its development through the work of its most important expositors. We will unpack the assumptions, principles, and social consequences of each model with respect to its understanding of human nature and of persons in relation. We will be ranging over a number of social philosophers, metaphysicians, scientists, and theologians in order to provide a comprehensive and detailed analysis of those models of community whose theoretical formulation and practical application shape our lives every day and set before us expectations and visions of what we might hope for in the way of relating to other persons. If we are to be more than victims of traditional modes of thought, then we need to know what those modes are and how they have influenced us. Only then can we appreciate the boldness of a relatively unconventional understanding of community and determine its suitability for our lives in the present.

NOTES TO CHAPTER 1

1. Martin Buber, "The Philosophy of Dialogue," in *Philosophical Interrogations: Interrogations of Martin Buber, John Wild, Jean Wahl, Brand Blanshard, Paul Weiss, Charles Hartshorne, Paul Tillich,* edited with an introduction by Sydney and Beatrice Rome. (New York: Holt, Rinehart and Winston, 1964), 20.
2. Martin Buber, *Paths in Utopia,* trans. R.F.C. Hull, introduction by Ephraim Fischoff (Boston: Beacon Press, 1958), 133.
3. John Macmurray, *Persons in Relation* (New York: Harper and Brothers, 1961), 159.
4. Colin Bell and Howard Newby, *Community Studies: An Introduction to the Sociology of the Local Community* (New York: Praeger, 1972), 15.
5. David W. Minar, *The Concept of Community: Readings with Interpretations* (Chicago: Aldine, 1969), 331.
6. Ellen Meiksins Wood, *Mind and Politics: An Approach to the Meaning of Liberal and Socialist Individualism* (Berkeley: University of California Press, 1972), 2–3.
7. Quoted in Raymond Plant, *Community and Ideology: An Essay in Applied Philosophy* (London: Routledge and Kegan Paul, n.d.), 75.
8. Buber, *Paths in Utopia,* 8.
9. Isabel Carter Heyward, *The Redemption of God: A Theology of Mutual Relation* (Washington, D.C.: University Press of America, 1982), 26.
10. Louis Dupré, *Marx's Social Critique of Culture* (New Haven: Yale University Press, 1983), 277.
11. Ibid.

2. The Atomistic/Contractarian Model of Community

GESELLSCHAFT AND THE SOCIAL CONTRACT

No discussion of models of community can ignore the monumental sociological study, first published in 1887, of Ferdinand Tönnies, called *Community and Society*, or in the equally well-known German, *Gemeinschaft und Gesellschaft*.[1] The underlying theme of the book was Tönnies' description (and generally negative evaluation) of Gesellschaft, or society, by which he understood those forms of association based on contract and composed of atomistic, individual entities. Tönnies' own predilection for Gemeinschaft, or community, by which he understood something much more akin to an organic unity, will be discussed later. In this chapter we need to take up the essential outlines of the Gesellschaft association, and then explore the ways in which it has been developed by a number of leading social, moral, and religious philosophers, including some who are currently quite influential in articulating an understanding of community for contemporary Americans.

Tönnies' concept of the Gesellschaft is intimately linked to the notion of the social contract, the agreement many social philosophers postulate as the basis for political association. In his study of the historical development of the Gesellschaftsvertrag, or 'social contract proper', J. W. Gough defines this particular kind of association as an agreement on the part of previously independent individuals living in a state of nature to band together to form an organized society.[2] Although most political discussion focused on what was assumed to be a logically subsequent contract (that by which the government of those banded together was established), the metaphysical assumptions about persons and their relations are more explicitly revealed in the references that are made to a logically prior contract (most probably an historical fiction) by which free individuals leave a state of unimpeded pursuit of self-interest in order to erect some kind of social bond with other equally free individuals.

As early as the Sophists in ancient Greece, the view existed that in a state of nature (which was another way of saying in accordance with the essence of human nature as such) "individual men moved freely in pursuit of their own ends" and when they created a civil society their "natural freedom was hampered by the laws."[3] Like Hobbes many centuries later, the Sophists believed that the move into society was stimulated by the fact that in the state of nature each person's freedom threatened every other person's, leaving all in a state of war toward each other. The only way to provide individuals with protection and security in this situation was by a mutually agreed upon contract of association. But this contract was, in comparison with "natural" man, arbitrary and conventional and thus not essential to the person's very being.

Plato and Aristotle placed greater emphasis upon man as a "naturally" social or political animal. They did not disagree with the notion that the state was established by contract, but they did argue that entering into social relations with others was not simply a way of self-protection, but, more importantly, a way of enhancing and developing one's highest natural faculties. (It has been argued that even with this shift of interest to man's "natural" social nature, Aristotle in particular still regards society as essentially a necessary means or condition for the individual's pursuit of what is best for him as an individual. Dorothea Krook has argued that Aristotle's ideal is the morally *self*-sufficient individual.[4] If this reading of Aristotle is correct, then the individualistic bias of the Sophist view remains uncorrected. Only the conditions for the realization of individual interest have altered.)

By the Middle Ages, the contract view of independent individuals in association was quite prevalent, even though it was most often applied to the development of government and not to the original social bond prior to the establishment of governmental authority. The notion of independent, free individuals voluntarily subjecting themselves to each other remained the basic understanding of community. There was a subterranean and conflicting view, found among some Christians, which had existed since the time of the earliest church, which tacitly challenged the prevailing view; but it expressed itself primarily in isolated monastic and religious communities which had little influence on the dominant structures of social and political life. (We will examine this view in more detail when we take up the mutual/personal model of community.)

According to the dominant view of community, in the state of nature which preceded formal society, persons "were solitary... merely isolated individuals."[5] By the end of the Middle Ages, "it was an accepted belief that the state originated in a contract of society, and since it is by contract that individuals enter into partnership together, this doctrine seemed to cohere well with the notion that in the 'state of nature' that preceded society the world was populated by entirely independent individuals."[6]

This linkage between individualism and contract was a logically necessary one. As Otto Gierke, in his *Natural Law and the Theory of Society 1500 to 1800*, has said, "when the theory of the social contract triumphed, and the unity of the People was referred to a contractual act, it became entirely impossible to escape from the circle of individualistic ideas."[7] This is the essence of what he calls the natural law theory, which found frequent expression in the period from 1500 into the nineteenth century. The guiding principle of this theory "was always, from first to last, individualism."[8] According to Gierke, the "fixed, first principle" of the natural law theory of society was the "priority of the Individual to the Group... because the state of society was universally held to be derived from a previous state of nature, in which it was supposed no real group had existed."[9] The individual in this state of nature "had been his own sovereign. Men were originally free and equal, and therefore independent and isolated in their relation to one another."[10] The essential function of the state was to secure for each individual his own good in a way that he could not secure so effectively by himself as long as he lived in isolation and had to be constantly defending himself against all the others. "The purpose of all social institutions was limited to the development of individual persons... the sovereign commonwealth was reduced, in the last analysis, to the level of an insurance society for securing the liberty and property of individuals."[11]

In this Gesellschaft or society, which emerges as persons begin to take greater rational control of their individual lives, the controlling agent is the individual in rational association with others. Such an association, or special-interest group, is, according to Tönnies, "based on a complex of contracts among its members."[12] The law of contracts "is the adequate expression of a relationship characteristic of the Gesellschaft per se... the transfer of such a part of freedom from one sphere of rational will to another."[13] This set of contracts gives the association an end or purpose "upon which all of the contracting parties have agreed."[14] The contribution that each makes to the association, Tönnies suggests in a telling image, "may be reckoned in atomlike units..."[15] The dominant metaphor for the relationship of these atoms to each other is that of the mechanical unity of a machine, a unity "per accidens," in which the concept of the person "is a figment, the product of scientific thought."[16] And the unity of the atoms within the machine is always a fragile one since "every person strives for that which is to his own advantage and he affirms the actions of others only in so far as and as long as they can further his interest. Before and outside of convention and also before and outside of each special contract, the relation of all to all may therefore be conceived as potential hostility or latent war."[17]

Tönnies' description of the Gesellschaft contains the main elements of the atomistic/contractarian model of community. Metaphysically, persons are essentially independent and isolated from each other. When they enter into a social contract it is primarily out of self-interest. Genuine freedom is believed to exist only in the state of nature prior to society and the social contract is a necessary evil if one wants to pursue one's self-interest with the least amount of interference from others. Yet even in society individuals are seen as essentially atomistic or monadic, desiring self-sufficiency as much as their power will permit them and always defensive against the inevitable collisions they can expect with other atoms.

This view of human nature and its form of relationship flourished in the seventeenth and eighteenth centuries in Europe, especially in Great Britain, which was, not coincidentally, in the throes of the Industrial Revolution. Market society was replacing medieval feudalism. The old bonds of tradition, loyalty to the manor, and to a controlled economy, were giving way to the exuberance of individuals shattering the barriers that had kept them in fixed classes and stations of life. Many of the most important social thinkers of this period, such as Thomas Hobbes and Jeremy Bentham, tried, as Raymond Plant has put it,

> to come to terms with the new world—with incipient market society, industrialization, specialisation and urbanisation

and attempted to provide an understanding of the nature of man and his place in the world which would justify the loss of the old communalities. This tradition of thought sought the basis of human association not in tradition, habit or custom but in contract and consent of free persons. The individual, emerging as he was during this period from the rigid status groups of feudal society was taken as the basic reality and all forms of social interaction were to be taken somehow as constructions out of the motives and desires of these palpable, free, self-conscious individuals who derived their freedom and consciousness of themselves precisely from the decline and loss of closer, communal forms of social relationship ... [The] natural law and contract view of human society was an attempt at a systematic level to make sense of social reality in terms of a system of concepts which took the individual as basic.[18]

All forms of human association which could not be grounded upon reason, or natural law, were declared to be obsolete and without foundation. Most traditional communities, with the exception of the family, found their way, as Robert Nisbet puts it, "into the lumber room of history."[19] But it must be emphasized that this disposal of the traditional community (which Tönnies calls Gemeinschaft) was "a necessary condition of the emancipation of the self-conscious, self-directing individual ... "[20]

THOMAS HOBBES

Nearly all commentators agree that the social philosopher who did more than any other to develop this notion of the atomistic, self-directing individual who enters into contracts with others for self-protection, was Thomas Hobbes (1588-1679). Plant calls him the "most gifted and astringent exponent" of a view which may be taken as a "paradigm case of the individualist's idea of the unity of human society as being both contrived and artificial."[21] Otto Gierke claims that Hobbes "pushed the premises of the natural-law school to their ultimate logical conclusions."[22] Dorothea Krook, commenting on Hobbes' *Leviathan*, has argued that its view of human nature "is the most cogent, the most impressive, and ... the most masterly" to be found "in the whole range of English moral philosophy."[23] And

Robert Nisbet concedes that Hobbes is the "greatest political theorist of the seventeenth century," whose theory of the modern state not one of his successors (Locke, Rousseau, Bentham, etc.) has departed from with respect to its fundamental perspective.[24]

Hobbes does have a metaphysical view of human nature and in its exposition he sets forth the essential elements in the atomistic/contractarian model of community (it was probably Hobbes that Edmund Burke alluded to when he said a century later that "nothing is harder than the heart of a metaphysician").[25] While much was done by Hobbes' successors to modify or domesticate some of his harsher views of human nature, the fundamental atomism of persons in their natural state and the contract character of their social relations remain dominant motifs in subsequent social philosophy in the liberal tradition.

The only entities Hobbes recognized "as being metaphysically real are individuals ... And the only forms of social relationship he was willing to accept are those that geometrically rigorous logic can establish as arising from the very nature of man, *individual* man, with his instincts and his reason."[26] Hobbes was trained as a mathematician. He belonged to an age in which the mathematical sciences, especially geometry, were seen as the ultimate norms of explanation. "Hobbes was in fact the first of the great modern philosophers who attempted to bring political theory into intimate relation with a thoroughly modern system of thought, and he strove to make this system broad enough to account, on scientific principles, for all the facts of nature, including human behavior both in its individual and social aspects."[27] These scientific principles suggested to Hobbes that the world was a mechanical system in which all that happens may be explained "with geometrical precision by the displacement of bodies relative to one another."[28] All reality, including human beings, was composed of essentially identical units of matter variously joined together to make bodies in motion. As Krook puts it, for Hobbes reality "is composed exclusively of discrete or mutually disconnected particular things. Nothing is 'given' in nature but discrete, disconnected particulars or singulars."[29]

The connections or relations between material things are, for Hobbes, really more the result of mental convention than facts in themselves. "All differentiation, all connexion, all meaning and order are created by the conceptual powers of the human mind."[30] Hobbes' commitment to a purely mechanical view of reality was not unrelated to the fact that the emerging industrial order was preeminently a mechanical order, depending upon the invention and utilization of machines. And the Newtonian world of atoms in motion was a mechanical world perfectly adapted to the world of the Industrial Revolution. Once having committed himself to the mechanical model, Hobbes felt compelled to apply it universally. This meant in particular applying it to persons, and especially to human forms of association. As Richard Peters, in his introduction to the *Leviathan* (1651), has said, "Hobbes was excited by the possibility of extending this assumption to man as well as to Nature. Geometry could reveal the ground-plan of human nature and could help Hobbes to set out the bedrock foundations of a secure commonwealth."[31] At the heart of this geometric approach was the conviction that reality was essentially composed of discrete atomic 'bits' of matter. He was a reductionist, like many other philosophers of his time. The 'ultimate' or final explanation of anything resided in its smallest, simplest, most basic parts. Having broken reality down into its most basic parts, Hobbes then had to build it back up again in order to explain the existence of entities that seemed to be more complex than simply isolated units.

Faithful to the mechanical analogy, Hobbes proceeded to develop his fuller understanding of human nature. Like many thinkers before him, he assumed that we can best understand the true or essential nature of persons by examining (or imagining) it in a state of nature. Like those in the natural law tradition, Hobbes believed that nature was more revelatory of the essence of human beings than was 'artificial' society. This assumption is a crucial one and one Hobbes nowhere justifies. It is certainly as conceivable that human nature is truncated, incomplete, and abstract in a state of 'pure' nature and only reaches fulfillment and completion, is true to itself, in a state of relationship with other persons. However, Hobbes assumes that we can find human nature at its most authentic only by looking at the person in nature prior to his association with others. Consistent with his geometric or mechanical metaphor, Hobbes begins his discussion of man by proclaiming that "life is but a motion of its limbs" and the human person is an automata (an engine that moves itself "by springs and wheels, as doth a watch) . . . for what is the heart, but a spring: and the nerves, but so many strings: and the joints, but so many wheels, giving motion to the whole body . . . ?"[32]

In the state of nature, he declares, persons are equal. What he means by this is simply that no man can claim anything which others cannot claim with equal 'right'. Then he makes a crucial and far-reaching assumption: "if any two men desire the same thing, which nevertheless they cannot both enjoy, they become enemies."[33] Hobbes seems to believe, as would those who embraced the free market society and its reliance upon individualism, that human beings are of such a nature that they are not disposed or inclined to share their enjoyment of objects with each other. An object is to be possessed or owned by one person who alone will determine whether and to what degree it will be shared with someone else. Hobbes cannot conceive that an object can be unowned and that many persons can enjoy it mutually without having the desire to possess it individually. Rather, Hobbes believes, we are so constituted by nature that we will "endeavor to destroy, or subdue one another" because others will always stand ready "to dispossess and deprive" us of the fruits of our labor, as well as of our lives and liberties.[34] From this "diffidence we feel toward each other," we seek to "master the persons of all men" till we see their power reduced enough no longer to threaten us.[35]

In addition, persons in a state of nature have no natural sympathy or love for each other. There is "no pleasure, but on the contrary a great deal of grief, in keeping company" unless one does so out of a greater fear of someone else's power to overawe and control all those coerced into association.[36] From these observations Hobbes draws his now famous conclusion: outside of society "there is always war of every one against every one."[37] This does not mean physical combat but, more importantly, a continual and basic disposition to war. Antagonism to the other isolated, independent atoms, the individual units that persons essentially are, is an authentic revelation and expression of their nature. In such a condition of attitudinal war, there is no society, no fellowship, no love, no friendship. This is a time marked by "continual fear and danger of violent death; and the life of man, solitary, poor, nasty, brutish, and short."[38]

While this natural state may be lamentable (can one doubt that Hobbes felt some anguish and regret that things should be such?), it is illegitimate to call it sinful or immoral because it precedes a state of sin or morality. "The desires, and other passions of man, are in themselves no sin . . . till they know a law that forbids them: . . . The notions of right and wrong, justice and injustice there have no place . . . They are qualities, that relate to men in society, not in solitude."[39] In the state of nature, "only that to be every man's, that he can get: and for so long, as he can keep it."[40] This is a law or right of nature: "the liberty each man hath, to use his own power . . . for the preservation of his own nature."[41]

Liberty, the virtue that would become so supreme in the liberal societies that base themselves upon the atomistic/contract model of association, is consequently defined by Hobbes as "the absence of external impediments: which impediments, may oft take away part of a man's power to do what he would."[42]

This definition may be unexceptional (given the dominance of the atomistic mindset for most people today), but it should be understood that it links logically with a notion of individual solitariness and defensiveness against others. One could define liberty with an emphasis upon the power to embrace others rather than the power to keep others at bay. But for Hobbes and those who would follow him down the path of possessive individualism, liberty is the power and right to possess whatever one can secure and hold. "Naturally every man has right to every thing."[43] From such a premise it is impossible to envision any form of human association which does not rest upon fundamental antagonism, fear, and the necessity for impediments to the unrestricted exercise of liberty; and that is exactly what we find when we move into Hobbes' understanding of the social order. The second law of nature states that in order to have peace (i.e. a state of successful defense of what one holds without actual fighting), a person will lay down his right to all things (asserted in the first law of nature) "and be contented with so much liberty against other men, as he would allow other men against himself."[44] This is a voluntary act and is performed solely out of self-interest, not out of any genuine compassion or concern for others ("of the voluntary acts of every man, the object is good to himself").[45] This voluntary, self-interested act is the first contract or covenant between persons and moves them from the state of nature into the first society or association.

But not even the contract is sufficient in and of itself to bond persons. To be credible, the contract must be backed by the sanctions of force: the force of a power external to the contracting parties. "There must be some coercive power, to compel men equally to the performance of their covenants, by the terror of some punishment, greater than the benefit they expect by the breach of their covenant ... and such power there is none before the erection of a commonwealth."[46] This commonwealth, or Leviathan, has as its primary end the preservation of individual security. "The final cause, end, or design of men, who naturally love liberty, and dominion over others, in the introduction of that restraint upon themselves, in which we see them live in commonwealth, is the foresight of their own preservation ... that is to say, of getting themselves out from that miserable condition of war, which is necessarily consequent . . . to the natural passions of men, when there is no visible power to keep them in awe, and tie them by fear of punishment to the performance of their covenants . . ."[47] Men move into society because they rationally calculate that it is in their individual self-interest to do so. It is not a move inspired or justified on moral grounds, unless morality is understood to refer solely to those acts which advance one's own natural rights (i.e., the right to self-preservation and security against the aggression of others).

Relations with others are only a means to an end. There is no virtue per se or any intrinsic or self-fulfilling pleasure to be found in relations of love and trust with others. In fact, trust exists only to the degree that it is backed by the power of sanctions against those who would violate it. Trust is essentially defined by the terms of the contract. "Covenants, without the sword, are but words, and of no strength to secure a man at all."[48] This contractual understanding of human relationship is so pervasive in Hobbes' philosophy that even when he pauses to discuss what he calls "grace" or the free gift of one man to another, he does so solely in terms of self-interest and rational calculation. It is what he calls a fourth law of nature that *a man which receiveth benefit from another of mere grace, endeavor that he which giveth it, have no reasonable cause to repent him of his good will. For no man giveth, but with intention of good to himself . . . if men see they shall be frustrated, there will be no beginning of benevolence, or trust; nor consequently of mutual help; nor of reconciliation of one man to another.*"[49] It would be difficult to imagine how in Hobbes' society any act of sacrifice for another, any act in which one acts solely for the other's benefit without prior consideration of how it will affect oneself, any act of what Christians call "agape," could ever find a place.

The controlling power of Hobbes' mechanical and materialistic metaphor of persons as individual, isolated, antagonistic atoms entering into association through rational calculation via contract is perhaps best caught in his allusion, when discussing why men will accommodate themselves to others in society, to the material construction of a building. "There is in men's aptness to society, a diversity of nature, rising from their diversity of affections; *not unlike to that we see in stones brought together for building of an edifice.*"[50]

If it were not for reason, essentially a tool of man's self-interest, the stones which men are would never contract for association. Reason is thus the salvation of men from their natural and more authentic state. Hobbes is really left with a paradox. Authentic human beings are essentially hostile to each other's interests. But to live solely in terms of this essential nature is to live suicidally. And so persons enter into society as a way of saving themselves from the consequences of their own nature. But society remains artificial, a construction whose bonds are held in place solely out of fear. It is only out of fear that men can achieve—in however poor, nasty, brutish, and short a way—the extension of their own self-interested purposes. To preserve themselves, persons must violate or transcend their own "natural" state by entering into relations which are forced and contrary to their essential nature, and yet without which they would perish.

Now it would hardly need to be remarked upon that Hobbes' picture of man's nature, both in and outside of society, is among the bleakest, starkest, and most negative one can encounter in the annals of social philosophy. Certainly, the social philosophers who follow him struggle to modify and ameliorate the harshness of his description. Nevertheless, I believe that with respect to Hobbes' basic assumptions about man's individuality, isolation, and self-interest, those in the individualistic, atomistic, and liberal tradition who follow him, including those who will have the greatest influence on the development of the market society, show little deviation or significant difference from this master of social architecture.

JOHN LOCKE

Of more direct significance to the American understanding of community was the work of John Locke (1632-1704), whose political philosophy is now generally conceded to have decisively influenced the founding fathers.[51] With Locke, we do discover a somewhat greater emphasis than in Hobbes on man's sociability, even in the state of nature prior to the creation of civil society. But I think it can be argued that his fundamental picture of persons as essentially isolated, individual, self-interested entities who must contract for relationship, is congruent with that of Hobbes.

Locke was not a metaphysician, although he was an astute philosopher and political analyst. He did not develop a full-blown picture of human nature, even though his work rests on an interpretation of it. What we can discover of his views of men in relation is taken primarily from his famous political tract, *The Second Treatise of Government* (1690). There the completely antagonistic, warring persons of Hobbes' state of nature are replaced by men "living together according to reason, without a common superior on earth with authority to judge between them" and this is "properly the state of nature."[52] There has been for many years a persistent debate among Lockean scholars as to how much weight Locke actually gives the social nature of persons *per se*. In the state of nature, Locke claims, persons live under a common natural law in "one community," and by virtue of this fact they are "distinct from all other creatures." And were it not, he says, for the "corruption and viciousness of degenerate men, there would be no necessity that men should separate from this great and natural community and by positive agreements combine into smaller and divided associations."[53] Within this community, persons are in a condition "of perfect freedom to order their actions and dispose of their possessions and persons as they think fit, within the bounds of the law of nature, without asking or depending upon the will of any other man."[54]

This is also a state of equality, "no one having more than another."[55] Locke even suggests, although he draws almost exclusively upon the Anglican theorist Richard Hooker in this particular respect, that natural equality is the foundation "of that obligation to mutual love amongst men."[56] Locke also quotes with approval Hooker's sentiment that in the state of nature, because men can supply each other with "things needful for such a life as our nature doth desire, . . . we are naturally induced to seek communion and fellowship with others."[57] These comments might lead one to believe that Locke is affirming that persons naturally seek each other's company in order to be fulfilled through fellowship. But I think that would be a misreading of his intentions. Locke certainly thinks persons are more predisposed to relationship even in a state of nature than Hobbes does, but the characteristics of persons living in a state of nature to which he gives the greatest emphasis do not always seem compatible with the reflections on human nature drawn from Hooker, which suggest mutuality or fellowship.

It is also important to note how Locke expresses his views on sociability. It is a rather curious way of stating the significance of mutual love, to refer to it as an obligation based upon equality. Love is not normally understood as an obligation, nor as initially dependent *upon* equality (though equality may be intended *by* love). Love, at least in the Christian tradition (agape), is a free, spontaneous act of grace, and occurs more often than not between unequals (the supreme example being that of God's gracious, forgiving love to his sinful creatures).

Instead of concentrating upon any kind of mutual affection which the state of nature might prepare and intend men for, Locke focuses, as had Hobbes, upon the characteristics of freedom and independence. In fact, it could be argued, it is our equal freedom to do as we wish that makes us both independent of and equal to each other. He defines freedom in this context as the individual's being "free from restraint and violence from others ... the liberty to dispose and order as he lists his person, actions, possessions, and his whole property ... and therein not to be subject to the arbitrary will of another, but freely follow his own."[58] The first law for such independent, equal, and free persons is to preserve themselves. Only when that obligation has been carried out can they look to the preservation of others.[59]

Why is it not possible to remain in the state of nature enjoying our freedom and independence, and helping others when our self-interest permits? The answer, for Locke, depends upon another right which occurs in man's natural state: the right to property and the need to protect it. Now Locke should not be seen, at least without qualification, as a defender of all that now passes in an advanced capitalist society for property. In fact, Locke is not far from Marx's labor theory of value in his understanding of property as that which accrues to the individual as a direct result of his labor. In the state of nature "every man has a property in his own person.... The labor of his body and the work of his hands ... are properly his. Whatsoever then he removes out of the state that nature has provided and left it in, he has mixed his labor with, and joined to it something that is his own, and thereby makes it his property ... For this labor being the unquestionable property of the laborer, no man but he can have a right to what that is once joined to, at least where there is enough and as good left in common for others."[60]

The traits of the laboring man that entitle him to the product of his labor are the traits of industriousness and rationality, the very traits that would mark emerging industrial and capitalist society. Unless a person knows that his labor will be protected, both in execution and with respect to its fruits, he will live in insecurity and fear. Thus private property is essential to the very nature of persons. Locke assumes, as the previous quotation indicates, that if labor is the work of individuals then there will always remain enough of the 'common' world for each to have sufficient ground or resources for his own labor. But whatever a person applies his labor to becomes his own private, individual possession. Individuals enter into society in order to protect their property. This move is done by contract or compact. The first such society is the conjugal one, between man and woman: the right to property is here determined as extending "to one another's bodies as is necessary to its chief end, procreation."[61] The terms in which Locke describes even this most organic and intimate of relations are those of voluntary rational decision, and right. Parents care for their children because the latter have a 'right' to be nourished and maintained. The father "is bound" to care for those he brings into the world and "is under an obligation" to remain with his wife "so that their industry might be encouraged and their interest better united to make provision and lay up goods for their common issue."[62]

The move from conjugal union into civil society proper occurs more explicitly because of the need to protect private property. "Man, being born ... with a title to perfect freedom and uncontrolled enjoyment of all the rights and privileges of the law of nature equally with any other man or number of men in the world, has by nature a power ... to preserve his property—that is, his life, liberty, and estate—against the injuries and attempts of other men ... "[63] By a rational free act, persons consent to or contract for a community of common protection with others, "where every one of the members has quitted his natural power, resigned it up into the hands of the community in all cases that exclude him not from appealing for protection to the law established by it.... Those who are united into one body and have a common established law and judicature to appeal to, with authority to decide controversies between them and punish offenders, are in civil society one with another; ... "[64]

The whole purpose of civil society is to avoid the inconveniences and dangers of having each person decide solely for himself how to protect or enhance his labor and possessions. If each person had to judge for himself what to do whenever his rights had been violated by someone else, the result would be chaos and perpetual war. In the state of nature the enjoyment of one's property

> is very uncertain and constantly exposed to the invasion of others; for all being kings as much as he, every man his equal, and the greater part no strict observers of equity and justice, the enjoyment of the property he has in this state is

very unsafe, very unsecure. This makes him willing to quit a condition which, however free, is full of fears and continual dangers; and it is not without reason that he seeks out and is willing to join in society with others who are already united, or have a mind to unite, for the mutual preservation of their lives, liberties, and estates, which I call by the general name 'property.' The great and chief end, therefore of men's uniting into commonwealths and putting themselves under government is the preservation of their property.[65]

The end of civil society therefore is a direct result of the essential individualism of the state of nature, namely, "to avoid and remedy these inconveniences of the state of nature which necessarily follow from every man being judge in his own case, by setting up a known authority to which everyone of that society may appeal upon any injury received or controversy that may arise, and which everyone of the society ought to obey."[66] In the state of nature men are obviously "partial to themselves" and their general self-interest leads to what Locke calls an "unconcernedness" about the needs of others.[67]

But the move into civil society is not without a price. Locke describes it as a 'divesting' of natural liberty, a 'putting on' of 'the bonds' of civil society, even though the result will be "comfortable, safe, and peaceable living one amongst another, in a secure enjoyment of their properties and a greater security against any that are not of it."[68] Even when they find in civil society a certain friendship and trust in one another,[69] their first concern remains that of securing themselves against others. Locke simply took it as self-evident that men will look out for their own private interest before considering anything or anyone else. This self-concern is a passion, a desire which precedes and sets the conditions and directions for rationality, and is an essential part of the atomistic/contractarian model of community. "Why passions should be assumed to be essentially egoistic—and even antagonistic—is not entirely clear, but perhaps the same [atomistic] metaphor, especially for example as used by Hobbes, provides a clue. The assumptions underlying the metaphor of matter in motion are atomistic, based on a model of separate and discrete particles whose relationships, such as they are, must ultimately take the form of collision."[70]

In this respect, Locke and Hobbes are not in significant disagreement. They both accept the atomistic model of individuality and while Locke can see some disposition toward sociability even in the state of nature, both he and Hobbes believed that the purpose of society as such was to protect individual interest, primarily property. This seemed far more self-evident to them than any claim that persons enter into society because it is in any sense a fulfillment of their nature or because sociability is intrinsically enjoyable and an end in itself. Locke in particular assumed that the common good would be preserved best by the protection of private interest. Nevertheless, both he and Hobbes, as Sabine has put it, "fastened on social theory the presumption that individual self-interest is clear and compelling, while a public or a social interest is thin and unsubstantial."[71]

To make the common or social good depend ultimately upon the protection of individual self-interest, to assume that atoms on a perpetual collision course will always collide in such a way that the good of the whole and each individual's good in particular will be advanced, was the hallmark of the free market age which followed Locke and Hobbes. As any student of political philosophy knows, there would be numerous and partially successful attempts to harmonize or adjust the civil society in order to alleviate the worst injustices caused by adherence to a strict atomistic/contractarian view. But the fundamental model of relationship would remain essentially unchallenged except by those who embraced an organic alternative (especially Hegel and later Marx). Before we turn to that alternative model, we need to see how the individualistic assumptions of the atomistic/contractarian mindset influenced later ages and still influence some of the most powerful and influential analyses of contemporary culture.

Jeremy Bentham. In the same year that saw a revolution across the Atlantic inspired to a large extent by the political ideas of Locke, another English philosopher by the name of Jeremy Bentham (1748-1832) wrote *A Fragment on Government* (1776), which inaugurated a philosophical movement known as utilitarianism. At the same time, he began a school of thought, known as liberalism, which drew upon Hobbes and Locke, and which has influenced political thought down to the present day. Both utilitarianism and liberalism carried on the tradition of individualistic thinking so prominent in Hobbes and Locke. Utilitarianism was essentially a moral philosophy and liberalism was its political application. Bentham expressed the moral underpinnings of utilitarianism, James Mill applied it to a philosophy of government, and Adam Smith developed its economic implications. But the motifs of individualism, atomism, and a contract understanding of relationship would remain essentially unchanged throughout the development of the liberal philosophy.

Douglas Long has said of Bentham that "his intention was to become the Newton of the moral (and social) sciences."[72] He intended "to design, to engineer, a structure of social and government authority to fit the known contours of the human personality."[73] This is an appropriate analogy. It was Newton who first reduced the world to atoms in motion subject to mechanistic law. Bentham simply took that model of reality as it had been suggested by Hobbes and applied it in a more rigorous way to the moral nature of persons. The metaphors that he used in this regard are indicative of the mechanical/atomistic mindset within which he worked. One finds throughout his work references to surveys, maps, and the accoutrements of architecture. Even when he shifts metaphors in the direction of the anatomy of the body, the ambience he creates is still mechanical. The body politic comes under the control of the master physician, whose job it is to oversee in the most scientific way possible the health of the body entrusted to his care. We should not be misled by this shift to what may seem a more organic understanding of persons in relation. The approach remains that of the scientist trying to determine the mechanics by which the body operates. In fact, it is the mathematical analogy which tends to win out, as we are reminded when we hear Bentham discuss the utilitarian 'calculus.'

According to the principle of utility, all men are governed by "two sovereign masters, *pain and pleasure.*" Every action and every measure of government is approved or disapproved "according to the tendency which it appears to have to augment or diminish the happiness of the party whose interest is in question."[74] The calculation of pain and pleasure is essentially an individualistic matter. Only one's own interests should be taken into account in determining the worthiness of an act and the determination will be an almost exclusively mathematical one. "Sum up all the values of all the *pleasures* on the one side, and those of all the pains on the other. The balance, if it be on the side of pleasure, will give the *good* tendency of the act upon the whole, with respect to the interests of that *individual* person; if on the side of pain, the *bad* tendency of it upon the whole."[75] There is no particular reason to consult other persons' summation of pleasure and pain, and their consequent deduction of what is good or bad for them. "What motives ... can one man have to consult the happiness of another? ... the only interests which a man at all times and upon all occasions is sure to find *adequate* motives for consulting, are his own."[76]

This radically individualistic stance ineluctably leads Bentham to a view of community as a "fictitious *body,* composed of the individual persons who are considered as constituting as it were its *members*. The interest of the community then is, what?—the sum of the interests of the several members who compose it."[77] There really is no community for Bentham other than an aggregation, a collection of atoms, each of which is essentially driven by self-interest. "It is in vain to talk of the interest of the community without understanding what is the interest of the individual."[78] Bentham did, it is true, reject the Lockean notion of a contract by which society came into being, but in Sabine's words, "his jurisprudence put a premium on extending contract as much as possible in the sphere of private relations."[79]

James Mill. James Mill (1773-1836) expressed similar sentiments in *An Essay on Government* (1825). A society should be composed of persons who act solely out of the rational pursuit of their own self-interest. But he concluded from this that only those deemed competent to know and act upon their rational self-interest should have any say in government. This meant, to Mill, only those with property. "Only adult males, age forty, with a substantial amount of property, qualify" because age and wealth are the best evidence of rationality.[80] A case could be made that once having accepted the fundamental assumptions about human independence and the need for some agency to protect what one has gained by power and reason, it follows necessarily that society will be governed, and all forms of personal relationship determined, by the alignment of power.

This has meant, and still means today, that the social order, having little or no significance of its own, the community having no rights or needs other than those of the individuals it is designed to protect, must always be subservient to and a reflection of the distribution of power as it prevails at any given time. Without power, the individual atoms in relation must depend upon the moral sentiments, the condescension, of those atoms *with* power. But in the atomistic philosophy there is no inherent moral sentiment of benevolence or condescension, nor any bond (whether of duty or of sentiment) between one atom and another. Thus, if one atom is to secure its place in the contracted society, it must always be prepared to do so on the basis of the countervailing power it can present to the other atoms. That is why atomistic/contractarian societies are so slow to respond to moral appeals for and by the historically disenfranchised (children, women, blacks, etc.) until and unless these groups gain power. Morality, in other words, being little more than the agreed upon adjustment of power by the powerful, is hardly swayed by the voices of those without power.

Adam Smith. In order to soften the implications of government by power (apart from reminding us that power is always rational), it became part of the individualistic, atomistic/contractarian philosophy to claim that if and only if each person pursues his self-interest in a rational way will the overall results turn out to be in the self-interest of everyone. In other words, if each of us works for his own self-interest, the clash of self-interests will produce results satisfactory to everyone in the long run. Adam Smith (1723-1790), in the world of economics, perhaps did more than anyone to make this view clear and it is to Adam Smith that so many of those who defend contemporary market society still return (perhaps not unmindful that Smith was, in fact, above all a moral philosopher, not an economist).

Smith had declared, following the atomistic and egoistic tradition, that each individual intends in producing or consuming goods to advance only his own interest. "He generally, indeed, neither intends to promote the public interest, nor knows how much he is promoting it ... he intends only his own security; and by directing that industry in such a manner as its produce may be of the greatest value, he intends only his own gain ... "[81] But this pursuit of self-interest is morally justified because the self-interested individual is "led by an invisible hand to promote an end which was no part of his intention ... By pursuing his own interest he frequently promotes that of the society more effectually than when he really intends to promote it."[82] The morality of self-interest is thereby justified on the grounds that the invisible hand (remotely, of course, God's, but for all practical purposes the rational, mechanical order of the universe which He created) will ensure that if I pursue my self-interest (lower prices for the goods I buy, higher for the ones I sell), and if your interests are identical for yourself, it is in my self-interest to produce many goods cheaply, inducing you to buy more, and for you to do the same thing. Thus we both produce goods at the lowest possible price and thus we both gain, even though we have each sought only our own individual good. "It is not from the benevolence of the butcher, the brewer, or the baker that we expect our dinner, but from their regard to their self-interest. We address ourselves, not to their humanity, but to their self-love, and never talk to them of our necessities, but of their advantages."[83]

In a market economy one can do as one pleases (freedom); but if one chooses to do that which no one else likes (e.g., produce a product or price it at a cost which discourages potential buyers), then one will necessarily suffer since one will lose income or else one will encourage competitors to produce the same product at a cheaper price or an alternative product more appealing to the consumer. In Adam Smith's time this was a perfectly adequate description of the economy as it actually worked. As Heilbroner has noted, in eighteenth century England, "business was competitive, the average factory was small, prices did rise and fall as demand ebbed and rose, and prices did invoke changes in output and occupation."[84] It was indeed "a world of atomistic competition ... in which each agent was forced to scurry after his self-interest in a vast social free-for-all."[85]

Jean-Jacques Rousseau. Before we look at the contemporary disciples of the atomistic/contractarian model of relationship, we need to acknowledge what some might regard as a glaring omission to this point in our examination of eighteenth century thinkers who dealt with the social contract theory. That omission is, of course, Jean-Jacques Rousseau (1712-1778), and his famous tract, *The Social Contract* (1762). Rousseau is a difficult thinker to classify. His philosophy contains strong elements of the atomistic view but he also departs from it, or seems to depart from it, at some significant points. For example, unlike Hobbes, though closer to Locke, Rousseau seems to believe that it is not just self-interest that drives men into society. There are, to be sure, natural sentiments (e.g., "self-love, the fear of pain, the horror of death, the desire for well-being") which keep men in a social order; but it cannot be doubted, Rousseau claims, that "man is sociable by nature, or at least made to become sociable," and can be so "only by virtue of other innate sentiments."[86]

Ellen Wood has argued that Rousseau can be understood as saying that man has a latent feeling for community even in the state of nature, but that this feeling must be made conscious and developed. This feeling for and idea of community in Rousseau is "at least as primary as individuality."[87] Unlike Hobbes and Locke, Rousseau seems to believe that men change their consciousness and personality for the better as they move from the state of nature into civil society. This at least is the ideal, although Rousseau can be implicitly critical of civil society as it now exists precisely because it does not encourage or bring out sufficiently persons' compassionate social sentiments. Instead, it violates "human sociality by institutionalizing acquisitiveness, competition, and a struggle for power. The ideal *social* contract that Rousseau prescribes would re-establish true sociality by institutionalizing natural compassion and the sense of community."[88]

Wood's interpretation of Rousseau can be shown, however, to stand in some tension with other comments Rousseau made about persons both before and after they enter into society. In *Emile*,[89] Rousseau says it is the individual's "weakness" which renders him social. "It is our common miseries which carry our hearts towards humanity."[90] In *The Social Contract*, Rousseau explicitly echoes the assumptions about freedom and security found in Hobbes and Locke, which, for them, create the conditions and motivations for entering the social order. " 'How to find a form of association which will defend the person and goods of each member with the collective force of all, and under which each individual, while uniting himself with the others, obeys no one but himself, and remains as free as before'. This is the fundamental problem to which the social contract holds the solution."[91] Notice here how central the idea of individual freedom is—to be as free from other wills as possible; and how important is the idea of the protection of one's own private goods. Rousseau even suggests later on in *The Social Contract* that the test of a political association is primarily a mechanical or statistical one: the increase in the number of its members. There is no mention or allusion here to a sense of solidarity, compassion, or union one with another. The government under which the "citizens increase and multiply most, is infallibly the best government."[92] And in a revealing injunction which recalls the atomistic, mechanical mindset so central to contract theories, Rousseau says to the social theorist, "statisticians, this is your problem: count, measure, compare."[93]

For Rousseau, the solution to the problem of individual wills clashing in a state of nature is their mutually agreed incorporation into a single general will. They would alienate their individual rights to the community and in so doing they would gain a sense of their unity with others and a true freedom from the incursions of others. Since each one gives himself, as it were, to everyone else, and to no one in particular, "he recovers the equivalent of everything he loses, and in the bargain he acquires more power to preserve what he has... Each one of us puts in the community his person and all his powers under the supreme direction of the general will; and as a body, we incorporate every member as an indivisible part of the whole... and by this same act that body acquires its unity, its common ego, its life and its will."[94]

Robert Nisbet is probably right, therefore, when he sees in Rousseau an ideal of independence of one individual from another but at the same time an almost complete dependence of all individuals upon the state.[95] In addition, I think we can see in this last quotation from Rousseau the beginnings of the organic/functional model of community, especially with respect to the notion that the individual becomes incorporated into a whole which is greater than himself, which whole is conceived along the lines of an organic body. For these reasons, while I believe there is still a strong trace of atomistic individualism in Rousseau, it is enough tempered by a different evaluation of persons in relation that it is not possible to fit him into a strict classification of atomistic/contractarian thinkers, despite the subject matter and title of his most famous work.

ATOMISM IN AMERICAN THOUGHT

It is probably a truism to claim that America has understood itself to a very large extent as an individualistic society and assumed that these two terms were not mutually imcompatible. "Individualism" in one form or another has been part of the American ideology from the time of the founding fathers (the framers of the Declaration of Independence and the Constitution, not the Puritans) to the present. There have been, to be sure, varying connotations placed upon the concept of individualism (Ralph Waldo Emerson's transcendental individual is not identical to Jefferson's rational one), but Americans resonate far more sympathetically to an ideology of individualism than to one of socialism or corporatism.

Initially, this individualism was understood primarily in political terms. The influence of John Locke on Jefferson's draft of the Declaration of Independence is obvious. The self-evident truths Jefferson enumerates include equality, liberty, and the right to pursue one's own individual happiness. Government is instituted essentially to secure these rights for individuals and democracy has historically been defended because it establishes the conditions for their protection. Not long after the establishment of our constitutional government, a journal devoted to the defense of the American idea sprang up, called *The United States Magazine and Democratic Review*. In one of its early articles, "The Course of Civilization," the author proclaimed that America's foundation is "the distinct existence of individual man in himself as an independent end... His instinctive convictions, ... his boundless capacity for improvement, conspire with all the indications of Providence, with the teachings of history... to make the doctrine of individual rights the greatest of political truths. Clearly to define and religiously to respect those rights, is the highest, almost the only duty of government."[96] This kind of individualism "supplied the nation with a rationalization of its characteristic attitudes, behavior patterns and aspirations."[97] And the essential implication of this notion of individualism, which was to mark American life and thought down to the present, was also expressed in the pages of the *Democratic Review*: "personal separation and independence were the beginning, as they will be the end, of the great progressive movement" of history to which America was making the greatest contribution.[98]

Alexis de Tocqueville. There has been no more astute and critical observer of American individualism than the much quoted Alexis de Tocqueville. It is de Tocqueville, in fact, who actually coined the word 'individualism' in the course of lamenting some of its implications as he saw them in early nineteenth century Europe. His criticism of individualism singled out that feature of it which "disposes each citizen to isolate himself from the mass of his fellows and to draw apart with his family and friends."[99] Democratic individualism "breaks the chain and sets each link apart." Individuals then soon "become accustomed to considering themselves always in isolation" and "imagine that their destiny is entirely in their own hands." This kind of individualism throws each person back "on himself alone and threatens finally to confine him entirely in the solitude of his own heart."[100]

What de Tocqueville feared was that this increasing isolation and sense of self-sufficiency would actually create the conditions for a more powerful and dominant state. Individualism might lead to the destruction of the virtue of public life, and "apathy toward the public weal" which would leave each person only to "the enjoyment of the feeble pleasures of privacy."[101] The state would increase in power as individuals withdrew from it. Although de Tocqueville himself preferred a return to some form of aristocracy, America, he believed, might escape these dire consequences because it had developed institutions which required the participation of the citizenry. Nevertheless, his somewhat negative view of individualism remained at least briefly in the dictionaries of America. Webster's 1847 *American Dictionary* defined individualism as "an excessive or exclusive regard to one's personal interest, self-interest; selfishness."[102]

It could be argued, however, that despite de Tocqueville's skepticism about individualism it remained the basic value of the growing American society down through the nineteenth century. It combined readily enough with the laissez-faire doctrine of the free market to reinforce most Americans' commitment to the principle that "self-reliance and enlightened self-interest, competition and association, were the conditions of liberty and progress."[103] As William Graham Sumner put it after the Civil War, as America was experiencing one of its greatest periods of economic growth, the individual "has all his chances left open that he may make out of himself all there is in him. This is individualism and atomism."[104]

The free contract relation with other individuals was the hallmark of association. Edwin Godkin, editor of *The Nation* and the *New York Evening Post*, defined the American system as one "in which all relations were regulated by contract and not by status."[105] At the end of the century, the great American entrepreneur Andrew Carnegie summed up this linkage between an individualistic political philosophy and the conditions of the free market by declaring that individualism alone, understood as competition between one individual and another in the market place, would bring wealth to society. If it were not for individualism and the unlimited right of the enterprising to pursue their own self-interest, the poor would never rise. "Even the poorest can be made to see this, and to agree that great sums gathered by some of their fellow citizens and spent for public purposes, from which the masses reap the principal benefit, are more valuable to them than if scattered among them through the course of many years in trifling amounts."[106] We can count, he proclaimed, on individualism to bring "peace on earth, among men of Good-Will."[107]

It was almost always the case, as Carnegie's statement reveals, that America's belief in individualism, even Herbert Hoover's "rugged individualism," was linked in some vague way with the belief, more often the hope, that as individuals depended upon themselves to look out for their own best interests, the social whole would be enhanced. It was the individual who would spend for public purposes and thus contribute to the common good. Socialism would simply not be necessary in America since essential social goods would be provided by the generosity of individuals. Even the rise of progressivism and the social gospel at the end of the nineteenth century did not threaten the basic tenets of the gospel of individualism. Teddy Roosevelt expressed it best when he declared that his brand of progressivism came "not to destroy but to save individualism [which he called the "fibre of our whole citizenship"] from socialism and plutocracy."[108]

ATOMISM TODAY

As America moves into the middle of the next to last decade of the twentieth century, the philosophy of atomism and contract, the foundation of individualism, is still very much alive. The persistence of the atomistic and individualistic assumptions in American life does not deny the simultaneous presence in American consciousness of a pull in the direction of community. As the debate alluded to earlier over whether Jefferson intended a more communitarian vision in his political philosophy than a strict adherence to Locke would indicate, there is, and perhaps always has been, a conflict in the American soul between acceptance of an unqualified individualism and a commitment to maintaining some kind of social consciousness. In a recent study, which one of its authors contends is an updating of de Tocqueville's own analysis of this conflict, the ambiguities and ambivalences of individualism in the American soul today are clearly revealed. Private life is increasingly experienced by devotees of individualism as devoid of meaning "when there is no longer any purpose to involvement with others except individual satisfaction."[109] There is for many Americans both a

> deep desire for autonomy and self-reliance combined with an equally deep conviction that life has no meaning unless shared with others in the context of community.... The inner tensions of American individualism add up to a classic

case of ambivalence. We strongly assert the value of our self-reliance and autonomy. We deeply feel the emptiness of a life without sustaining social commitments. Yet we are hesitant to articulate our sense that we need one another as much as we need to stand alone, for fear that if we did we would lose our independence altogether. The tensions of our lives would be even greater if we did not, in fact, engage in practices that constantly limit the effects of an isolating individualism, even though we cannot articulate those practices nearly as well as we can the quest for autonomy.[110]

At this point in my own study, I am attempting to define and elaborate the underlying philosophy of individualism in the context of an atomistic/contractarian model of community. In the final chapters, I will define and elaborate an alternative vision of community which attempts to articulate just those practices referred to above which express our need for one another and which transcend the ambiguities of individualism. But the strength and persistence of the atomistic basis of individualism must be acknowledged. In this regard, it is extremely significant that it can be found—at least implicitly, and in some cases explicitly—in elaborate defenses of capitalism which are intended to reconcile its assumptions and principles with those of the Christian tradition. It can also be found in the works of two of the most famous, and quoted, moral philosophers in America today.

George Gilder. One of those who defend capitalism in religious terms is the economist George Gilder. Following the election of Ronald Reagan to the presidency of the United States in 1980, Gilder's name became well known. Gilder cannot be classified as a great thinker. Nevertheless, he deserves examination because of the tremendous influence his views presently exert upon persons in positions of great political and economic power in America. His book *Wealth and Poverty*, published in 1981, has become virtually a bible to many of those who, in the 1980s, have done much to reshape American economic policy, not least of whom are the President of the United States, Mr. Reagan, and his former budget director, David Stockman. Gilder expounds many of the economic principles, couched in highly moral, even quasi-metaphysical, language, which the president has embraced. His book sets forth, nearly a century after its last

American incarnation, a new version of the Gospel of Wealth. At the heart of Gilder's religious defense of capitalism is his abiding faith in the creative capacity of the individual, nourished by the rhythms of ultimate reality itself. "The essence of the universe is creative consciousness, continually generating new energy and thought."[111] Each man (and in Gilder's examples, it is most often a man) has the moral responsibility to utilize his potential for exploiting this creative consciousness. This, Gilder claims, is the only way to be faithful to human nature. Man must dare, risk, and challenge himself and the world around him if he is to advance and tap "the underlying and transcendant [sic] order of the universe."[112]

But the corollaries of risk and daring are chance and uncertainty: the willingness to go beyond rational calculation, "beyond the ken of ordered rational processes."[113] Only in this way will we be able to invent new things and open up the future to new possibilities. "Any attempt to reduce the world to the dimensions of our own understanding will exclude novelty and progress. The domain of chance is our access to futurity and to providence."[114] This means in practice that individuals must be left free to take their own chances, to make their own way, to risk and create on their own.

Gilder is highly suspicious of any kind of social planning, especially for the poor, because such planning inevitably eliminates risk and chance and thus destroys the essential conditions for creativity, which, once destroyed, sap the very essence of human nature. A social welfare economy which attempts to insure its citizens against the dangers of failure in the creative world of risk is really a moral hazard. "Shifting, diffusing, equalizing, concealing, shuffling, smoothing, evading, relegating, and collectivizing the real risks and costs of economic change—is to desensitize the economy.... To nationalize insurance is to upset the balance between risk and security.... The particular moral hazards of various policies accumulate into a collective danger of national sclerosis, an economy that is closed to the necessarily risk-fraught and unknown future."[115]

It is the individual entrepreneur, the free, risk-taking individual, who will save society from the sclerosis threatened by welfare and social planning. In Gilder's philosophy of community, only capitalism, which depends on the freedom of the individual to plan his own course of action in the market, can save society and at the same time be faithful to human nature and the laws of the universe. The "crucial rules of creative thought can be summed up as faith, love, openness, conflict, and falsifiability."[116] Faith means a willingness to risk because one believes risk will be rewarded, love means a willingness to offer one's gift (e.g., one's product) on the market in the belief that it will be useful or desirable to others, openness refers to taking one's risks in the public market, conflict means a competition with others through which the best and cheapest goods will be made available, and falsifiability means simply that one waits upon the market, the free choices of other individuals, to determine whether one has risked wisely. Fortunately, the essential rules of capitalism are in miraculous conformity to the rules of creative thought: economic innovation and progress require "faith, altruism, investment, competition, and bankruptcy."[117] And the reason capitalism succeeds is because "its laws accord with the laws of the mind. It is capable of fulfilling human needs because it is founded on giving, which depends on sensitivity to the needs of others. It is open to faith and experiment because it is also open to competition and bankruptcy.... It is the only appropriate system for a world in which all certitude is a sham."[118]

In such a system the freedom of the individual entrepreneur must be sacred. Without that freedom, there is no risk and without risk there is no motive to give to others so that one might gain from their desire to take one's gift. "Giving is the vital impulse and moral center of capitalism; give and you will be given unto is its fundamental law."[119] But such giving requires that capitalist entrepreneurs have "the freedom and power to consummate their entrepreneurial ideas," and this means, specifically, that they alone have the right to decide what they shall do with the gains they have received for the risks they have taken. In a statement that could have been taken almost verbatim from Carnegie's "Gospel of Wealth," Gilder asserts that "entrepreneurs must be allowed to retain wealth for the practical reason that only they, collectively, can possibly know where it should go, to whom it should be given."[120]

Like most modern defenders of the capitalist system, Gilder assumes that there will be a correspondence between the self-seeking pursuits of individual entrepreneurs and a generosity toward others. Capitalism, he believes, "is good and successful... because it calls forth, propagates, and relies upon the best and most generous of human qualities."[121] In this sense Gilder departs somewhat from the worldview of Adam Smith, who simply believed that an invisible hand would make a society of self-seeking individuals work for the benefit of all. But Gilder's departure from Smith is based upon his curious identification of seeking one's own good with giving generously to others. The equation rests heavily on Gilder's religious faith in creativity and risk. By risking one's investment, as one embodies the creative principle of the universe, one is giving to others even as one is seeking something for oneself. To give to others because they are in need bypasses the crucial element of creative risk. It does a disservice not only to the giver, who thus violates his own nature, but also to those who are in need, because it eliminates their opportunity to take their own creative risks. "Our greatest and only resource is the miracle of human creativity in a relation of openness to the divine. It is a resource that above all we should deny neither to the poor, who can be the most open of all to the future [a fact which must surely be of great comfort and inspiration to them], nor to the rich or excellent of individuals, who can lend leadership, imagination, and wealth to the cause of beneficent change."[122]

F.A. Hayek. Gilder's defense of individualism as somehow ontologically linked to the public good is reminiscent (except for the use he makes of Adam Smith's view of human nature) of the work of another of capitalism's most articulate and spirited contemporary defenders, F.A. Hayek. In his now famous "Individualism: True and False," Hayek argued that the true capitalistic individual is not the isolated, self-contained, rationally calculating individual of Rousseau, whom he (along with Nisbet) sees as a precursor of socialism and collectivism. Like Adam Smith and the Bible, Hayek believes that men are not capable of infallible rational decisions. They are finite beings characterized essentially by self-love. This does not mean egotism but it does mean for Hayek, if not for the biblical tradition, that man is a "very irrational and fallible being" who can "effectively comprehend" only the "facts of the narrow circle of which he is the center," and thus the needs for which he can effectively care "are an almost negligible fraction of the needs of all members of society."[123] But because no one can know my interests better than I do, the best social system is one in which each person (e.g., Gilder's entrepreneurial man) "is allowed to try and see what he can do."[124] Capitalistic individualism is the system in which "bad men can do least harm," "an interpersonal process in which anyone's contribution is tested and corrected by others," a "voluntary and spontaneous collaboration of individuals."[125]

Such a system faces its greatest danger from an attempt to coerce or dictate forms of association ostensibly for the common good. Like Gilder, Hayek believes that any attempt to spread the gains of some across a spectrum that includes everyone else is fundamentally unjust and unhealthy. In an individualistic system the rewards an individual should receive should correspond "to the relative utility of the results of his efforts to others... the objective results rather than... their subjective merits."[126] "We must face the fact that the preservation of individual freedom is incompatible with a full satisfaction of our views of distributive justice."[127] To the argument that such a system may well leave someone, who has less to offer that is of utility to others, worse off than a system based on some kind of distributive justice, Hayek, like Gilder, responds by claiming that "the hard discipline of the market... still leaves him at least some choice... and it is better to have a choice between several unpleasant alternatives than being coerced into one."[128] Hayek is quite explicit and emphatic in defense of the central characteristic of capitalistic individualism: freedom of individual choice. The condition of freedom is "so essential that it must not be sacrificed to the gratification of our sense of justice."[129]

There is a certain honesty in these claims which cannot be ignored. In their defense of individual rights, especially the right to enterprise and its rewards, Gilder and Hayek are willing to admit the existence and necessity of injustice. I believe that what they see as a trade-off between justice and freedom within the atomistic/contractarian model can be seen in other models of community as unnecessary, or at least not as obvious or blatant. But the defenders of capitalistic individualism give such significant priority and emphasis to the individual's right to work out his own destiny (and enjoy or suffer the consequences by himself), that they must regard any attempt to spread the reward and pain of risk as a fundamental violation of human nature.

Michael Novak. The defense of capitalism in both Gilder and Hayek often calls forth religious and metaphysical language, somehow linking it to the fundamental principles of reality as such. Apparently nothing less is at stake, for the defenders of capitalistic individualism, than the reality of human nature in correlation with the fundamental principles of the universe. Convinced that Christian claims about human nature are best represented by a democratic capitalism, Michael Novak has brought his theological skills to a defense of capitalism in his recent book *The Spirit of Democratic Capitalism.*

Like Gilder and Hayek, Novak sees a fundamental link between capitalism and the spirit of individualism. In fact, he seems to go even further than they do in extolling as a virtue the pain and isolation of individualism. The alienation that is so often lamented by those who criticize the atomistic/contractarian scheme is regarded by Novak as the necessary price one must pay for being free. "Of course free persons will feel alienation! The opposite would be to feel so connected as not to be free. To appropriate one's own liberty is to learn—sometimes against one's will, forcibly—to be detached from all things."[130] Such a claim almost suggests that Novak longs to return to a state of nature (as in Hobbes) where the social bond has not yet been established. But fortunately, present democratic capitalism "permits individuals to experience alienation, anomie, loneliness, and nothingness. Democratic capitalism is also constantly renewed by such radical experiences of human liberty... Each experiences a solitariness and personal responsibility which renders him (or her) oddly alone in the midst of solidarity. It is because individuals... are able to raise questions about all schemes of community, order, purpose, and meaning, and able to choose in darkness—that individuals have inalienable rights."[131]

At the heart of this otherwise strange defense of isolation, loneliness, and nothingness is Novak's commitment to the religious principle that men live in a state of sin. "In the world as it is, humans as they are are often and unavoidably enmeshed in lies, betrayals, injustices, and sinful energies of every sort... [To] treat any society of this world as 'a Christian society' is to confound precious hope with a sad reality."[132] But the greatest virtue of man's sinfulness, paradoxically, is that it leads the Creator, who hates sin, to permit it "for the sake of liberty."[133] In other words, liberty is so precious a good, so ontologically valuable, that it must be preserved even if the price for doing so is individually a sense of alienation and socially a sense of inequity in the distribution of goods and services. Besides, Novak protests, inequalities are built into nature. Therefore the "inequalities of wealth and power" in capitalism are "not considered evil in themselves. They are in tune with natural inequalities which everyone experiences every day."[134] But the gains of economic development, which depend upon exploiting these inequalities, far outweigh the losses. The freedom of individual enterprise—but perhaps more significantly, the freedom to shower one's wealth upon others in the form of moral compassion—make inequality truly justifiable.

Novak is not, of course, unmindful of or unconcerned about the importance communities or associations have in the life of capitalistic individuals. But the kinds of communities which play a role in capitalism are primarily those constructed on the atomistic/contractarian model. They are communities of "free persons in voluntary association," not, Novak notes specifically, the nostalgic communities of Gemeinschaft. While Novak can wax eloquent about the relation of community to the will of God ("what is most real in human life, of highest value, most godlike, is a community of persons"),[135] the assumption on which he builds his analysis is that community is essentially a contract relationship between individuals which permits them to cooperate with others to achieve their own essentially individualistic ends. His prime example of a community is revealing. It is the modern corporation. The corporation, Novak rightly notes, is social: "it holds that economic activity is fundamentally corporate, exceeding the capacity of any one individual alone.... This cooperative principle is essential to a capitalist economic system."[136] Novak claims that life in the corporation has created a "new type of human being, neither an individualist nor a collectivist."[137]

But he seems to assume that self-reliance and independence are the hallmarks of corporate activity, or at least that community and independence are correlative. Such an assumption makes sense in the contractarian model but not in the organic or mutual models. How else could Novak say in the same sentence, referring to some early pioneers, "they took pride in being free persons, independent, and self-reliant; but the texture of their lives was cooperative and fraternal"?[138] The examples of community which Novak brings up almost always seem to be characterized by cooperative activity but not by the joy of simply being together for its own sake or living for other persons. His communities are ones that individuals go into and out of, depending on desire or need at any given time. They tend to be focused on goals and tasks. He refers to the community of "colleagueship, task-oriented, goal-directed, freely entered into and freely left," as a particularly good model of community.[139] But again one misses any sense here of mutuality ("they may not have much emotional attachment to each other").[140] The antidote to the pains and perils of too much capitalistic individualism is essentially, for Novak, an association of "teamwork, and collaboration, oriented by tasks and goals, voluntarily entered into."[141] In the end, the spirit of democratic capitalism, and its religious defense, services the cause of brotherhood primarily "by recognizing that the most precious of all common goods is the individuality of each person, and that the best way to increase the common good is to empower people through differentiated systems."[142] The spirit of individualism and the contract relation with others for more effective teamwork remain very much alive at the heart of Novak's system, and no matter how set around it has been with the symbols and rhetoric of community, they recall for us the endurance of the spirit first expressed in the modern age by Thomas Hobbes.

We can conclude our survey of contemporary adherents of the atomistic/contractarian model of community by looking briefly at two American moral philosophers, John Rawls and Robert Nozick, whose works have taken academic citadels by storm and whose views are having a much greater than usual impact on the public as well. Their visions of society and their ways of getting to it differ from each other. Their arguments are highly sophisticated and elaborate, and I do not intend to make anything like a full-scale critique of their work. But what I do think needs emphasis is the degree to which the assumptions of the atomistic/contractarian model remain alive in their thought and thus continue to influence a new generation of social thinkers.

Robert Nozick. Nozick has perhaps gone further than any other contemporary moral philosopher of stature in defending a strong sense of individualism and a correspondingly minimal notion of the state. The state, for Nozick, in a distinct echo of Hobbes, is justified only if it is "limited to the narrow functions of protection against force, theft, fraud, enforcement of contracts, and so on."[143] The justification of society is really the protection of the individual and his rights. Like Locke, Nozick believes that in a state of nature individuals possess the basic rights of life, liberty, and property. In addition, Nozick claims, there are no rights but those of individuals. "Individuals have rights, and there are things no person or group may do to them without violating their rights."[144] "Individuals are ends and not merely means; they may not be sacrificed or used for the achieving of other ends without their consent. Individuals are inviolable."[145] There are no rights which accrue to a society of individuals that are not there in the individuals prior to association ("individuals in combination cannot create new rights which are not the sum of preexisting ones").[146] "Of course, if individuals *choose* to confer rights upon the groups to which they belong, they have every right to do so. Nevertheless, it is from individuals that rights always proceed and to them that they must ultimately devolve."

This leads Nozick, as it did Bentham, to the conclusion that the community of persons has no moral status or good over and above that of the individuals who comprise it. It does not make sense, therefore, to talk about people sacrificing their interests for the sake of the community. "There are only individual people, different individual people, with their own individual lives.... Talk of an overall social good covers this up ... [and] does not sufficiently respect and take account of the fact that [the individual] is a separate person.... There is no moral outweighing of one of our lives by others so as to lead to a greater overall *social* good. There is no justified sacrifice of some of us for others."[147] If this statement is taken in an absolute sense, of course, there is no justification whatsoever for Christian agape, and even a minimal notion of Christian community would have to be ruled out on the basis of Nozick's principles.

Because of his emphasis on the fundamental rights of individuals, Nozick comes to two significant conclusions affecting his understanding of community. The first is that any sense of association and justice must be derived exclusively from a process of rational agreement (or contract), not from some prior conception of a desirable *end-state*; and the second is that any community will be based upon the free, voluntary choices of those who decide to constitute it.

With respect of the first point, Nozick argues that justice, or a justified system of entitlements, is defensible only when it is "constituted by the individual aims of individual transactions. No overarching aim is needed, no distributional pattern is required."[148] The uncoerced choice of each individual is the bedrock on which any system of justice must be based. It will not do to put the needs of individuals ahead of their rights. I have no right, even in the name of need (my own or others'), to compel from other individuals what they do not choose to give. In a deliberate reversal of the famous Marxian dictum, Nozick sums up his position by saying "From each according to what he chooses to do, to each according to what he makes for himself (perhaps with the contracted aid of others) and what others choose to do for him and choose to give him of what they've been given previously (under this maxim) and haven't yet expended or transferred... *from each as they choose, to each as they are chosen.*"[149]

On the basis of nonnegotiable individual rights, Nozick does develop an outline of possibilities for human community. While many critics have derided Nozick for selfishness and narrow-mindedness egoism, I believe a case can be made that he is open to the possibility of a wide variety of communities, including those in which altruism, love, benevolence, sharing, and compassion play a role. In fact, his commitment to unfettered free choice leads him necessarily to accept the results of any set of free choices by free individuals contracting together, whether those choices range from selfish interest-groups to altruistic bands of loving brothers and sisters. "... [I]n a free society people may contract into various restrictions which the government may not legitimately impose upon them. Though the framework is libertarian and laissez-faire, *individual communities within it need not be*, and perhaps no community within it will choose to be so."[150]

This openness to a variety of social relationships, while it leads to constant experimentation and "a wide and diverse range of communities which people can enter if they are admitted",[151] is nevertheless based upon Nozick's fundamental assumption that persons do not naturally (as a result of their essential nature) need to be in mutual, loving relationships in order to be themselves or to fulfill their natures. There is not, in fact, one best of all possible worlds adequate to all human beings. People are different, including differences in "spiritual quests, and the kind of life they wish to lead.... There is no reason to think that there is one community which will serve as ideal for all people and much reason to think that there is not.... There is a wide range of very different kinds of life that tie as best."[152]

In addition to his belief that no form of community is objectively any better or more suited to human nature than any other, Nozick also seems to believe that all of these communities must presuppose the contract form of relationship. That is, no matter how diverse the kinds of communities, no matter how much caring and love might be present in any one of them, they all are to be entered into (and departed from) on the basis of individual choice. What this leads to is the question of whether the notion of mutuality is a dominant or subordinate factor in Nozick's scheme. I think the answer is clearly that it is subordinate. As I suggested at the outset, each model of community will probably find a place for most of those aspects of human life that are also in the other models. But what will distinguish the models to a large extent is the hierarchy or relationship these factors will have to each other. I think that in Nozick's model we can see the primary role still played by the atomistic/contractarian assumptions about the inviolability of individual free choice and the fundamental separateness and difference between individuals, a separateness and difference that can be bridged only if the bridging is done by rational contract and not because of a fundamental need in human nature to live in and for other persons.

John Rawls. Although he disagrees with his Harvard colleague about the way by which a conception of a just society is to be reached, and about what would constitute the principles of such a society, John Rawls, in his *A Theory of Justice*, shares Nozick's fundamental individualism and reliance upon the contract form of relationship with others. His position, as Raymond Plant has put it, develops a "sense of *solidarity* in society but basically from an individualistic point of view."[153] Society, for Rawls (as for Gilder, Hayek, Novak, and Nozick), is essentially an association of *cooperation*, not a community of mutuality. Rawls himself is quite explicit about his theory being a continuation of the contract tradition: "My aim is to present a conception of justice which generalizes and carries to a higher level of abstraction the familiar theory of the social contract as found, say, in Locke, Rousseau, and Kant."[154]

Prior to any social contract, Rawls assumes the fundamental priority of individual rights, the essential one being equal respect. On this basis, Rawls asks us to consider a process by which free, essentially autonomous and rational individuals go behind a veil of ignorance (where they no longer know what their own station in life will be nor what their interests and abilities are) and determine together what principles of justice they would wish to be governed by when they emerge from the veil. As is now well known, one principle of justice as fairness that Rawls claims will emerge from behind the veil is the "difference principle," which holds that "the social order is not to establish and secure the more attractive prospects of those better off unless doing so is to the advantage of those less fortunate."[155]

But what interests us more at this point than the principles themselves are the assumptions Rawls makes about the individuals who decide upon them. First and most important,

Rawls insists over and over that as individuals enter the veil of ignorance they must be "mutually *disinterested* [my underlining] ... not taking an interest in one another's interests."[156] Rawls insists that this does not mean that individuals in the original position are egoists but simply that a social order must *assume* the essential *self-interestedness* of the individuals who will comprise it. "Each desires to protect his interests, his capacity to advance his conception of the good."[157] Even our duty to help others is limited to those situations where we "can do so without excessive risk or loss to oneself; ..."[158]

I do not want to suggest that Rawls has a Hobbesian view of a person's fundamental antagonism to others. In fact, his theory of justice is driven by a conviction of the importance of working for the benefit of the least advantaged in the social order. But his understanding of that order is essentially contractarian, and thus assumes the essential individualism of that model. When people do come together in a just way, it will be primarily through cooperation, not mutuality. Rawls defines society as "a cooperative venture for mutual advantage ... typically marked by a conflict as well as an identity of interests."[159] Cooperation is essentially justified because it is more effective in securing individual purposes than is trying to go it alone ("social cooperation makes possible a better life for all than any would have if each were to try to live solely by his own efforts").[160]

Even when Rawls talks about the importance of friendship and mutual trust between persons, it is always on the basis of a prior contract of association binding them together through obedience to duty, rules, and obligations. As persons live up to their obligations, and only then, do others form friendly feelings toward them. Once a person's capacity for "fellow feeling" has been realized by participating in the just association, "then as his associates with evident intention live up to their duties and obligations, he develops friendly feelings toward them, together with feelings of trust and confidence."[161]

I think the order here is important. It reveals the ultimacy in Rawls of the atomistic, individualisitic standpoint. This ultimacy eventually and necessarily continues to conflict with Rawls' explicit interest in affirming what he calls the social union or the "tie of community."[162] Rawls does want to support the view that

> human beings have in fact shared final ends and they value their common institutions and activities as good in themselves. We need one another as partners in ways of life that

are engaged in for their own sake, and the successes and enjoyments of others are necessary for and complementary to our own good; ... [thus] we are led to the notion of the community of humankind the members of which enjoy one another's excellences and individuality elicited by free institutions, and they recognize the good of each as an element in the complete activity the whole scheme of which is consented to and gives pleasure to all.[163]

But this sense of community is still, I believe, a cooperative society into which individuals enter because they find it to their individualistic advantage to do so. There may be an enjoyment they experience in the achievements of others, but this enjoyment follows from others *first* accepting the terms of association on the basis of contract. In addition, the institutions valued as good in themselves are so valued because they interfere least with the pursuit of self-interest. The real question is whether the disinterest in others that characterized the original position can lead smoothly to a social union characterized by mutual interest. As Milton Fisk has asked, "Can the atomism of his original position provide [an] adequate ... framework for community"?[164]

Fisk believes, and I think he is correct in this, that Rawls' concept of human nature winds up in a shambles precisely because his original disinterestedness never gets adequately connected to the bonds of friendliness which he wants to see in the social union to which the contract is supposed to lead. If fellow feeling is contingent, as I have suggested it is in Rawls, then it is not an *essential* part of human nature and thus cannot form the foundation for a genuine community of mutuality. If fellow feeling is essential to human nature, then the description of the original position is misleading at the very least. As Fisk says, "Mutual disinterestedness and the awareness that one has fellow feeling toward unspecified fellows cannot be combined to form a coherent conception of human nature .... Thus on the basis of the atomistic human nature of Rawls' original position we derive, not surprisingly, atomistic conclusions that are not sufficient for community and seem incompatible with it."[165]

Benjamin Barber has also singled out Rawls' uneasy alliance between what he calls the Hobbesianism of the original position and the Kantianism of Rawls' genuine enthusiasm for some kind of social union or community. But as if on the top of a ridge separating the valley of private society and perfect union, Rawls seems continually in danger of plunging down one side or the other, able to traverse the terrain comfortably only by descending to the valley of private society and interest theory (the Hobbesian path), or sliding down the other side into the valley of perfect union and superogatory mutualism (the trans-Kantian trail, as it were). No doubt he would like to remain on the ridge ... [but] he cannot, and the Hobbesian and Kantian in him are never really made compatible.[166]

Rawls' difficulty is, I believe, in large measure traceable to the ambivalence in the atomistic/contractarian position generally. As a theory of human association it emerges in order to explain the obvious and necessary relationships that prevail among persons. But it generally starts from an individualistic bias in which monadic persons in their essential nature are in some sense set apart from each other in an original state (e.g., the state of nature) prior to their entering into these relationships. While many social philosophers from Locke on have claimed some kind of social sentiment even in the state of nature, the dominant characteristic of persons remains their self-interest and consequent disinterest in others, a disinterest or diffidence to which even the feelings of union, or fellow feelings, remain subordinate.

INDIVIDUALISM, THE FREE MARKET, AND COMMUNITY

One of the reasons why the individualistic bias has remained dominant is the coupling of individualism with the principles of capitalism or the free market model of economic relations. This model requires—so the defenders of capitalism continually remind us—conditions of competition, private ownership of property, and above all, "genuine independence of economic units" and its corollary, self-reliance.[167] The market necessarily places "the constant competitive struggle for self-assertion and self-advancement in the center of the stage."[168] If this concern for the self and its interests starts the play of human relations already at center stage, it is hard to see how a genuine community of sharing, self-sacrifice, love, and altruism could ever find a place except somewhere to the rear of the stage or, perhaps, off-stage or in the private spaces of the wings. The only context for relationships that go beyond mere utilitarian contract is the limited space on the stage: that is, the necessity to recognize that the stage will hold only so many self-interested individuals and that eventually they must begin to take account of each other.

As Robert Paul Wolff has put it in summarizing the philosophy of individualistic liberalism, "It is as though society were an enclosed space in which float a number of spherical balloons filled with an expanding gas. Each balloon increases in size until its surface meets the surface of the other balloons; then it stops and adjusts to its surroundings."[169] The balloons, the expanding atoms of a mechanical, contract-based social order, do not feel for each other, they do not live for each other, they do not find their essential nature fulfilled only in communion with each other. As competitors for space and the limited resources necessary for self-advancement, the atoms must always be on their guard against others. Whatever communities of love and trust emerge from these conditions must necessarily, therefore, be fragile, contingent, and derivative. They cannot complete or fulfill human nature: they can, at best, provide a diversion or an enjoyment for it over and above what it needs to be itself.

There are many prophetic voices which have arisen over the years to lament the consequences of the atomistic/contractarian view of relationships. They usually identify the experience of alienation as central to life lived in an individualistic, capitalistic society. As Erich Fromm, perhaps the most popular of these critics, has said, "Modern society consists of 'atoms' (if we use the Greek equivalent of 'individual'), little particles estranged from each other but held together by selfish interests and by the necessity to make use of each other."[170] But if we are, as Fromm claims, essentially social beings, then living as atoms will necessarily alienate us, not just from each other, but more importantly, from our own essential nature. (We will explore some of the consequences of this alienation in our examination of Karl Marx, who was among the first to try, through an organic model of relationship, to overcome the deficiencies of the atomistic model.)

In addition to alienation, capitalistic individualism leads to such other maladies as loneliness, impersonality, and the self-defeating quest for privacy. As Philip Slater, in his indictment of competitive capitalism, has put it, "We seek more and more privacy, and feel more and more alienated and lonely when we get it."[171] The greatest irony of all, as Slater and others have pointed out, is that in our search for privacy and the space to be alone in order to develop our self-interest and exercise our freedom of choice, we become more and more vulnerable to conformity and determinism by others and by the state. We find our private and public lives diverging more and more, with the private sphere becoming more and more restricted. De Tocqueville had warned of this danger but it still exists. "[T]he temptation to give power away is very strong in Americans because of our individualistic heritage. We're always wanting to give power to leaders so we can do our own thing and not be bothered by the demands of collective commitment.... Cooperation is so irksome to individualistic natures that they spend half their political lives giving power to centralized government and the other half fearing for their personal liberties, without ever considering the contradiction."[172]

The contradiction results in a dualism between the social self and the private self. A person's social inclinations wind up getting expressed in and through his political obligations (to vote, pay taxes, and contribute to the institutions to which he belongs). His subjective inclinations get expressed by his freedom to do as he pleases outside the boundaries, or within the interstices, of the social order. But the great irony is that his social self becomes less and less free while his private self becomes the basis for the only kind of mutuality with other persons he can have. In the model of atomistic individualism, the public world, the world of contracts in which a person's freedom is allegedly preserved, is a world separated or abstracted from the individual's most personal and subjective intentions. The public interest is an aggregate or sum of private interests (consistent with the mechanical aspect of the atomistic model) and it must be dominant over each individual interest: the public interest must be "represented and objectified by a power external and alien to the mass of private individuals,"[173] whether by Hobbes' Leviathan or Locke's representative government. And because of this it becomes necessary for individuals to carve out some private space within society to express their 'true' freedom. "[B]ecause liberal doctrine assumes an antagonism between private and public, individual and community, the individual freedom it calls for can paradoxically be achieved only at the price of subjection to an external, alien public power, a power ultimately inimical to individual liberty and autonomy."[174] Individualism sows the seeds for totalitarianism.

The result in practice is often a resentment by individuals of the machinery of the state, which is empowered to carry out the obligations of the social contract and to implement the demands of the social order. People resent being taxed to provide social services to the poor and needy, and yet in their private freedom they are often extremely generous to needy individuals if they can give to them directly from their own pockets. But the dualism between the social and the private self eventually causes an estrangement, an alienation in the individual. His social and private inclinations are usually at war with each other. He becomes more and more determined by the structures of the social order, and more and more retreats into private pursuits in order to actualize the freedom that remains to him. But as Slater has pointed out, this retreat into privacy is itself often taken hostage by conformity. Individuals enact their freedom by using their discretionary income to buy superficially different objects, but usually the same objects (cars, barbecue grills, videotape recorders, suburban homes, etc.), distinguished only by color or brand names.

These decisions to consume become in the end so predictable that social man becomes the prey of the social scientist, who applies to his allegedly free decisions the tools of analysis appropriate to objects under the sway of causal law. Freedom gained in one area soon becomes freedom lost in another. This view of human nature "frees the individual to a great extent from human authority by subjecting him to the impersonal authority of mechanistic social forces."[175]

Ellen Wood has, I believe, captured the necessary link between this denial of freedom within the context of individualism's assertion of it and a mechanical or atomistic view of human relations. She claims that it is a social scientist's dream to have a view of society "as a smoothly operating mechanism consisting of a network of externalized, perhaps institutionalized, social interactions (an image to which the concept of the market is so eminently suited), in which man's freedom consists in the relatively unobstructed enjoyment of his role."[176] But should we have expected anything else when persons are essentially understood as atoms in mechanical relation to each other, as beings whose subjective need for and enjoyment of each other is never more than contingent or a necessary evil? Once having begun with the atomistic notion of the person, you must inevitably (unless you become inconsistent or qualify your position beyond recognition) wind up with a mechanized view of society. "Thus," as Wood concludes,

> the atomization of society seems again to be the condition for man's subjection to "autonomous" social laws. In fact, it can be argued that the most essential statistical procedures on which much of contemporary social science depends are possible only on the basis of a particular conception of community. Apparently, the very mathematical possibility of these procedures rests on the implicit assumption that men are bound together, not by interpersonal relations, but by a network of independently existing social forces which act upon each of them in isolation.[177]

That there are other ways to view persons in relation and their freedom will be seen now as we move into a model of community, the organic, which explicitly challenges the fundamental assumptions about human nature which constitute the atomistic/contractarian model.

NOTES TO CHAPTER 2

1. Ferdinand Tönnies, *Community and Society (Gemeinschaft und Gesellschaft)*, trans. and ed. Charles P. Loomis (East Lansing: Michigan State University Press, 1957).
2. J.W. Gough, *The Social Contract. A Critical Study of Its Development* (Oxford: Clarendon Press, 1936), 2.
3. Ibid., 8.
4. Dorothea Krook, *Three Traditions of Moral Thought* (Cambridge: The University Press, 1959); see Chapter III, "Self-Sufficiency for Love: Aristotle's *Nicomachean Ethics*."
5. Gough, *The Social Contract*, 40-41.
6. Ibid., 45.
7. Otto Gierke, *Natural Law and the Theory of Society 1500 to 1800*, translated with an introduction by Ernest Barker, vol. I (Cambridge: The University Press, 1934), 46.
8. Ibid., 96.
9. Ibid.
10. Ibid.
11. Ibid., 113.

12. Tönnies, *Community and Society*, 214.
13. Ibid., 179.
14. Ibid.
15. Ibid., 69.
16. Ibid., 173.
17. Ibid., 77.
18. Plant, *Community and Ideology*, 30–31.
19. Ibid., 31.
20. Ibid.
21. Ibid.
22. Gierke, *Natural Law and the Theory of Society 1500 to 1800*, 52.
23. Krook, *Three Traditions of Moral Thought*, 94.
24. Robert Nisbet, *The Social Philosophers. Community and Conflict in Western Thought* (New York: Washington Square Press, 1982), 23–24.
25. Ibid., 25–26.
26. Ibid., 26.
27. George H. Sabine, *A History of Political Theory* (New York: Henry Holt, 1946), 457.
28. Ibid.
29. Krook, *Three Traditions of Moral Thought*, 100.
30. Ibid., 105.
31. Richard S. Peters, Introduction to the Collier Books Edition, Thomas Hobbes, *Leviathan, Or the Matter, Forme and Power of a Commonwealth Ecclesiasticall and Civil*, ed. Michael Oakeshott (New York: Collier Books, 1962), 9.
32. Hobbes, *Leviathan*, 19.
33. Ibid., 98.
34. Ibid., 99.
35. Ibid.
36. Ibid.
37. Ibid., 100.
38. Ibid.
39. Ibid., 101.
40. Ibid.
41. Ibid.
42. Ibid., 103.
43. Ibid.
44. Ibid., 104.
45. Ibid., 105.
46. Ibid., 113.
47. Ibid., 129.
48. Ibid.
49. Ibid., 118.
50. Ibid.
51. The influence of Locke on the founding fathers, especially on Thomas Jefferson, is still generally accepted despite a recent scholarly

flap surrounding the claims made by Garry Wills in his book on Jefferson, *Inventing America*, that the primary drafter of the Declaration of Independence was far more indebted to the communitarian views of the Scottish enlightenment, through the moral philosophy of such men as Francis Hutcheson and Thomas Reid, than he was to the work of Locke. Wills argues that Hutcheson's emphasis upon community and the social bonds of affection ultimately had more influence on Jefferson's mind than did Locke's emphasis on individualism and property rights. Wills's case rests on his belief that Hutcheson relies far more heavily on the sentiments of sociality than does Locke and that these sentiments are more crucial to Jefferson than the Lockean views of property and individualism. The critical reaction to Wills's claim indicates that his argument has failed to convince a large number of Lockean and American history scholars. The parallels between Locke's language in the *Second Treatise* and the Declaration of Independence are simply too many and too close to qualify the traditional belief that Locke was a decisive influence on the thinking of Jefferson, and by extension, upon the majority of political thinkers at the time of this nation's founding. See Garry Wills, *Inventing America: Jefferson's Declaration of Independence* (Garden City, N.Y.: Doubleday, 1978). Two representative criticisms can be found in Ronald Hamowy, "Jefferson and the Scottish Enlightenment: A Critique of Garry Wills's *Inventing America: Jefferson's Declaration of Independence*" (*William and Mary Quarterly*, vol. 36, 3d ser., (1979) 503–23); and Harry V. Jaffa, "Inventing the Past: Garry Wills's *Inventing America* and the Pathology of Ideological Scholarship" (*The St. Johns Review* (Autumn, 1981): 3–19.

52. John Locke, *The Second Treatise of Government*, edited with an introduction by Thomas P. Peardon (Indianapolis: Bobbs-Merrill, 1952), 13, sec. 19.

53. Ibid., 72, sec. 128. A somewhat dated but still very fair discussion of the debate regarding the degree to which Locke tried to provide more emphasis on a natural communal inclination than did Hobbes can be found in J.W. Gough, *John Locke's Political Philosophy*, 2d ed. (Oxford: Clarendon Press, 1973), especially chapter II, "The Rights of the Individual," and chapter IV, "Locke's Theory of Property." Gough argues that in the end, Locke did not draw a sharp distinction between the good of the community and that of individuals. "For him the one was the sum of the other, and though it is true that he was more concerned in some contexts with the particulars and in others with the total, he equated the public good with the preservation of the property (i.e. the lives, liberties, and estates) of individuals ... He thought in terms of a society and government of property-owners, whose interests would naturally coincide" (p. 38).

54. Ibid., 4, sec. 4.
55. Ibid.
56. Ibid., 5, sec. 5.

57. Ibid., 11, sec. 15. The quotation is from Richard Hooker, *The Laws of Ecclesiastical Polity*, lib. i., sec. 10.
58. Ibid., 32–33, sec. 57.
59. Ibid., 5–6, sec. 6.
60. Ibid., 17, sec. 27.
61. Ibid., 27, sec. 44.
62. Ibid., 45–46, sec. 80.
63. Ibid., 48–49, sec. 87.
64. Ibid.
65. Ibid., 70–71, secs. 123-124.
66. Ibid., 50, sec. 90.
67. Ibid., 71, sec. 125.
68. Ibid., 54, sec. 95.
69. Ibid., 61, sec. 107.
70. Wood, *Mind and Politics*, 49, n. 2.
71. Sabine, *A History of Political Theory*, 529.
72. Douglas Long, *Bentham on Liberty: Jeremy Bentham's Idea of Liberty in Relation to His Utilitarianism* (Toronto: University of Toronto Press, 1977), 208.
73. Ibid., 212.
74. Jeremy Bentham, *A Bentham Reader*, ed. Mary Peter Mack (New York: Pegasus, 1969), from *An Introduction to the Principles of Morals and Legislation*, 85–86.
75. Ibid., 97.
76. Ibid., 135.
77. Ibid., 86.
78. Ibid.
79. Sabine, *A History of Political Theory*, 654.
80. Currin V. Shields, "Editor's Introduction," James Mill, *An Essay on Government*, edited with an introduction by Currin V. Shields (New York: Liberal Arts Press, 1955), 38.
81. Adam Smith, *An Inquiry into the Nature and Causes of the Wealth of Nations*, edited, with an introduction, notes, marginal summary and an enlarged index by Edwin Cannan, with an introduction by Max Lerner (New York: Modern Library, 1937), 423.
82. Ibid.
83. Adam Smith, quoted in Robert L. Heilbroner, *The Worldly Philosophers* (New York: Simon and Schuster, 1961), 40.
84. Heilbroner, ibid., 43.
85. Ibid.
86. Jean-Jacques Rousseau, *Emile*, from *Oeuvres Complètes*, IV, 599–600, as quoted in Ellen Wood, *Mind and Politics*, 79.
87. Wood, ibid., 81.
88. Ibid.
89. Rousseau, *Emile*, Book IV, 29, as quoted in Maurice Cranston, "Introduction," Rousseau, *The Social Contract*, translated and introduced by Maurice Cranston (Baltimore: Penguin Books, 1968), 29.

90. Ibid.
91. Rousseau, *The Social Contract*, 60.
92. Ibid., 130.
93. Ibid.
94. Ibid., 60–61.
95. Nisbet, *The Social Philosophers*, 39.
96. *The United States Magazine and Democratic Review*, vol. 6 (1839): 212–14, quoted in Yehoshua Arieli, *Individualism and Nationalism in American Ideology* (Cambridge: Harvard University Press, 1964), 191.
97. Ibid., 345.
98. Ibid., 192.
99. Alexis de Tocqueville, *Democracy in America*. The Henry Reeve text, as revised by Francis Bowen, now further corrected and edited with introduction, editorial notes, and bibliographies by Phillips Bradley, foreword by Harold J. Laski (New York: Alfred A. Knopf, 1945), 98–99.
100. Ibid.
101. Arieli, *Individualism and Nationalism in American Ideology*, 196.
102. Ibid., 198.
103. Ibid.
104. Ibid.
105. Ibid., 20.
106. Andrew Carnegie, "The Gospel of Wealth," in *The Gospel of Wealth and Other Timely Essays*, ed. Edward C. Kirkland (Cambridge: The Belknap Press of Harvard University Press, 1962), 15–16, 28–29.
107. Ibid.
108. Quoted in Arieli, *Individualism and Nationalism in American Ideology*, 341.
109. See Robert Bellah et al., *Habits of the Heart: Individualism and Commitment in American Life* (Berkeley: University of California Press, 1985), 150.
110. Ibid., 151.
111. George Gilder, *Wealth and Poverty* (New York: Basic Books, 1981), 263.
112. Ibid., 254.
113. Ibid.
114. Ibid., 255.
115. Ibid., 111–13.
116. Ibid., 265.
117. Ibid.
118. Ibid.
119. George Gilder, "Commentary," *The Heroes of Growth*, vol. III, no. 8; in *Newsweek*, November 1981.
120. Ibid.
121. Ibid.
122. Gilder, *Wealth and Poverty*, 268.
123. F.A. Hayek, "Individualism: True and False," in *Individualism*

and Economic Order, Gateway Edition (Chicago: Henry Regnery, 1972), 11, 14.
124. Ibid., 15.
125. Ibid., 11, 15, 16.
126. Ibid., 21.
127. Ibid., 22.
128. Ibid., 24.
129. Ibid., 30.
130. Michael Novak, *The Spirit of Democratic Capitalism* (Washington, D.C.: American Enterprise Institute, 1982), 53.
131. Ibid., 55.
132. Ibid., 68.
133. Ibid., 82.
134. Ibid., 84.
135. Ibid., 338.
136. Ibid., 131.
137. Ibid., 134.
138. Ibid., 135.
139. Ibid., 136.
140. Ibid., 137.
141. Ibid., 138.
142. Ibid., 226.
143. Robert Nozick, *Anarchy, State, and Utopia* (New York: Basic Books, 1974), ix.
144. Ibid.
145. Ibid., 30–31.
146. Ibid., 90.
147. Ibid., 33.
148. Ibid., 159.
149. Ibid., 160.
150. Ibid., 320.
151. Ibid., 307.
152. Ibid., 309–10.
153. Plant, *Community and Ideology*, 42.
154. John Rawls, *A Theory of Justice* (Cambridge: The Belknap Press of Harvard University Press, 1971), 11.
155. Ibid., 75.
156. Ibid., 13.
157. Ibid., 14.
158. Ibid., 114.
159. Ibid., 126.
160. Ibid.
161. Ibid., 470.
162. Ibid., 526.
163. Ibid., 523.
164. Milton Fisk, "History and Reason in Rawls' Moral Theory," in *Reading Rawls: Critical Studies on Rawls' A Theory of Justice,* edited with an introduction by Norman Daniels (New York: Basic Books, 1975), 65.

165. Ibid., 67.

166. Benjamin Barber, "Justifying Justice: Problems of Psychology, Politics and Measurement in Rawls," in Daniels, ed., *Reading Rawls*, 318.

167. William Roepke, "Ordered Anarchy," in *The Capitalist Reader*, ed. Lawrence S. Stepelevich (New Rochelle: Arlington House, 1977), 38.

168. Ibid., 62.

169. Robert Paul Wolff, *The Poverty of Liberalism* (Boston: Beacon Press, 1968), 141.

170. Erich Fromm, *The Sane Society* (New York: Rinehart, 1959), 139–40.

171. Philip Slater, *The Pursuit of Loneliness. American Culture at the Breaking Point*, rev. ed. (Boston: Beacon Press, 1976), 13.

172. Ibid., 164.

173. Wood, *Mind and Politics*, 152.

174. Ibid., 159.

175. Ibid., 177.

176. Ibid., 181.

177. Ibid., 184.

3. The Organic/Functional Model of Community: Part One—Social Visions from Hegel to Marx and Some Sociologists

ORGANISM AND THE SOCIAL WHOLE

The emergence of a model of community which would provide an alternative to the atomistic/contractarian model of liberal philosophy followed both from theoretical difficulties in the atomistic model and from the social consequences of trying to live by its principles. Its greatest theoretical failing, first expressed in metaphysical form by the most influential philosopher of the nineteenth century, G.W.F. Hegel, was its lack of appreciation for the wholeness and interrelatedness of reality. It failed to do justice to the felt unity of reality and to the dynamic dimension of life itself. From Hegel on, many social philosophers would come to regard reality as a single whole composed of lesser wholes organically related to each other and to the larger whole of which they were parts. Under Hegel's influence, many of those who wrote at the end of the nineteenth and the beginning of the twentieth century attacked the atomistic, mechanical philosophy of society and urged in its place a theory of community in which the social whole took precedence over the individual part.

We will examine the nature of the organic concept of community as it took shape in Hegel and, under his influence but for different political purposes, in Marx. We will also examine the way in which some important sociologists at the beginning of the century employed the organic model as part of their conceptual understanding of human association. Their work was, outside of philosophy, the most important in the scholarly community to address itself to an understanding of persons in relation. Through their work (especially that of Tönnies and Cooley) the organic metaphor of community gained legitimacy in social theory and became part of a much wider but often unconscious model of how persons relate. The reliance upon organic imagery has since become almost universal among social theorists, except those who still believe the atomistic/contractarian model best fits the social order. Because of the strength of the organic model (which is not to be denied even when its deficiencies are pointed out), it needs to be explored in some depth if the advantages of the mutual/personal model are to be appreciated.

The most developed metaphysical view of organic relations has been that of Alfred North Whitehead. After an examination of his organic philosophy, we will turn to an exploration of the ways in which the organic model has influenced contemporary philosophy of biology (much of it under the influence of Whitehead) and of systems theory. Because biological science and the philosophy of biology have played a major role in defining and shaping the organic model of relationship, it is necessary to see how its categories of explanation affect its understanding of persons in relation. We will evaluate this work from the point of view of the self as an agent who may be more than a biological organism. In particular, we will find the organic notion of the systems theorists and the unified hierarchical notion of Edward Pols, to be a way of integrating the notion of the self as agent (which is central to the mutual/personal model) with the notion of the self as organism. This will provide us with a point of departure for and a smooth transition to Macmurray's development of the mutual/personal model of community, which will include, but in significant ways go beyond, a more limited notion of persons as organisms.

In the process we will note two very important but different uses of the organic metaphor. The first is what I will call the narrow or restricted use, in which "organism" is used in a reductionist way to understand persons as simply complex biological organisms. In this narrower use of the organic metaphor, dimensions such as freedom to initiate action and a consciousness of one's intention are generally eliminated through a reduction of persons to the level of nonpersonal entities. In the second use of the organic metaphor, which I will call the broader or open-ended use, persons are understood to have consciousness, intentionality, and some degree of freedom. In these specific ways they are to be understood differently from (even though they are ontologically continuous with) other organisms such as plants and most forms of animal life. The category of the "system" or the "hierarchy" will be used to explain how various levels of organic life can be made compatible with a higher, more uniquely personal level in which freedom, intentionality, and consciousness control lower levels. I will argue that if this second use of the organic metaphor is developed in the direction of a nonreducible, basic concept of persons as agents, then the essential difference between conceiving of community as mutuality (persons in relation) or as organism tends to diminish, if not disappear entirely.

But even if the broader use of "organism" is developed, some crucial problems will still remain in the organic model as it is perceived from the perspective of the model of mutuality. These difficulties will center around the following issues:

1. Does an "organism" subsume persons in relation: is the relationship itself an organism greater than the individuals in relation? If so, what protects the uniqueness and individuality of the persons who enter into relation with each other (and not, as it were, into relation with something called "the relation")?

2. Is it necessary, in order to avoid a dualism between persons and the rest of nature, to resort to a form of panpsychism in which some kind of mentality is ascribed to all levels of reality? Can a theory of persons retain that which is unique to their level of being and at the same time not create an ontological dualism between them and the rest of nature?

3. Is there a way to avoid regarding the state as the organism to which all individual organs must ultimately be subject? Does the organic model have any internal checks against totalitarian notions of the state? If the state is an organism, how can persons not be seen as merely functional organs whose purpose is to serve it?

4. Does a consistently developed organic model have any room for an abiding, substantial self, or is it compelled logically to find its basic entities or selves at the microscopic level? If the latter is true, then how does the organic view avoid regarding personal selves as simply complex, not basic, unities built up out of more basic, and thus more authentic, more primordial entities?

5. Does the organic model have any room for or emphasis on the nurturing of intentions of living for others, or is it primarily concerned to encourage self-development and self-creation?

A full explication of the organic model will occur as we examine the various writers who have employed and developed it. As we begin our analysis of it, however, we need to note some of the general characteristics of viewing entities (large and small) as organisms. John Macmurray has, I believe, fairly summarized the essential elements in the organic category.[1] The underlying characteristic of an organism is its totality: it is to be taken as a unified whole which is not simply the sum of its parts but is itself a basic unity comprising and in an interdependent relationship with its parts. Beyond this, the organism has six basic traits. (1) It is alive, or grows over time, and its parts contribute to the growth process by becoming differentiated and coordinated. (2) The differentiation of the parts, their specific functionality, must not impair the unity of the totality or the organism taken as a whole— the differences must be complementary and harmonious. (3) The growth process in higher level organisms will combine reproduction with variation. There must be a balance between reproduction of a similar species with variation of particulars within the individuals of that species. (4) The unity of differences within the organism will most often be represented as a balance of harmony and expressed in aesthetic terms. (5) Becoming or process, rather than unchanging static completeness, is central to the organic understanding of growth. Organic life never "is" at any one moment. It is always becoming. (6) Organisms have something like a goal toward which they are directed (or in the case of higher organisms, toward which they seem to direct themselves). This has been called the teleological dimension of the organic model. Growth is not random but seems in some sense determined by a final end. One of the crucial questions facing the organic model is whether within its own terms it can satisfactorily distinguish between the kind of teleology appropriate to an acorn (which seems destined to become an oak) and the self-conscious, free self-direction of which persons seem capable. But clearly, the reference to some kind of telos or goal distinguishes the organic entity from the mechanical monad central to the atomistic model.

A seventh characteristic, not mentioned by Macmurray but certainly present in higher level organisms, is that of hierarchy. These organisms display a kind of structure in which higher levels subsume and control lower levels while remaining dependent upon and in constant interaction with them. This hierarchical structure or system can provide an opening for the presence in some kinds of organisms of a self-controlling dimension. It is through this opening that some contemporary philosophers of biology believe a link can be forged between the organic model and what we are calling the mutual/personal model which claims an important and irreducible distinction between the kind of free choices persons make and the kind of goal-directed behavior found in the lower level organisms.

Edmund Burke. As far back as Edmund Burke, who wrote in reaction to the excesses of the French Revolution, the significance of society as in some sense greater or larger than the individuals who comprise it has been asserted in social philosophy. Society was too large and complex to be treated, according to Burke, as a simple contract relationship between essentially atomistic individuals. "The nature of man is intricate; the objects of society are of the greatest possible complexity; and therefore no simple disposition or direction of power can be suitable either to man's nature, or to the quality of his affairs."[2] Because of the complexity of man's nature, Burke argued, we need to recognize in society the place of affection, and not just of rational will, and, consequently, the place of communities built upon ties of affection, custom, and habit. "We begin," he said, "our public affections in our families. No cold relation is a zealous citizen. We pass on to our neighborhoods, and our habitual provincial connections. These are inns and resting-places. Such divisions of our country as have been formed by habit ... were so many little images of the great country in which the heart found something which it could fill. *The love to the whole is not extinguished by this subordinate partiality.*"[3]

Burke is suggesting that human nature is not fulfilled simply in relations of cold rationality and calculation so essential to the atomistic/contractarian relation. There is something in the human heart and will which requires the inns and resting-places of affinity: the likeness of family, habit, and tradition. And these smaller communities are a necessary part of the larger community, the nation or commonwealth, which binds them together into a unified whole. It is natural, in this context, to resort to organic imagery. For what is more interrelated than an organism? There is a whole, the organism taken as a single entity, and there are parts, the organs, which have reciprocal relations both to the whole and to each other. Burke himself was interested in defending a social conservatism which would preserve the traditions and bonds that had been built up over centuries and which could withstand the rational assault of liberal philosophy which would tear them down in the name of individualism and freedom. He was not interested in developing a metaphysics of community.

G.W.F. HEGEL

A philosopher who did attempt a major metaphysical system built upon the notion of the organic whole was G.W.F. Hegel. It was Hegel, I believe, who gave the atomistic/mechanical view a profound metaphysical challenge. Although his student Marx was to attack that view primarily because of its devastating effects on the lives of those who were destroyed by those who thrived on it, Hegel provided the basic theoretical categories for the organic model as an alternative to the atomistic model.

Hegel departs from the atomistic model root and branch. His fundamental metaphysical premise is that reality is fulfilled only in and through the whole, not in and through the parts alone. The thrust of his entire philosophy is to explicate the way in which the Unity of the Whole is attained by the self-development of the Absolute. The Absolute, or Spirit, is the Whole of Reality. There is nothing outside of it: Hegel is so radical in this claim that he goes beyond classical rationalism and identifies the Whole with its parts, not statically but dynamically, through a time-process and the development of self-consciousness by the Whole in and through its historically continuous parts.

Hegel's stress on the unity of the Whole leads him to emphasize the interrelatedness of reality. It is not possible for one thing to stand in monadic isolation from other things. All things (events and objects) are part of the self-development of the Absolute's knowledge of itself as Absolute. In this respect Hegel stands diametrically opposed to any sort of ultimate dualism between kinds or levels of reality. In fact, in his theory of knowledge, Hegel assumes that to know something in the most complete way is to have that thing become part of the knower. That is why, ultimately, the Absolute must take each and every thing up into itself (without destroying its individuality in the process) through the movement Hegel calls 'aufhebung,' or transcending and taking up, preserving and annulling at the same time.

This notion of unity achieved through incorporation of many things into One determines Hegel's notion of freedom, and ultimately of the individual's relation to the state. If true unity can be found only when duality and opposition are overcome, then freedom can be achieved only when the free subject no longer has anything over-against it, opposing it. True freedom is the achievement of being in and for oneself. This can be realized only in and by the Absolute, but its constituent parts can realize their freedom to the degree that they give themselves fully to the Absolute. This is obviously a very different view of freedom than that found in the atomistic/contractarian philosophy. There, the ideal of freedom was doing as one pleased without interference from others. In Hegel, freedom means becoming one with others so that there is no opposition of will, and ultimately it means that "otherness" will disappear as all become one in the single One, the Absolute.

This notion of freedom leads Hegel to the view that only as one identifies himself with larger, more inclusive wholes does he gain in freedom. As long as he understands his freedom to consist in narrowing the range of his action so that he can do what he wants with the least amount of obstruction, he becomes, in fact, less free. If the unity of the Whole is the final fulfillment of each of the individuals which comprise it, then the achievement of being in and for oneself can occur only when one identifies oneself with the greatest possible whole. Only that which is Absolute, that which is the whole of all wholes, can be truly free because only it has nothing over-against it and thus can truly be in and for itself, since there is nothing else for it to be 'in' or 'for'.

On the basis of this logic, Hegel inevitably is led to extol the moral supremacy of the state over the individual. But it is only on an atomistic/mechanical level that we would view this supremacy as a diminution of freedom or as a loss of the individual. For Hegel it is a gain of freedom and the fulfillment of the individual because apart from the Whole the individual is nothing and freedom an illusion. It follows that the Absolute will be manifested in greater degree in the larger rather than the smaller Whole. Thus the state or the social community has a moral and metaphysical supremacy which the individual in isolation lacks. Morality reaches its culmination in the largest possible community.

We are here at the opposite end of the political spectrum from individualistic liberalism. Persons do not enter into a necessary evil through contract relations with other equally free individuals who also give up part of their freedom in order to gain the benefits of increased security. Rather, in Hegel they enter into a positive good through subsuming their individual morality under that of the community as a whole in order to gain greater freedom and fulfillment. The new notion of Hegel, as Charles Taylor puts it, "displaces the centre of gravity, as it were from the individual on to the community, which is seen as the locus of a life or subjectivity, of which the individuals are phases. The community is an embodiment of *Geist*, and a fuller, more substantial embodiment than the individual. . . . These ideas only appear mysterious because of the powerful hold on us of atomistic prejudices, which have been very important in modern political thought and culture."[4]

From the atomistic point of view, this understanding of the community as including the individual in the movement toward greater freedom must appear as the germ of totalitarianism, in which the individual becomes nothing more than a pawn of the state. But such a view misunderstands Hegel's claim. The state is not over-against the individual but is instead his fulfillment. The state is the "substance" of individuals, their very essence, their telos or final end. "Everything that a man is he owes to the state; only in it can he find his essence. All value that a man has, all spiritual reality, he has only through the state."[5]

It is precisely at this point that Hegel uses the imagery of the organism in a not fully successful attempt to save his view from being interpreted as totalitarian. Only on an atomistic view would one set up an opposition between state and individual, as end and means. In an organic model, "the state is not something abstract, standing over against the citizens; but rather *they are moments as in organic life*, where no member is end and none means . . . "[6] The metaphor of the organism is perfect for Hegel's purposes. The organism does not stand in opposition to its organs: it is what it is as a unitary whole only in and through its organs. And its organs do not see the organism as a barrier to their activity: it is only in and through their participation in the organism that they can function and have life at all. Apart from the organic whole, they are lifeless, functionless, isolated monads.

Hegel says in the *Logic*, "the limbs and organs, . . . of an organic body are merely parts of it: it is only in their unity that they are what they are, and they are unquestionably affected by that unity, as they also in turn affect it. These limbs and organs become mere parts, only when they pass under the hands of the anatomist, whose occupation, be it remembered, is not with the living body but with the corpse."[7] When Hegel discusses the state, it is usually with this explicit imagery of the organism in mind. The state is a self-reproducing organism marked especially by complexity of organization. He says of the state that "this organism is the development of the Idea to its differences and their objective actuality" and of its members as "functions and spheres of action."[8] These spheres of the state are not "independent, self-subsistent," but are rather "determined by and dependent on the aim of the whole," and in this sense the state has the same characteristic "as that in accordance with which the so-called 'parts' of an animal organism are not parts but members, moments in an organic whole, whose isolation and independence spell disease."[9] These parts of the state, he says on another occasion, "are organic moments in a whole."[10]

One important implication which Hegel drew from his understanding of the state as an organism was that the state could itself be treated as an individual. "The state is an individual, unique and exclusive, and therefore related to others."[11] The unity of the state is the unity of "a single self."[12] The importance of this implication is that while affirming the fulfillment of individuals who comprise the state, Hegel can also subsume their uniqueness by incorporating it into the single individual of the state itself. There is something in the organic model of relationship that permits the largest organism, in this case the state, to reduce the significance of its parts (while not denying its dependence on them) to a status of something other than basic or irreducible. If the state is itself an organic individual, then those individuals who comprise it cannot have the same degree of metaphysical primacy or authenticity that it has. This fact will lead us to question the ability of the organic model to account in the fullest possible way for personal uniqueness and the irreducibility of persons' relation to each other, and not simply their relation to a greater whole in which they are members or moments. It also indicates why this particular development of the organic model can lead to its own form of totalitarianism, despite Hegel's attempt to avoid it.

THE ORGANIC MODEL AND SOME SOCIOLOGISTS

Ferdinand Tönnies. Following Hegel, the organic metaphor came to dominate the work of some prominent sociologists who were beginning to stand alongside the social philosophers as analysts and evaluators of persons in community. The influence of the organic model of community today is due in large part to the work of these sociologists, who helped fix the metaphor in the scientific disciplines and extend it to the popular mind.

No one's work stands out more clearly in this regard than that of Ferdinand Tönnies, whose analysis of the Gesellschaft, or atomistic/contractual society, we had occasion to examine in our introduction to that model of community. Tönnies' massive study *Community and Society*, or *Gemeinschaft und Gesellschaft*, was not only a critique of the impersonal, rational, atomistic relations of the Gesellschaft society, but was, more importantly perhaps, a defense of the Gemeinschaft community. And the metaphor of organism determines his understanding of that community in a thorough and decisive way. The contrast between the Gesellschaft and the Gemeinschaft is clearly drawn by Tönnies as a contrast between a mechanical structure and an organic life. "Gemeinschaft should be understood as a living organism, Gesellschaft as a mechanical aggregate and artifact."[13]

Like Hegel, Tönnies defines the organic community as that which is "related to the totality of reality and defined in its nature and movements by this totality."[14] The mechanical form of analysis is simply incompetent to grasp this organic whole. "The tendencies and inevitableness of organic growth and decay cannot be understood through mechanical means. In the organic world the concept itself is a living reality, changing and developing as does the idea of the individual being."[15] This is especially true of human relationships which are "living organisms."[16]

Tönnies believes that the organic relation between persons is more basic and ultimately more natural than the artificial constructs of the Gesellschaft society. Gemeinschaft is present from birth: it is "all intimate, private, and exclusive living together."[17] Gesellschaft, on the other hand, is "public life—it is the world itself," and one moves out from the natural bonds of Gemeinschaft, experienced first in the family, into Gesellschaft, "as one goes into a strange country."[18] This kind of imagery certainly suggests the unnaturalness of the mechanical society. Gemeinschaft has tradition, history, and nature on its side. Gesellschaft is the product of the modern age. It has arrived with urbanization and rationality. It marks the individual's break from nature and organic ties. Tönnies is, nevertheless, convinced that although it is no longer the dominant form of association for modern persons, only Gemeinschaft "is the lasting and genuine form of living together."[19]

Tönnies calls Gemeinschaft the natural form of association because it represents "a perfect unity of human wills as an original or natural condition," the common root of which is (as he says in strongly biological imagery) "the coherence of vegetative life through birth and the fact that human wills . . . remain linked to each other by parental descent and by sex."[20] In fact, in the natural, biological relations of parent to child, husband to wife, and brothers to sisters, we find "the embryo of Gemeinschaft."[21] From this embryo develop the later forms of Gemeinschaft: of locality, and of mind, the latter representing for Tönnies "the truly human and supreme form of community,"[22] also called friendship. Friendship has to some extent transcended kinship and neighborhood, and comes into being because of "similarity of work and intellectual attitude."[23] This unity creates a common faith or spiritual bond, and includes the capacity for free choice. (In this sense, Tönnies admits, friendship goes beyond the level of lower organic life wherein such freedom is not normally found.)

At the heart of the Gemeinschaft community is "a special social force" or "reciprocal, binding sentiment" called understanding or sympathy, "which keeps human beings together as members of a totality."[24] This "love" or "concord," as Tönnies also calls it, is both a natural and a willed sense of organic unity with others. It precedes and is more lasting than the kind of unity established by rational calculation based on utilitarian considerations as common to the atomistic, mechanical society so clearly contrasted by Tönnies to Gemeinschaft.

The community established by concord or common will takes on a life of its own and exists in "the endless community of life of its members."[25] It goes back to the "original unity of natural wills" called understanding. Persons who live in such a community are living in "a product of nature," not a product of artifice. They experience its power in their laws, folkways, and mores, and through these they know that the significance of the community has "absolute and eternal validity for its members."[26] They know the community's will is "prior to all individual spheres of will and as involving all of them. Thus, freedom and property of men exist only as modifications of the freedom and property of the commonwealth."[27] Tönnies is here echoing the Hegelian notion that the organic whole must have a priority over (even while it is the fulfillment of) its individual organs or parts.

What needs to be stressed is that Tönnies, like Hegel, believes that only through some such organic metaphor is the monadic independence and ultimate isolation of the atomistic association to be overcome. In the Gesellschaft, persons "are essentially separated in spite of all unifying factors."[28] There is no natural unity of wills: "here everybody is by himself and isolated, and there exists a condition of tension against all others."[29] But in the Gemeinschaft, conceived as a living organism, "the forms of will ... stand in such an organic relation to another that there always exists before and beyond them a totality which expresses itself in them and has a relation to them; the relation between the whole and the parts is primary, the one from which all others must be derived."[30] The relationship between persons in the Gemeinschaft can be understood "only in terms of a whole that is innate in all of them."[31] Only through such an understanding can we grasp the unity of persons, even while each one pursues his own interests. The key to such an understanding is precisely that of an individual organ's contribution to the organic whole. "As long as they [persons] can still be considered as a unity, even exchange between them is only a manifestation of their functions, i.e., *of their existence as organic modifications* [emphasis mine], and of their natural unity."[32]

In the end, Tönnies reminds us of no one so much as of Edmund Burke. Both were conservatives, lamenting the destruction of tradition and "natural" bonds which had held persons together in the period before the rise of liberal, rational, social philosophy. It is not simply coincidental that Tönnies finds the models for Gemeinschaft in family life, rural village life, and town life, and the models for Gesellschaft in the later development of city life, national life, and cosmopolitan life. In all these latter forms of association, something of the natural unities of relationship has been lost, even while some advances have been made through exploitation of rational, as opposed to natural, will.

The one dimension of personal relationship that Tönnies does not discuss is that of mutuality. That is, he does not consider the possibility that the deepest forms of human relationship may not be based on kinship, proximity, or similar interests, but may, instead, be based on a love for the other in his or her otherness, as a stranger or alien to one's own immediate interests. It is not always the case that the bonds of love are woven the tightest between organically related persons. There are many occasions when love must make an effort to leap beyond the barriers of biological or organic relations in order to embrace those who are, from the organic point of view, foreigners and strangers: who share little "naturally" with one but who, in the very fact of their otherness, call forth a desire for mutuality. The difficulty with Tönnies' analysis of human community through the organic metaphor is that it places a premium on factors over which the individual has little intentional control. In Tönnies' Gemeinschaft one can almost feel the walls of natural distinctions and boundaries closing in. Unless there is either a much broader use for the organic metaphor or a different but inclusive metaphor of mutuality, the bonds of relationship within the Gemeinschaft threaten to become too narrow, too biological, to account adequately for that dimension of human intentionality and freedom which strains to build upon but go beyond the "natural" and the organic.

Charles H. Cooley. Shortly after the turn of the century an American sociologist, Charles H. Cooley, wrote a number of works which gave great prominence to the organic model for understanding human community, anticipating what contemporary sociologists call functionalism: that is, the theory that assumes that the parts of a society are like the functional parts of an organism. In his book *Social Process*, Cooley stated that "if we take society to include the whole of human life, this may be truly said to be organic, in the sense that influences may be and are transmitted from one part to another part, so that all parts are bound together into an interdependent whole."[33]

Cooley was quite explicit that this organic interdependence meant that individual persons "may be regarded, without the slightest strain on the facts, as organs of the whole, growing and functioning under particular conditions, according to the adaptive process.... The total life being unified by interaction, each phase of it must be and is, in some degree, an expression of the whole system."[34]

Like Hegel, Cooley believed that one must start with the primacy of the whole: "the real thing is a total organic process not separable into parts."[35] From this starting-point the sociologist could move to an acceptance of the principle that "the relation between society and the individual [is] an organic relation. That is, we see that the individual is not separable from the human whole, but a living member of it, deriving his life from the whole through social and hereditary transmission as truly as if men were literally one body."[36] At the same time, and in accord with the Hegelian principle that parts and whole are reciprocal in influence, Cooley stated that "the social whole is in some degree dependent upon each individual, because each contributes something to the common life that no one else can contribute."[37] The conclusion to which the sociologist is then driven is that in society we have "in a broad sense of the word, an 'organism' or living whole made up of differentiated members, each of which has a special function."[38]

In his discussion of what he called "primary groups" or intimate face-to-face associations, Cooley said that in addition to helping shape the social nature and ideals of individuals, these groups also represented "a certain fusion of individualities in a common whole, so that one's very self... is the common life and purpose of the group."[39] While it is not clear that Cooley had ever read Hegel, the Hegelian sense of the fulfillment of individuals in a greater whole is echoed by Cooley's reference to a sense of "we" as the sense of social wholeness: "it involves the sort of sympathy and mutual identification for which 'we' is the natural expression. One lives in the feeling of the whole and finds the chief aims of his will in that feeling."[40]

Faithfully reflecting Macmurray's characterization of the organism, Cooley believes that the wholeness of the primary group provides for differentiation and competition among the parts, provided that they do not work against the unity of the whole. The unity of the primary group "is always a differentiated and usually a competitive unity, admitting of self-assertion and various appropriate passions; but these... are socialized by sympathy and come, or tend to come, under the discipline of a common spirit."[41] Human nature, in fact, cannot be fulfilled except in and through these primary group relationships. "In these, everywhere, human nature comes into existence. Man does not have it at birth; he cannot acquire it except through fellowship, and it decays in isolation."[42] The ideal for individuals is to live in a "moral whole or community wherein individual minds are merged and the higher capacities of the members find total and adequate expression."[43]

Despite his frequent talk of merging the individual into the social whole, Cooley resisted a complete reduction of persons to the level of nonpersonal organisms. Opposed to individualism, Cooley stressed that the ideal society "must be an organic whole"[44] in order to provide an ideal beyond that of individual self-interest. He did not want to sacrifice what Guy Swanson has called "the sturdy integrity" of persons.[45] But the question remains whether his emphasis upon organic organization ("a system of co-ordinated activities fitted to the conditions"[46]) is adequate to an understanding of persons who have more than functional relations to each other. If persons are truly, as Cooley said, one body, then the independence which persons require who freely seek relation with each other—not simply in order to find support for their own ends, or for functional cooperation in a common task, but for its own sake—may not be fully compatible with an organic model. Like Tönnies, Cooley did not explore all the ramifications of his organic imagery as it might affect the kind of personal relations which go beyond those of "natural" feelings of sympathy, kinship, or affection, or those of social and functional cooperation. The dangers of applying a model which is equally at home in the nonpersonal world of plants and animals, as surely the common use of "organism" would be, are not discussed or examined.

R.M. MacIver. A contemporary of Cooley, R. M. MacIver, did attempt to analyze the organic model for sociology and made some interesting suggestions about its potential weaknesses. In his study *Community*, MacIver defined a community as "the common living of social beings"[47] and further asserted that there "are no individuals who are not social individuals, and society is nothing more than individuals associated and organised."[48] Nevertheless, MacIver warns, the social relations between individuals must not themselves be taken to exist "somehow outside the beings they bind together, as railway-couplings are outside the carriage they connect."[49] If we do think in this way, then we are led erroneously to believe that society is greater than the sum of its parts and in some way independent of its parts. Now neither Hegel, Tönnies, or Cooley made the second of these two errors, but MacIver suggests both are endemic to the organic analogy for society.

MacIver acknowledges that when people first came to reflect on community life, "it was very natural" that they should have been "struck by certain features of it wherein it resembled the life of an individual animal or organism, the persistence of the whole though members pass away, the division of function between the members serving the welfare of the whole, the dependence of every member on the 'corporate' unity of the whole. From the observance of these and other resemblances . . . it was only a step to the 'explanation' of society in terms of an organism, and the establishment of a complete and intricate analogy."[50]

While not denying some resemblance, MacIver denies that society is an organism in the strict sense. The one essential difference between a community and an organism is that an organism is or has "a single centre, a unity of life, a purpose or a consciousness which is no purpose or consciousness of the several parts but only of the whole."[51] But a human community, composed of individual persons, "consists of myriad centres of life and consciousness, of true autonomous individuals who are merged in no such corporate unity, whose purposes are lost in no such corporate purpose. . . . A community does not act in unity like an organism, or maintain itself like an organism, or grow like an organism, or reproduce like an organism, or die like an organism. The central difference renders the whole analogy vain."[52]

MacIver notes that we do not normally include consciousness in the case of animal organisms or cells. And it is precisely because "it is exceedingly difficult to speak of cells or organs as having purposes" that the analogy between an organism and a human community fails to convince. A community is "a unity of self-determining members seeking in a common life the same kind of fulfillment."[53] If we cannot speak of cells, or of any kind of less-than-personal life as self-determining, then we cannot employ the organic model for human community. We will return in our discussion of Macmurray to the strength of MacIver's argument, but its significance at this point is twofold. It marks from within the sociological tradition a warning against too hasty a use of the organic metaphor and it throws down a challenge (which will be taken up by Whitehead and a number of biologists influenced by him) to find a way of doing precisely what MacIver says cannot be done: namely, to attribute self-determination and consciousness to even the "lowest" levels of nature. Through panpsychism the Whiteheadian process view of organism will attempt to undercut MacIver's primary objection to the extension of the organic model to all of reality, including personal community.

MacIver insisted that "no metaphor derived from any other form of unity can describe for us the unity of society."[54] Community "can be understood only by itself."[55] But this claim will be challenged on the grounds that it is potentially or actually dualistic: it sets up levels of reality that are not continuous with each other and thus introduces metaphysical bifurcations and dichotomies into what should be a continuous whole. The response to the challenge to MacIver, a response which I believe is to be found in the systems theory and the hierarchical model as well as in Macmurray's work, will have to show both that MacIver is essentially right in declaring that human community is not to be understood simply or exhaustively through an analogy drawn from the nonpersonal level of reality, and that the understanding of human community is not dualistic or discontinuous with the other levels of existence.

The essential question will become whether or not the organic metaphor is broad enough to encompass what MacIver calls a single centre or a self-determining consciousness which is more than, or in some way different from, the essential constitution of the cells of a plant or even of an animal. If fascination with the organic model leads to the reduction of persons and of persons in community to the level of plants and animals, then something essential to what it means to be human has been removed.

In addition, if the organic metaphor is read in a narrow or restricted way, persons may have to be regarded as essentially living *only* in a functional or cooperative relation to each other. While it is true that we do play important roles for each other in social life, the question is whether there are forms of relationship which are *more than* functional and cooperative. Are there occasions when we reach out to others, not simply to cooperate with them in the performance of a common task or because we share some "natural" affinity, but because we, of all the creatures that exist, have the capacity and sometimes the intention to embrace another simply because he or she is there as 'other'? Is the kind of mutuality in which two or more persons enjoy each other's friendship simply for its own sake capable of being embraced within an organic model? As long as the model relies primarily on notions of functionality and natural ties, it can provide the infrastructure or condition for mutuality but not its substance.

KARL MARX'S VISION OF COMMUNITY

There is no doubt that the appeal to the thought of Karl Marx underlies many visions of community that are either contemplated or are actually being implemented by thousands of people in the world today. Whether the visions are realistic or the implementations faithful to Marx himself is not something we can pursue in great detail here. What we are interested in discovering is what place Marx has in his model of community for relationships of love and mutuality, and whether the organic framework within which he placed these relationships is completely adequate in explaining them. If the thought of Marx is to be appealed to by those who build a more human community, including those who believe that Christian insight can complement the visions of orthodox Marxists, then his thought needs to be explored for its explicit and implicit understanding of what a human community is and could be.

There seems little doubt that Marx did indeed work with a concept of social reality that was intrinsically organic. Bertell Ollman and Melvin Rader have probably done more than any other scholars of our time to justify the claim that Marx employed an organic model for the social order (and perhaps even for reality as a whole—though Marx was notoriously uninterested in the speculative task of trying to develop a full metaphysics). Ollman calls Marx's philosophy one of "internal relations,"[56] and Rader argues that Marx employed an "organic totality" model for understanding society.[57]

Ollman makes his case for the internal relations model in Marx by contrasting it specifically to the mechanical or atomistic/contractarian model we examined in the previous chapter. This latter model leads the scientist, having started with a belief that all entities are logically independent of one another, to explain their interaction through a strict use of the cause-effect relationship. One entity will always precede and thus cause effects upon or in relation to other entities. This leads inevitably to economic or social determinism since there is no reciprocal relation between the entities.

Both Rader and Ollman believe Marx is saved from the deterministic implications of a base-superstructure model (one which holds that culture and other creations of human action are causally determined by more basic economic factors) by his use of an organic, reciprocal, and hierarchical model of "inner-relation." Marx, according to Ollman, sees "all conjunction as organic, intrinsic to the social units with which he is concerned and part of the nature of each. . . . On this view, interaction is, properly speaking, *inner*action (it is 'inner connections' which he claims to study)."[58] When discussing the relation between the elements of the economic order, Marx says that "mutual interaction takes place between" them. "Such is the case with every organic body."[59] No strict cause and effect relation is possible here since relations are internal to each other: when a relationship alters, all the factors in the relationship also alter.

Only an organic model which assumes a unified totality in which the parts are internally related to each other and to the whole, is adequate to grasp Marx's insight. Ollman is quite explicit about the organic nature of Marx's thought. In outlining this philosophy of internal relations in Marx, Ollman echoes many of the characteristics of the organism with which we began this chapter. He says: "Marx's subject matter comprises an organic whole; the various factors he treats are facets of this whole; internal relations exist between all such factors; reciprocal effect predominates and has logical priority over causality; . . . the concepts Marx uses to refer to factors convey their internal relations."[60] Ollman even extends his claim to Marx's view of reality as a whole, not just to the social order.

This holistic view means that Marx assumes an identity between entities before he looks at their differences. Identity "is the relation between mutually dependent aspects of a whole before differences are noted."[61] The whole is the "structured interdependence of its relational parts—the interacting events, processes and conditions of the real world—as observed from any major part."[62] This view is fully faithful to the thought of Hegel, who perhaps had more influence on Marx than any other single thinker. When Ollman claims, on behalf of Marx, that "only the procedure that moves from the whole to the part, only the prior acceptance of the identity of each part in the whole, permits adequate reflection on the complex changes and interaction that constitute the core qualities of the real world,"[63] he is implicitly linking Marx and Hegel in an identical understanding. "Marx never wavered from the relational conception bequeathed to him by Hegel."[64] It could even be argued that Marx and Hegel take the latter's famous notion of "aufgehoben" (to annul and preserve at the same time) and give it an organic meaning. For both, it seems to mean any kind of process by which a higher quality supersedes a lower by transforming its nature and incorporating it in a higher level of development. Both "thought that action of this sort is the essence of organic development, applying to both individuals and societies. To this extent they agree."[65]

Functionality. One of the most important characteristics of the organic whole in Marx is the functionality of its parts. That is, each part has significance and individuality to the degree that it functions in a particular way within and for the whole. The philosophy of internal relations holds that the identity or difference between the parts depends on their *functional* similarity or diversity. "Through its internal ties to everything else, each factor is everything else viewed from this particular angle, and what applies to them necessarily applies to it, taken in this broad sense. Thus, each factor has—in theory—the potential to take the names of others (of whatever applies to them) when it functions as they do . . . "[66] This means that it is only in practice, in use, that differences between individual entities become important. That which ultimately distinguishes one individual from another within a philosophy of internal relations is the particular function it performs within a specific context. When the context changes, the self-identity, the differentia, of the individual also changes. Whether this is enough of a sense of individuality to ground a mutual relation between two abiding, distinct persons will have to be examined.

The reciprocal action of the individual parts determines, in any given context, what function each is playing. And it is only an organic metaphor which can capture this kind of reciprocity and interaction. Engels explicitly connects this kind of reciprocal action with Hegel and says that it is what he and Marx are calling the "organic body."[67] In Ollman's paraphrase, "to explain change in the physical world by referring to the reciprocal action of its parts is said to be the same thing as presenting the world as an organic body."[68]

While rejecting what he believes are Ollman's somewhat excessive claims for the theory of internal relations (he does not believe, for instance, that Marx applied this to the whole of reality),[69] Melvin Rader essentially supports the view that Marx worked primarily within the context of an organic model of society. Like the organism outlined in Macmurray's characterization, Rader's "organic totality" is a differentiated and dynamic structure rather than a static unity, or at the opposite extreme, "a mere heap or collection."[70] The organism is " 'well-balanced' or in 'dynamic equilibrium' if it has not only achieved homeostasis but has established a *modus vivendi* between its inner play of forces and its external environment. In this inward adjustment and outward adaptation it is continually in the process of development. This is true of organisms at every level, whether plants, animals, or human mind-bodies; and if 'organism' is extended to include societies, the organic life-process applies to 'social organisms' too."[71]

While admitting that Marx's use of the organic model is less explicit than his use of a base-superstructure model (which is exploited by later Marxists to defend a strict causal determinism of economic forces), Rader believes that the organic totality model does more justice to Marx's explanation of historical development than any other model. Nevertheless, he admits that Marx often used the base-superstructure model alongside and in contradiction to the more inclusive organic model.[72]

Hierarchy. Placing the notion of a hierarchy (the notion of a unified whole in which the 'higher' elements control the lower but without disturbing the unity of the whole) at the heart of the organic model, Rader can claim that the model enabled Marx to stress both the interdependence of the factors in society and the fact that some factors, on occasion, play a more important role than others. The organic whole remains fairly constant while the hierarchical structure enables change with variation to take place within it. The reliance upon the fundamental image of society as an organism is carefully detailed by Rader, echoing the similar argument in Ollman. For example, in the Preface to the first edition of *Capital*, Marx says that "the present society is no solid crystal, but an organism capable of change, and it is constantly changing."[73] In the Afterword to the second edition he quotes, apparently with approval, a reviewer's remark that "the scientific value of such an inquiry lies in the disclosing of the special laws that regulate the origin, existence, development, and death of a given social organism and its replacement by another and higher one."[74] And, as Rader notes, the book abounds in organic metaphors, such as "cell-forms" of the economic structure, the "metabolism" of the work process, and the growth of a social embryo in the "womb" of the old social order.[75] He even goes so far as to suggest that Marx's organic model of society, with respect to the way in which "wholes exercise a configuration control over sub-wholes, and sub-wholes function (a) in sub-ordination to their controlling agency, (b) in supraordination to their own parts, and (c) in co-ordination with other parts on the same level as themselves,"[76] is identical to the organic model of a nervous system, thereby eliminating any fundamental distinction between these levels of reality. Organic hierarchy "operates with respect to both biological and social organisms, whether it be the action of a nervous system or a complex socio-economic order."[77]

Perhaps the most explicit statement by Marx on society as an organism comes from the *Grundrisse*:

> "While in the completed bourgeois system every economic relation presupposes every other in its bourgeois economic form, and everything posited is thus also a pre-supposition, this is the case with every organic system. This organic system itself, as a totality, has its pre-suppositions, and its development to its totality consists precisely in subordinating all elements of society to itself, or in creating out of it the organs which it still lacks. This is historically how it becomes a totality."[78]

This means that for Marx a society is, in Rader's words, "a total functional integration in which each element is what it is because of its relations to the other elements and to the whole.... The interdependence of part and part, and part and whole, is the very mark of an organism."[79] While it was certainly not part of Marx's intention, this understanding of society could lead (and some would argue has led in many contemporary communist states) to a totalitarian view of society in which the individual has no significance other than that assigned to him by the state. If one pushes the notion of society as an organism too far, the organic whole can take on a personality of its own to which all its subsidiary parts must be subservient. While Marx, in his development of the notion of self-realization (as we shall see) tried to guard against this danger, it is one that emerges almost necessarily when the logical implications of an organic model are developed.

This was precisely MacIver's point: that if the organic whole is treated as an individual, having a substantial identity similar to that of the individual persons who comprise it, then, because it is larger, stronger, and more enduring than any one person or any group of persons, it can command their subservience. It is not simply coincidental that in many Marxist societies today, the state has practiced totalitarianism and justified it on the grounds that it has a right (both moral and theoretical) to demand the sacrifice of the individual to the needs of "the society" as manifested in the state. The danger of functionalism is that if it treats individuals solely in terms of their functionality, then they become secondary to that which they are serving as functions. When that happens, and when the state determines that they are no longer serving a useful function, they have no independent worth, no non-functional integrity, on which to fall back. They become merely replaceable organs within a body which can go on functioning as long as new organs replace the old. As organs (and nothing more), the old organs, once removed from their sphere of productivity, are useless, meaningless, and worthless.

Another very important consequence of this functional interdependence is the elimination of any kind of dualism between the various parts of nature. The relations between various levels of nature are simply the relations between the various levels or structures of a single, unitary organism. "Marx thinks," according to Rader, "in terms of wider and wider structures of organic wholeness. The psycho-physical individual is an organic structure, the society of which he is an organic member is a wider structure, [and] nature of which mankind and its social formations are organic parts is a still wider structure."[80]

Teleology. Another crucial feature of an organic model is its emphasis on the teleology of the organism and its parts. In this context, teleology simply means that the organism does not behave randomly nor are its parts (or organs) randomly in relation to each other. There seems to be in the organism a goal, telos, or end for which it exists and toward which its parts are directed. In his recent study of Marx, Allen Wood fastens upon the teleological dimensions in his thought and interprets them in a decidedly organic way. He defines teleological explanations as those which are connected with "goal-directed systems.... We explain some element or aspect of such a system teleologically when we show how it manifests or contributes to the persistent tendencies which characterize the system, and provide reasons for thinking that this element or aspect exists *because* it manifests or contributes to those tendencies."[81] What is most significant about this understanding of teleology (for Wood) is that it need not refer to the intentions of human beings or superhuman agents. It is an explanation drawn essentially from living organisms. Wood argues that Marx's historical materialism relies precisely upon this latter kind of teleological explanation, by showing how social relations "manifest or contribute to" a community's tendency "to make efficient use of its productive powers."[82]

Even more significantly, Wood argues, Marx extends his use of the organic, teleological form of explanation to his understanding of the world. "For Marx the world is a system of organically interconnected processes characterized by inherent tendencies to development, and subject periodically to radical changes in organic structure."[83] The best way to understand this world is through dialectical theory, "which views its subject matter organically, traces the hierarchical structure of its subject matter through the stages of its concreteness and explains the systematic changes in this structure by the development tendencies inherent in it."[84] The dialectical relationship between the parts of the organic whole avoids the problem of determinism in a linear fashion, and thus bypasses or at least exists alongside a strict causal model of base-superstructure.

If Wood is correct, and his interpretation is certainly consistent with the organic totality model of Rader and the internal relations model of Ollman, then Marx would be committed to viewing change, including that brought about by human beings, as controlled in some sense by a final end which may or may not reside in the self-conscious choices of human agents. If Marx applies his organic model in a way which eliminates the distinction between persons and lower levels of organic life, then it would be hard for him to maintain that persons contribute to organic processes by free acts which cannot be fully explained in terms of the kind of organic reciprocity which is equally at home in the processes of a biological cell. If Marx does want to insist that persons make some kind of unique contribution to history, a contribution not *completely* determined by interaction with all the other elements of reality, then he must appeal in some way to a model which goes beyond the narrow or restricted understanding of the organism. We shall see whether in fact he is able to do this and to justify his belief in personal freedom.

While sharing much in common with Hegel, Marx does not hold, as the former did, that the present development of the organism of the state is the highest expression of "Spirit" or Reason to date. Instead, Marx uses the organic metaphor to claim that the present state of society is "diseased." There is, in capitalistic society, a disunity which is threatening the health of the organism as a whole. It is a disunity marked by contradictions that ultimately endanger the unity of the whole social organism, and in particular of the human persons who constitute its most important organs. One could argue that the whole burden of Marx's work is to diagnose the pathology of the unhealthy social organism and prescribe a remedy in terms of revolutionary praxis aimed at removing its alienating conditions.

One of the reasons that Marx departed from Hegel in viewing the social organism as diseased, as something other than the fullest embodiment of Spirit in history, is that Marx rejected Hegel's interpretation of Spirit's march through history as essentially a conceptual one. He wanted to turn Hegel on his head and to see the development of history as the fulfillment of material needs, especially those of human beings trying to fulfill what he called their "species being." This leads Marx to his specific understanding of persons and of the goal or telos of their behavior.

Social Being. True to organic imagery, Marx was unalterably opposed to an atomistic understanding of human beings. All his life he protested against the "isolation of the individual, ... the dissolution of mankind into monads, ... the world of atoms."[85] Instead, persons must be seen always in their relations to others. Marx goes so far as to say that "the human essence is no abstraction inherent in each single individual. In its reality it is the ensemble of the social relations."[86] If this is taken literally, then a person is not "an" entity, but a relation, or more accurately, a whole set of relations. This is different from saying that a person is someone who enters into relationship. If Ollman and Rader are correct, then Marx meant literally to say that persons are only relations viewed from a certain perspective and within a certain context.

By "activating their own essence," Marx insists in his commentary on James Mill, persons create a human community, which Marx calls "their social being." [87] This community is not outside or over-against the individual but is "the nature of each individual, his own activity, his own life, his own enjoyment, his own wealth... Men, not in the abstract, but as real, living, particular individuals, *are* this nature. It is, therefore as they are."[88] In the *1844 Manuscripts*, Marx reiterates his belief in the social nature of human beings. Communism is described there as "the complete return of man to himself as a social (i.e. human) being... my *own* existence *is* social activity, and therefore that which I make of myself, I make of myself for society and with the consciousness of myself as a social being."[89] With the ending of alienation, man can return to his true social being. Only then will society cease being an abstraction over-against the individual and become instead the fulfillment of his nature. "The individual *is the social being*. His life, even if it may not appear in the direct form of a *communal* life in association with others—is therefore an expression and confirmation of social life."[90]

Marx's stress on the social nature of human beings does not detract from his equally strong stress on the continuity between human and nonhuman being. Nature is not dualistically split, for Marx, between radically different levels such as human and less-than-human. This at least would have to be the logical implication of a fully worked out philosophy of internal relations or organic totality, since any sharp bifurcations in reality would sever the identity of the parts and the unity of the whole. Engels expresses this belief in the continuity of nature when he says that "the science of the most general laws of all motion... must be valid just as much for motion in nature and human history as for the motion of thought."[91] In another context, Marx calls man "a natural object, a thing, although a living conscious thing."[92]

What we need to explore is the degree to which Marx considered the significance of being a "living conscious thing" as taking the person beyond strictly organic categories of explanation. If the organic totality category is absolutely determinative of and applied in a rigorously consistent way to Marx's view of human nature, then one would have to conclude that Marx has little basis on which to claim that persons occupy not only an organic level of reality but a superorganic one as well. In the end, I believe, the evidence will show that Marx was ambivalent and perhaps inconsistent on this score inasmuch as he did, in fact say things about the relations between persons that do not, strictly speaking, fit within the organic totality or internal relations model.

If man's social nature is nothing more than his organic interdependence with other persons and the rest of nature, then obviously sociality is not unique to persons. The cells in one's body would have the same kind of sociality (as Rader implicitly suggests when he claims that the organic model of the nervous system is identical to the organic model of a complex socio-economic system). If Ollman's theory of internal relations is pressed hard enough, the relations of persons to each other within the social order are simply the relations of organs distinguished from each other solely by the particular function each plays within that specific context, but ultimately they are identical with each other. If Wood's analysis of Marx's use of teleological explanation is correct, then persons have no more control over their destiny than an acorn has over its eventually becoming an oak tree. If this narrow reading of the organic model is truly Marx's, then the great advance that the organic model has made over the atomistic model will be limited to seeing interdependent relations established between elements of reality, and will not extend to seeing persons as somehow more than functionally cooperative organs participating in a greater whole.

Eugene Kamenka, a well-established scholar of Marx's thought, has argued that Marx, like Hegel, ultimately winds up sacrificing the uniqueness and individuality of persons within the whole of organic society. He accepts the claim that Marx employed an organic framework of explanation within which all changes are merely the "interaction of the minor systems within the whole."[93] While rejecting Hegel's absorption of all elements into *Geist*, Marx winds up, in effect, by absorbing all elements into a single, completely self-sufficient organic totality, or what Kamenka calls a deterministic monism which is materialist rather than idealist.

Freedom and Individuality. Like Hegel, Marx believes that genuine freedom means total *self*-determination. "To be free is to be determined by one's own nature. To be unfree is to be determined from without."[94] But the only thing that can be completely free, consistent with this definition, is a single whole which has nothing outside it and which contains everything within itself. This is Hegel's *Geist* and it is also, according to Kamenka, Marx's single Man, not individual men but one all-embracing Man. "It is no accident that Marx is forced to take all social institutions, even non-human objects, into man himself, forced to reconcile Subject and Object by obliterating the distinction between them . . . In the name of . . . the continuity of human and non-human events, Marx has reduced everything to Man."[95]

Self-determination ultimately leads to the disappearance not only of conflict but of the very differences between "one man and another."[96] Kamenka must be logically correct if one follows the argument of Ollman regarding the identity of the parts in a philosophy of internal relations to its logical conclusion. And Kamenka is correct as well in noting that this conclusion follows from a narrow organic model which is consistently elaborated.

And yet, Kamenka's argument fails to do justice to another, obviously inconsistent, set of claims Marx makes about individual persons. By stressing the notion of freedom as self-determination, Marx, for the most part, has little place for an act in which one individual gives himself up or lives for another individual. Istvan Meszaros, in his influential study of Marx's theory of alienation, has pointed out that for Marx "nothing is worthy of moral approval unless it helps the realization of human life-activity as internal need."[97] What this means specifically is that individual fulfilllment will consist in the "self-determined and externally unhindered exercise of human powers."[98] This means, at least in one sense, that true human freedom (an internal need) is the *independence* of one person from another, and in another sense the *use* of relations with other persons in the service of individual self-fulfillment. As Marx says, "A *being* only considers himself independent when he stands on his own feet; and he only stands on his own feet when he owes his *existence* to himself. A man who lives by the grace of another regards himself as a dependent being."[99]

This kind of language does not fit easily into a fully organic framework in which the mutual interdependence of all individuals is the essential characteristic, or into an internal relations theory in which each part is functionally *identical* to the others. Nor does it fit into Kamenka's claim that if Marx were perfectly faithful to his organic model, he would have to reduce all men to one Man. But it is consistent, I think, with Marx's stress on *cooperation* between individuals within the social order. What is often overlooked in the attention given to Marx's emphasis on sociality or man's social being is that this emphasis really rests on the necessity of cooperation in the pursuit of *individual ends*. What this means is that individuals pursue in practice in a cooperative manner ends which they have previously and to some extent privately determined for themselves. Marx does not rule out the possibility that these individual ends can include a primary concern for the welfare of the other person but neither does he explicitly affirm this concern or give it any kind of ontological priority or status. Obviously, individual ends that are most likely to be achieved with the cooperation of others will be most successful and therefore, ideally, most likely to be chosen by individuals. The social nature of human persons resides primarily in the fact that if they are wise they will choose their ends so as to maximize social cooperation in their accomplishment. But this kind of functional cooperation between individuals is not the same as their living for each other in mutual love. It is only on rare occasions that Marx rises above the notion of cooperation in order to hint at a kind of relationship which is based on the genuine enjoyment of others for their own sake, and not simply on the way in which they can function to increase one's own enjoyment or self-determination.

Whenever Marx appeals to cooperation between individuals as illustrative of their social being, it almost always means functional cooperation. That is, two or more individuals function for each other in such a way that the needs of each are fulfilled. It is far more efficient for a group of persons to act together to build a ship than it is for each to try to do it alone. Now, in one sense this is a social act and expresses the social nature of persons. But in another sense it is an act in which the worth or meaning of the persons involved depends almost entirely upon their functionality, upon their productivity or effective contribution to the work at hand. In such a cooperative endeavor there need never occur any kind of relationship among the workers which transcends functionality. It is interesting to note that Marx never discusses at any length the existence or place of communities based upon the desire of persons to be together with others regardless of whether each is contributing to a common task. The stress upon functional cooperation is, ultimately, a form of individualism because it presupposes that persons cooperate in order to realize more effectively individual and private ends, not to enjoy the presence of other persons for its own sake or to serve their needs simply because they are needy.

This reliance upon a residual kind of individualism (understood as being realized only in relation to others) comes out particularly in Marx's tendency to define "social," as in *The German Ideology*, as the "cooperation of several individuals, no matter under what conditions, in what manner, and to what ends."[100] People cooperate, it seems, because they need each other for individual fulfillment, often simply at a biological level. People live in relationship to each other because "their needs—therefore their nature—and the manner of satisfying them creates between them reciprocal links (sexual relations, exchange, division of labor)." [101] It is particularly revealing that Ollman, in discussing this aspect of Marx's thought, insists that sociality is essentially based on one's need for others "and what they can do to aid him in the realization of his powers ... This glue binding man to man is also referred to by Marx as natural 'necessity' ... and 'interest'." [102] Marx does not believe competition or independence will be sufficient to achieve self-fulfillment, but the question is whether he sees in personal relationships any value which goes beyond the value of functional cooperation in achieving individual ends.

Marx's language is redolent with imagery of "appropriating" and "using" other persons. My association with others, Marx says in the *1844 Manuscripts*, is "an organ for *expressing* my own *life*, and a mode of appropriating *human* life."[103] This means that the objective world and the objects within it—including, presumably, other persons—become for the individual "the *objectification of himself*, become objects which confirm and realize his individuality, become *his* objects."[104] Objects in this sense are "indispensable to the manifestation and confirmation of [man's] essential powers ... A being which is not itself an object for some third being has no being for its object ... and ... an unobjective being is a *nullity*—an *un-being*."[105] As Ollman puts it, "each person is himself object and sense content for other people, just as they, being equally parts of nature, serve in this capacity for him."[106]

Objects seem to have value to the degree that they can be "the confirmation of one of my essential powers. ... The meaning of an object for me goes only so far as *my* senses go (has only a meaning for a sense corresponding to that object)."[107] Man's social being is his being when it is expressing its power and possibilities to the fullest. This means when each individual is able to appropriate objects to himself in the fullest possible way, when "the senses and enjoyment of other men have become my own appropriation."[108] This seems to mean that human beings, in communist society, will essentially function as means to the end of others' self-fulfillment. "As communist objects, human beings possess those necessary attributes which enable others to achieve complete fulfillment through them."[109]

In this way, true freedom and individuality are linked. Only in communism, a fully cooperative society, will the individual discover the freedom "to assert his true individuality," which is "man at the height of his powers and needs, thoroughly and intensively cooperating with his fellows, and appropriating all of nature. Free activity is activity that fulfills such powers, and freedom, therefore, is the condition of man whose human powers are thus fulfilled; . . . "[110]

It is just at this point that we find Marx developing his fullest view of human "community." For a community is that social arrangement of persons in which "each individual [has] the means of cultivating his gifts in all directions; only in community, therefore, is personal freedom possible . . . In a real community the individuals obtain their freedom in and through their association."[111] While this notion of community certainly underlines the importance of social bonds, the emphasis seems to be upon the way in which those bonds are ultimately means to the end of individual self-determination or freedom. There is no mention here of what ends that freedom will serve. There is, in particular, no hint that persons may or should (in order to fulfill their species being) use their freedom *for* others, or that communal relations with others might be an end in itself rather than a means to individual ends.

It may not be stretching the point to say that, at least in these passages, Marx seems to understand the significance of communism as the removal of alienating and artificial barriers to individual self-realization. Communism understands that an atomistic free-for-all is ultimately fatal to individual self-development. Egoism cannot be the road to ego strength. Only by becoming aware of their "need" for others, can individuals recover the means for their own fulfillment. But this, Marx seems to warn, is not the same as love. "The individuals' consciousness of their mutual relations will . . . become something quite different [than in capitalism], and, therefore, will no more be the 'principle of love' . . . than it will be egoism."[112] Community, therefore, exists and is justified to the degree that it permits individuals to experience the greatest amount of self-expression possible. What is left out of this account is whether that self-expression includes the intention to live for others, to serve their needs altruistically, and to love them for their own sakes in the bonds of mutuality.

Self-Fulfillment and/or Mutuality? But, unfortunately for consistency, Marx says some other things about persons in relation which suggest that there are times when they will go beyond the freedom simply to express themselves and *will* find fulfillment in and through the fulfillment of others. In an alienated society, Marx says in the notes on James Mill, I will have produced "for myself and not for you," just as you will have produced for yourself and not for me.[113] "Each of us sees in his own product only his own selfish needs objectified, and thus in the product of another he only sees the objectification of another's selfish needs independent and alien to him."[114] But what if we produce in a truly human way, as will occur in communist society? Here Marx makes some startling claims (at least as compared to what he has said in his other writings). To be sure, he admits, I will have produced in such a way as to objectify my individuality and in so doing "enjoyed an individual expression of my life and ... have had the individual pleasure of realizing that my personality was objective ... "[115] But, I would, over and above that expression of my own individuality, have had the "direct enjoyment of realizing" through your enjoyment or use of my product, "that I had both satisfied a human need by my work and also objectified the human essence and therefore fashioned for another human being the object that met his need."[116]

By serving this function for you, I would have been "acknowledged and felt by you as a completion of your own essence and a necessary part of yourself and have thus realized that I am confirmed both in your thought and in your love." And, finally, "in my expression of my life I would have fashioned your expression of your life, and thus in my own activity have realized my own essence, my human, my communal essence. In that case our products would be like so many mirrors, out of which our essence shone."[117]

In this highly significant passage, we can see an interweaving of the theme of self-fulfillment with the hint of a theme of producing in order to serve the other person for his or her own sake. Marx certainly does not want still another dualism to creep into philosophy, this time between self-need and the need of others. He is clearly affirming his belief that only by producing for others (or at least recognizing that I can produce most appropriately in cooperation with others) can I produce most satisfyingly for myself. But beyond that, I think, Marx may here be suggesting, in a way he does not elaborate, here or elsewhere, that I can actually work intentionally for you and in so doing, not alienate myself nor frustrate my own sense of fulfillment or the realization of my human essence.

If this is a correct reading of this important passage from Marx's comments on James Mill, then we have to conclude that he is not as faithful to or as consistent with a fully elaborated organic totality or internal relations model as Rader and Ollman have sketched them. If Marx had subjected persons in relation to a fully developed organic model, then he would have had to reduce their relationship to an entirely functional one (assuming he did not want to develop any kind of metaphysical "split" between persons and other "lower-level" organisms). They would have been simply organs functionally serving each other's needs and the need of the whole organism (the society) of which they were a part, just as the heart and lungs are interlocked in a reciprocal net within the body as a whole.

Within a strict organic scheme, the insistence upon the self-fulfillment of each individual organ sorts poorly with the insistence upon the identity of each with the others, distinguished only by functional differences. But Marx seems to want to maintain both positions. Persons ultimately achieve self-fulfillment only by learning that they are organically interrelated with everything else in a single organic whole. And yet there are hints that even within the whole, persons may transcend their telos of self-development in order to concern themselves with the self-development of others.

Where Marx leaves us, therefore, is with a confused and incomplete rendering of persons in relation, in community, through an organic model. He both relies upon that model and transcends it. But when he transcends it, he does so without a fully developed metaphysics to guide him. This is, of course, historically understandable, committed as he was to the praxis of overcoming the atomism of the capitalist and individualistic model of community. By comparison to that model, an organic model was a thousandfold superior. It had the advantage of understanding the interdependence, the essential sociality, of persons, nature, ideas, and social and economic structures. What Marx was not able to do was to show us how, within an organic model, a place for persons in relation, especially for relationships of love and mutuality, can be secured. He was so focused upon the need to remove the barriers to self-determination and self-fulfillment, particularly the barrier of atomistic egoism, that he did not explore what might or should be the ends persons freely choose on the basis of their new freedom and sense of fulfillment. There is also an open question of whether, within an organic framework, there is enough of a sense of individual difference and self-identity to permit the pursuit of mutuality for its own sake between loving persons.

A cooperative society, an ensemble of functional relations between persons, may well be the necessary basis or infrastructure for relations of loving mutuality. But in and of themselves, organic and cooperative relations are not necessarily mutual. For mutuality, persons must love others for their own sakes: they must see their freedom, individuality, and self-identity as gifts to be offered to the other for the sake of the other. Mutuality means regarding the other as a "Thou" like oneself, not as an "It" to be cooperated with because it is functionally necessary to do so in order to be self-realized. Mutuality means that persons find in their loving relationship an end in itself, not a functional relationship serving some greater good. I believe that Marx was aware to some extent of this kind of mutuality. But I also believe that the way in which he used an organic model of community did not permit him to say all that could or should be said about such mutuality, in large part because he did not work out in a completely consistent way all the metaphysical implications of such a model. Whether, when those implications are fully elaborated, we can get closer to a sense of mutuality is what we now need to explore in the extensively developed metaphysical system of Alfred North Whitehead's philosophy of organism.

Notes to Chapter 3

1. See John Macmurray, *Interpreting the Universe* (London: Faber and Faber, 1933), chap. V, "Biological Thought and Organism," 84–102.
2. Quoted in Robert Nisbet, *The Social Philosophers*, 56.
3. Ibid., 57.
4. Charles Taylor, *Hegel and Modern Society* (Cambridge: Cambridge University Press, 1979), 85, 87.
5. Ibid., 86.
6. Ibid.
7. *Hegel's Logic* (Being Part One of the *Encyclopaedia of the Philosophical Sciences (1830)*), trans. William Wallace, with a foreword by J.N. Findlay (Oxford: Clarendon Press, 1975), 191–92.
8. *Hegel's Philosophy of Right*, trans. with notes by T.M. Knox (Oxford: Oxford University Press, 1967), 164, n. 269.
9. Ibid., 180, n. 278.

10. Ibid., 210, n. 324.
11. Ibid., 174, n. 271.
12. Ibid., 180, n. 278.
13. Tönnies, *Community and Society*, 35.
14. Ibid.
15. Ibid., 36.
16. Ibid., 37.
17. Ibid., 33.
18. Ibid., 34.
19. Ibid., 34-35.
20. Ibid., 37.
21. Ibid.
22. Ibid., 42.
23. Ibid., 43.
24. Ibid., 47.
25. Ibid., 214.
26. Ibid.
27. Ibid.
28. Ibid., 65.
29. Ibid.
30. Ibid., 139.
31. Ibid., 140.
32. Ibid., 141.
33. Quoted in Albert J. Reiss, Jr., ed., *Cooley and Sociological Analysis*, introduction by Robert Cooley Angell (Ann Arbor: University of Michigan Press, 1968), 6.
34. Ibid.
35. Charles Horton Cooley, *Human Nature and the Social Order*, rev. ed., with an introduction treating of the place of heredity and instinct in human life (New York: Charles Scribner's Sons, 1902, 1922), 15.
36. Ibid., 35.
37. Ibid.
38. Ibid.
39. Cooley, *Social Organization*, in *The Two Major Works of Charles H. Cooley*, with an introduction by Robert Cooley Angell (Glencoe, Ill.: Free Press, 1956), 23.
40. Ibid.
41. Ibid.
42. Ibid., 30.
43. Ibid., 33.
44. From *Social Process*, quoted in Reiss, *Cooley and Sociological Analysis*, 124.
45. Guy Swanson, "To Live in Concord with a Society: Two Empirical Studies of Primary Relations," in Reiss, *Cooley and Sociological Analysis*, 99.
46. Ibid., 68.
47. R.M. MacIver, *Community: A Sociological Study* (London: Macmillan, 1917), 24.

48. Ibid., 67.
49. Ibid., 69.
50. Ibid., 70.
51. Ibid., 71.
52. Ibid.
53. Ibid., 74.
54. Ibid., 123.
55. Ibid., 124.
56. Bertell Ollman, *Alienation. Marx's Conception of Man in Capitalist Society*, 2d ed. (Cambridge: Cambridge University Press, 1976).
57. Melvin Rader, *Marx's Interpretation of History* (New York: Oxford University Press, 1979).
58. Ollman, *Alienation*, 17.
59. Karl Marx, "Introduction," *A Contribution to the Critique of Political Economy*, trans. N.I. Stone (Chicago: 1904), 292; quoted in Ollman, *Alienation*, 17.
60. Ollman, *Alienation*, 131.
61. Ibid., 266.
62. Ibid.
63. Ibid., 267–68.
64. Ibid., 35.
65. Rader, *Marx's Interpretation of History*, 95.
66. Ollman, *Alienation*, 23.
67. From Engels, *Dialectics of Nature*, quoted in Ollman, *Alienation*, 282, n. 14.
68. Ibid.
69. Rader, *Marx's Interpretation of History*, 89.
70. Ibid., xxi.
71. Ibid., 86.
72. Ibid., 77.
73. Quoted in ibid., 57.
74. Ibid.
75. Ibid., 57–58.
76. Ibid., 76.
77. Ibid.
78. Quoted in Rader, *Marx's Interpretation of History*, 58. From *Grundrisse*, trans. Martin Nocolaus (London: Penguin, 1973), 278.
79. Ibid., 58–59.
80. Ibid., 61–62.
81. Allen W. Wood, *Karl Marx* (London: Routledge and Kegan Paul, 1981), 104–6.
82. Ibid., 105.
83. Ibid., 208.
84. Ibid., 208–9.
85. Quoted in Rader, *Marx's Interpretation of History*, 222.
86. Karl Marx, 'Theses on Feuerbach," in Karl Marx and Friedrich Engels, *On Religion*, introduction by Reinhold Niebuhr (New York: Schocken Books, 1964), 71.

87. Karl Marx, "On James Mill," in *Karl Marx: Selected Writings*, ed. David McLellan (Oxford: Oxford University Press, 1977), 115.
88. Ibid.
89. Karl Marx, *Economic and Philosophic Manuscripts of 1844*, edited with an introduction by Dirk J. Struik. Trans. Martin Milligan (New York: International Publishers, 1964), 135, 137.
90. Ibid., 138.
91. From Engels, *Dialectics of Nature*. Quoted in Ollman, *Alienation*, 54.
92. From Marx, *Capital*. Quoted in Ollman, *Alienation*, 27.
93. Eugene Kamenka, *The Ethical Foundations of Marxism* (New York: Frederick A. Praeger, 1962), 98.
94. Ibid.
95. Ibid.
96. Ibid., 99.
97. Istvan Meszaros, *Marx's Theory of Alienation* (London: Merlin Press, 1970), 185.
98. Ibid., 186.
99. Marx, *Economic and Philosophic Manuscripts of 1844*, 144.
100. Quoted in Ollman, *Alienation*, 104.
101. Ibid.
102. Ibid.
103. Marx, *Economic and Philosophic Manuscripts of 1844*, 140.
104. Ibid.
105. Ibid., 181-82.
106. Ollman, *Alienation*, 79.
107. Marx, *Economic and Philosophic Manuscripts of 1844*, 140.
108. Quoted in Ollman, *Alienation*, 106.
109. Ibid., 107.
110. Ibid., 115.
111. Karl Marx and Frederick Engels, *The German Ideology*, Part One, edited and with introduction by C.J. Arthur (New York: International Publishers, 1970), 83.
112. Ibid., 118.
113. Marx, "On James Mill," *Karl Marx: Selected Writings*, 120.
114. Ibid.
115. Ibid., 122.
116. Ibid.
117. Ibid.

4. The Organic/Functional Model of Community: Part Two—The Metaphysics of the Organic Community from Whitehead to Systems Philosophy

ALFRED NORTH WHITEHEAD

There is a growing consensus among those persons who are still interested in, or are gaining a renewed interest in metaphysical speculation, that the work of the early twentieth century philosopher Alfred North Whitehead is among the most important written in the past 100 years. His thought has remained outside the boundaries of popular knowledge (with the possible exception of his writings on education), both because metaphysics itself has been suspect for the past half-century and because his own mode of expression is so terribly obscure. Nevertheless, I believe, as do a growing number of theologians and philosophers, that Whitehead's metaphysical scheme is one of the most significant and challenging of our time.

This belief is based on the conviction that Whitehead's metaphysics is the most comprehensive and coherent account of reality taken as a whole, that has ever been written. While I am convinced that it is not completely adequate (in particular with respect to its understanding of persons in relation), I do believe that its explanatory power and scope, as well as its coherence and rigorous logic, require it to be taken with the utmost seriousness.

Its single most important characteristic is its systematic attempt to subject reality to a single, organic pattern of explanation. In the process, it rejects one of the most important assumptions of traditional philosophy: that of dualism in a variety of forms. Since Descartes, modern philosophy generally has accepted a split or division in nature between such radically different "things" as body and soul, reason and emotion, and the natural and supernatural. One of the greatest strengths of Whitehead's philosophy is its repudiation of these dualisms without the sacrifice of the realities which they represent (albeit inadequately).

With respect to the particular issue we are considering, the understanding of persons in relation, or community, Whitehead's speculative metaphysics develops one of the most sophisticated, logically constructed, and comprehensive schemes available today through which to understand persons in a nondualistic relation to the rest of reality. And the metaphor through which this scheme is elaborated is that of the organism. It can be argued that in Whitehead we find the fullest and most challenging development of an organic model of community. This does not mean that Whitehead simply repeats in different language the work of Hegel or Marx.[1] Whitehead's organic philosophy is a creative advance beyond the work of his predecessors. But in the process of developing his philosophy, he comes to some different and much more problematic conclusions about persons than can be found in earlier organic thinkers. Nevertheless, his work clearly represents an organic model of community and because of the extraordinarily complex and comprehensive way in which he worked out his organic philosophy, it must be examined in some detail if we are to understand both the persistent difficulties in that model as well as its greatest strengths.

In his monumental book, *Process and Reality*, published in 1929 and based on his Gifford Lectures (at the conclusion of which, according to legend, only six persons remained to hear him out), Whitehead calls his metaphysical scheme "the philosophy of organism."[2] It is devoted to the perennial philosophical task of reconciling the One and the Many, that is, to bringing into union within a single explanatory system both the plurality of the world of many things and its unity. There are unquestionably many individual entities. But these entities are also united in some ultimate way. Both of these facts about reality must be represented in any adequate metaphysical scheme. The philosophy of organism tries to do just that. I will outline the way in which this happens without reliance (except where it is unavoidable) on Whitehead's unusual and occasionally confusing language.

"Abide with me; Fast falls the eventide." In these words from the old familiar hymn, Whitehead finds formulated "the complete problem of metaphysics."[3] There is in the universe both stability (the first line) and change (the second line). The task of metaphysics is to bring them together into a unity without incoherence and without sacrificing one to the other. Traditionally, Whitehead argues, philosophy has concentrated upon the stability of the universe and ignored its equally important change or flux. It must now focus its attention upon the fact that, as Heraclitus saw thousands of years ago at the dawn of philosophy, "all things flow." Only a philosophy that can hold together in one organic whole both flux and permanence is truly co-herent, literally "holding or sticking together."

The principles of coherence by which Whitehead tries to do justice both to flux and permanence, to the many and to unity, are those of Creativity, Many, and One. Creativity is "the universal of universals characterizing ultimate matter of fact. It is that ultimate principle by which the many, which are the universe disjunctively, become the one actual occasion, which is the universe conjunctively. It lies in the nature of things that the many enter into complex unity."[4] There are many individual 'things' but they all come together, are functionally implicated in one another, in a single universe. The universe is literally one interconnected whole: there is no ultimate disjunction, dualism, or what Whitehead calls "bifurcation," in it.

While there are many entities in it, the universe for Whitehead, as Victor Lowe has put it, "is a *connected* pluralistic whole. No monist ever insisted more strongly than he that nothing in the world exists in independence of other things... Independent existence is a myth, whether you ascribe it to God or to a particle of matter in Newtonian physics, to persons, to nations, to things, or to meanings. To understand is to see things together, and to see them as, in Whitehead's favorite phrase, 'requiring each other.' A system which enables us to do this is 'coherent.' "[5]

Actual Occasions. The fundamental realities of the universe which exemplify both togetherness and diversity are entities called "actual occasions" (or "actual entities"). They are "the final real things of which the world is made up. There is no going behind actual entities to find anything more real."[6] They include everything in the universe from "God . . . [to] the most trivial puff of existence in far-off empty space."[7] Every fact in the universe is an actual entity (though they differ in function and importance). And their essential characteristic is that they are pulses, moments or "drops" of experience, "complex and interdependent,"[8] not static, mechanical atoms, individually identical and isolated. They are not inert substances, themselves the unchanging subjects of change. Actual entities (better conveyed, I think, by the word "occasions") are transient experiences, processes of feeling or enjoyment, each unique and individual though absolutely interconnected with all the others, either dependent on them for their internal constitution or available to subsequent ones for their enjoyment.

It is crucial to the philosophy of organism that all actual entities be of the same generic character in order to preserve the unity and coherence of the whole. "The presumption that there is only one genus of actual entities constitutes an ideal of cosmological theory to which the philosophy of organism endeavours to conform. The description of the generic character of an actual entity should include God, as well as the lowliest actual occasion . . . "[9] This is not, it should be understood, the identity of the parts so prominent in Ollman's theory of internal relations (which he attributes to Marx) but it is based on a similar intuition, namely, that in an organic whole there cannot be radically different kinds of entities unless one is ready to pay the price and accept an incoherent form of dualism which severs reality into irreconcilable parts.

The importance of the actual occasion in Whitehead's philosophy is that it is the locus of both unity and diversity: it is where the many become one and add to the many. This is not as paradoxical as it might sound. An actual entity is a "concrescence" of many things into a single unified whole. "Concrescence" is the name for the process in which the universe of many things acquires an individual unity in a determinate relegation of each item of the 'many' to its subordination in the constitution of the novel 'one'."[10] "Concrescence" (a term, incidentally, which Whitehead took from the organic field of biology) literally means a growing together, especially of parts originally separate. The 'one' in this case is the actual entity: it is novel because it is new. It is the way in which the principle of Creativity brings novelty into existence. This happens through a process of unification in which elements from already existing actual entities are "felt" or brought together into a new unity by the emerging actual entity.

While it is not strictly accurate as an analogy, you might think of your hand with all its fingers and thumb as widely separated from each other as possible. Each of these appendages can be thought of as already existing entities. Then, as you start to close your hand in order to make a fist, you might think of this process as a growing together of what is past in order to make a new, and novel, entity (the fist) which is, in a sense, a new "one" which has come into being through the concrescence of the "many" out of which it is constituted. The universe (the hand) of many things (fingers and thumb) acquires an individual unity (the fist) in a determinate relegation (it is this particular fist, not fists in general, that comes into being) of each item of the 'many' to its subordination in the constitution of the novel 'one' (the fingers and thumb are no longer separate and individual items once they have 'become' the fist).

The principle of Creativity requires that each instance of concrescence be an instance of the realization of value. That is, each actual occasion, in its unification into a single whole of the many which have preceded it waiting for unification by subsequent entities, is the achievement of a felt unity. And the experience of a felt unity is the experience both of self-realization and of value simultaneously, because value and feeling are identical. "An actual occasion is a concrescence effected by a process of feelings ... This process of the integration of feeling proceeds until the concrete unity of feeling is obtained."[11] This concrete unity of feeling is the experience of perceiving or valuing the world in a new way, in a way unique to this particular integration of feelings in this particular entity. This unity of feeling is called "the satisfaction" of each entity. It is "the attainment of the private ideal which is the final cause of the concrescence.... The many feelings ... are transformed into a unity of aesthetic appreciation immediately felt as private."[12]

With the principle of Creativity, the concrescence of the many into one is the basis for Whitehead's claim that the world is itself a process of self-realization, growing out of previous processes and each new one adding a novel unity, a new value, to the world. While the experience of satisfaction is private, once it has been achieved, the complete experienced unity, the product which is the completed concrescence or the entity itself, becomes available as an element, or datum, to be integrated into the unification process (each one guided by feeling and driving toward a satisfactory unity of feeling) of other emerging novel entities. The privacy of the satisfaction in a single entity becomes shared (once it has perished or completed itself) with all other entities-in-process. The concrescence is the "production of novel togetherness" and the achievement of concrescence makes possible the production of future novel togetherness. In this way all entities are implicated in a single one and each one becomes implicated eventually in all future ones. "[T]he potentiality for being an element in a real concrescence of many entities into one actuality is the one general metaphysical character attaching to all entities... and every item in its universe is involved in each concrescence."[13] Creativity keeps the process moving, as it were. And the world is the process of the realization of Creativity in and through actual entities.

Organism. "Organism" is the term which best captures this sense of process. Process is essential to the meaning of an organism: it is always becoming, or in a process of growth (see pp. 65–66 on the outline of the organic model). And it is governed by a teleology, in which the telos of the growth process determines the stages leading up to its realization. This organic process covers the growth and the actual occasion itself. Whitehead explicitly says that "each actual entity is itself only describable as an organic process.... It is a process proceeding from phase to phase, each phase being the real basis from which its successor proceeds towards the completion of the thing in question."[14] And its process is determined by its aim at satisfaction, or the integration of its elements (feelings) into a single satisfying unity.

The world which is made up of actual entities is also an organism, a macroscopic process as compared to the microscopic process of the single actual entity. This macroscopic whole (the world), Whitehead calls a community. "The community of actual things is an organism.... It is an incompletion in process of production."[15] That is, it is not complete as long as there are actual entities still undergoing their microscopic processes of completion and adding to the world new data to be incorporated into the internal processes of subsequent entities. "Thus each actual entity, although complete so far as concerns its microscopic process, is yet incomplete by reason of its objective inclusion of the macroscopic process."[16]

With this bare outline of Whitehead's general metaphysical principles, we now need to see what effect they have on his understanding of the character of the actual occasion itself and consequently of persons (both singly and in relation), since persons will have to be either themselves occasions or, as Whitehead argues, groups of occasions. This closer look at the actual occasion will serve as a basis for raising some important questions about the organic model of community (as Whitehead explicates it). These will include the following :

1. If persons are not basic unities (being societies of occasions), and if the basic unity (the occasion) is itself not a unity until its process of becoming is at an end, does this understanding permit an adequate notion of persons which would seem to require of them some kind of ongoing unity as they enter into ongoing relations with each other?

2. Is Whitehead's commitment to a similar generic character for all entities (in order to avoid dualism), and its resulting "panpsychism"—in which some kind of mentality and feeling are ascribed to even the "lowliest" of occasions—an adequate basis for understanding those things that generally have been taken to be the distinguishing marks of persons (e.g., consciousness, intentionality, and freedom of action)?

3. Is Whitehead's emphasis upon the self-realization of each entity (its subjectivity) consistent with or an adequate basis for a notion of mutuality in which one person seeks out another and in some sense lives for it and not for itself?

4. Does the notion of organic interconnectedness, in which each entity comes into being through the contributions of others and, when it perishes, serves a function in the unification of all subsequent others, a sufficient basis for a notion of the person as having some kind of worth intrinsic to itself, and not completely dependent on its *literal* inclusion *of* its predecessors and *in* its successors?

As we shall see, Whitehead has a way of dealing with each of these questions. However, there remains a justifiable sense of unease or dissatisfaction with his responses which, in turn, will suggest that either a broadened notion of organism or another more inclusive model of persons in community is necessary in order to capture fully our experience of living in loving mutuality with others.

The Inclusiveness of the Occasion. By examining the nature of the actual occasion, we can appreciate the force of Whitehead's claim that it is the final reality of which the world is made up. For literally *in* the occasion Whitehead wants to find a place for all those things that historically have been kept metaphysically apart by dualism. If actual occasions are ultimate facts of the universe, then nothing can exist apart from them. It follows that everything (from mentality to brute matter) must be contained within them. In one bold metaphysical stroke Whitehead claims that dualism is overcome through the notion of the actual occasion. The actual entity, as a process of unification of many previously individual things, reconciles or brings together (concresces) those things which previously philosophy had thought to be dualistically separate, such as reason and emotion, mind and matter. As a process of unification, the actual occasion *is* this concrescence. This leads Whitehead to say that every occasion is generically the same as every other occasion, no matter where it is found (in far-off empty space or in the brain of a genius). Mentality, for example, is not added to some occasions of a certain kind but must be present in all occasions, even if in some it is functionally trivial (Whitehead attributes a mental pole to all occasions).

Whitehead is careful to point out that the actual occasion does not exist prior to the concrescence nor does it endure after the concrescence has been completed. It *is* the concrescence. This point is difficult to grasp because it violates one of the most persistent effects of using subject-predicate language. Most of the time when we talk about an object, we say "it" exists and point to "it" as being "there." When we talk this way, we assume a kind of enduring, unchanging, substantial "thing" which is the object-in-itself, to which many things can happen but which, in its essential nature, does not change. Our subject remains the same while its predicates change. We might think of a chair which gets a new coat of paint every year, perhaps has its wood slats replaced from time to time, and even receives a new (but identical looking) seat. Our language suggests to us that we are dealing with the same chair throughout this process of change, only the predicates describing its color, wood, seat, etc. having altered. But Whitehead suggests that this kind of talk about objects is misleading and implicitly dualistic because it requires us to believe in two incompatible things simultaneously: i.e., an unchanging subject of change, and the changes which "it" undergoes. The relation between the subject and its predicates is thus not explained, only presupposed.

What Whitehead wants to put in place of such subject-predicate language is a (possibly counterintuitive) notion of a subject which, in one sense, "is" its changes. Or to put it differently, the subject is the process by which it comes to be. "[H]ow an actual entity *becomes* constitutes *what* that actual entity *is*.... Its 'being' is constituted by its 'becoming.' This is the 'principle of process'."[17] Whitehead uses the terms "subject-superject" to convey this difficult idea. The actual entity is "both process and outcome."[18] Its outcome is its satisfaction, or superject, that at which the process is aiming. The concrescence is the building up of the satisfaction through the process of becoming. But until the satisfaction is reached, the entity is not complete (or determinate). And until it is determinate it is not yet a full subject, but only a subject-in-the-making. The satisfaction "closes up the entity" and gives it full being: until that moment the entity is not fully a subject but a subject-superject, a *process* aiming at becoming a full subject. In fact, the subject only becomes complete at the moment when it ceases becoming. And when it ceases becoming, it loses its subjective life and becomes an object (determinate and complete) which is now and only now ready to be used as data for and by subsequent entities. "[F]or the philosophy of organism, the subject emerges from the world—a 'superject' rather than a 'subject'. The word 'object' thus means an entity which is a potentiality for being a component in feeling; and the word 'subject' means the entity constituted by the process of feeling, and including this process."[19]

One result of this view is that the subjective life of an entity ceases once its process of becoming is over. And it is over at the precise moment when it is first fully a complete being. But it must cease becoming, end its subjective life, if it is to have any effect on subsequent entities during their processes of becoming. This has the interesting consequence that an entity cannot act upon or affect another entity until it has "perished," i.e., completed its subjective existence. It also means that, while it can be influenced during the course of its process of becoming by all past entities, it cannot enter into ongoing relations with them (since they are already "perished") or with subsequent occasions (since it will be "perished" by the time they begin their subjective processes of becoming—otherwise it could have no effect on them). Whitehead explains this situation by appealing to a principle which holds that contemporaries cannot prehend each other ("contemporary events happen in *causal* independence of each other"). That is, no two occasions, contemporaneously experiencing the subjectivity of becoming, can prehend or be affected by each other. Ironically, in this sense two contemporary occasions have no direct organic relation to each other. In this way, Whitehead seems to preserve their individuality but it is at a high price: individuals-in-the-making, subjects, cannot affect each other or have any kind of mutual relation. Real causal effect occurs only between past and present, not between two present entities.

Another consequence of Whitehead's view of actual occasions is that they do not exist prior to, above, or underneath the process by which they become entities. The entity really "emerges" from and does not precede the process by which it becomes an entity. This way of viewing the actual entity leads Whitehead to the somewhat startling conclusion that the "feeler is the unity emergent from its own feelings; and feelings are the details of the process intermediary between this unity and its many data."[20] In this case the feeler would correspond to the notion of an already unified or complete being. But since such unity is the *outcome* of the process, and not something which exists prior to the process guiding and controlling it, it is not possible to talk about the subject as unified or complete until the process of its becoming is at an end.

One obvious objection which Whitehead anticipated to this rather revisionary view of the subject is: how is the process to be guided if there is no "guider" present at the outset? His answer was to suggest that the process of concrescence occurs through what he calls a "prehension" or a grasping, by which the entity brings into itself those elements of the past available to it for integration into a single unified satisfaction. Prehensions are essentially feelings or valuations which the entity has toward its data. It can feel these positively (and include them in itself) or negatively (and eliminate them from feeling). The details of how this is done need not concern us here. But one of the prehensions ingredient in each occasion is what Whitehead calls its "subjective aim."

The Subject and Subjective Aim. The concrescence of the actual entity is "dominated by a subjective aim which essentially concerns the creature as a final superject. This subjective aim is this subject itself determining its own self-creation as one creature."[21] It is an aim which Whitehead believes God (another actual entity) gives each actual entity at the beginning of its process of concrescence. By means of the subjective aim, the process has a "purpose" or "telos" by which it can decide the mode of prehension (that is, what to accept and reject in its particular form of integration). It points the occasion, in John

Cobb's words, "toward an ideal possibility for its satisfaction ... in terms of gradations of possible realization ... during the successive phases of the occasion's self-actualization, as it compares and harmonizes the data it has received from the world, it also modifies and adapts its subjective aim."[22]

The question that arises at this point is whether the subjective aim has become, in effect, a subject. We know that the final subject (the entity itself) does not actually achieve its full being, its completeness, until its process of becoming a subject is at an end. Therefore, the entity cannot be the controller of its own destiny since "it" does not really exist as such until it has been created by the process of becoming. Does this mean that the subjective aim is, then, the "subject" which controls the destiny of the entity which it is guiding? No, because only entities are real: the subjective aim is only a component in the entity: entities are the final real things of which the world is made up. Therefore, we seem to be faced with the peculiar problem of trying to conceive an entity simultaneously as the outcome (superject) of its process and as the determiner (subject) of its process. Whitehead adamantly refuses to retreat into the traditional philosophical view which holds that in some sense a process of change must be guided by a subject which endures "underneath" or throughout that process as its guider or determiner. As a result, he has to fall back upon what seems, at least to common sense, a counterintuitive position.

One recourse which Whitehead had at this point was to draw upon a notion of genetic unity to describe the unity of the occasion from its initial to its final phase. This genetic notion, or ephocal theory of becoming, holds that there is no real sweep of time from the "beginning" of an entity's subjective process to its "end" in the satisfaction. The entity's internal process can be genetically analyzed or divided (that is, with respect to its component parts) but not temporarily divided (with respect to determining which parts came "before" or "after" others). As Whitehead says, in discussing Zeno's famous paradox of how something can complete a given distance if in each move it makes it moves half the distance of the prevous move, "in every act of becoming there is the becoming of something with temporal extension; but ... the act itself is not extensive, in the sense that it is divisible into earlier and later acts of becoming which correspond to the extensive divisibility of what has become."[23] In other words, the act of becoming cannot be divided into earlier and later phases even though the completed entity has "temporal extension," i.e., has taken time to become.

Whitehead's argument at this point becomes rather obscure, and seems to me to avoid the nagging difficulty of how a subject with enough identity and completeness to determine its own destiny can be present at the beginning of the process by which this identity and completeness are to be determined. However, if we remember the organic metaphor of his philosophy, we might better appreciate what Whitehead is trying to do. Keeping in mind that it is a metaphor, the organism seems to bear a striking resemblance to the occasion with respect to genetic division. In any organism it makes little sense to ask which organ comes prior to others: the growth of the organism as a whole is clearly dependent upon the reciprocal interaction of the various organs, but not particularly upon the temporal priority of some to others. But this similarity to an organism (a similarity so significant that Whitehead, as we know, called his philosophy one of organism) simply raises our basic question in a different form. Can an organism in and of itself guide or control its own destiny? Used in the broad sense to cover persons, we might be willing to say that, of course, it can. But are we as willing to say that an organism at the level of plant life has the same capacity?

When we raise the question in this way, Whitehead has a ready answer. If the analysis of the actual entity is correct, then it must apply to the entities that make up all levels of reality, and therefore even the entities at the level of plant life must exhibit the characteristics of entities at the level of human beings. This is the basis of Whitehead's famous panpsychism, a view which attributes "psyche"or mind to everything, at least to some degree. We will explore some of its implications shortly but at this point we need only to see that it is a necessary doctrine if Whitehead is to avoid dualistic distinctions between some levels of reality and others. If all entities have the same characteristics, then the analysis of the genetic make-up of the occasions in a plant will be the same as the analysis of the occasions in the brain of a human being. If there is no problem attributing some kind of control of the occasion to itself in the human being's brain (though this is precisely what I think is questionable), then there is no trouble making the same kind of attribution to all occasions throughout nature.

Societies and Mutuality. So far, we have been discussing actual entities or occasions as the basic unities of reality. From this it might be assumed that persons are actual entities.

Technically speaking, this is not correct. While I believe that the analysis of the unity of an occasion ultimately casts doubt upon the unity of a person, for Whitehead persons are not single occasions. Instead, he insists, persons are *societies* of occasions. What he means by this is that persons as we know them seem to endure or persist throughout lengthy periods of time. Occasions do not so endure (lasting perhaps 1/100th of a second each). But occasions which influence each other (by the perished ones being prehended or "ingressed" into the emerging ones in accordance with some common trait or character) are in a social relation. This relation is determined by temporal contiguity and succession. (It is important to remember here that contemporary occasions do not influence each other.) A society is therefore an interconnected set of occasions (a "nexus," in Whitehead's language) exhibiting a common characteristic exemplified in each occasion within the nexus and dependent upon its exemplification in the previous occasions.

A person is a society of occasions. And only persons, not occasions, can endure over time, even though no two occasions in a chain of inheritance exist at the same time. The latest occasion is really the last occasion in a serial order, but it has prehended all the previous occasions in that order or society and thus exemplifies all their essential characteristics as they have prehended them from still previous occasions. Now in some societies, there is a "dominant" occasion or presiding personality. This occasion is extraordinary because it is the center of consciousness for those societies that possess it. It can occur only in very high grade societies and is particularly present in the human brain. The brain, Whitehead contends, is so coordinated "that a peculiar richness of inheritance [from the train of occasions making up that society] is enjoyed now by this and now by that part; and thus there is produced the presiding personality at that moment in the body."[24] Thus we have a living person.

We should notice that Whitehead's notion of a living person is not basic, that is, it is not the notion of a fundamental unity. Its unity is really composite, made up of the more basic unities of the actual entities whose path of inheritance constitutes the person. Thus, the unity of the person will be at least as problematic as the unity of its most basic part, in this case the actual entity. But as we have seen, some difficult questions can be raised about the unity of the actual entity, especially about whether it can be seen as controlling its own destiny from the outset of its existence. If the actual entity's unity is not firmly established, it is not clear that a society of such entities can have any greater, more established unity. And so, we have to ask once again of Whitehead's scheme whether it can adequately handle the notion of a person as a basic unity capable of entering into enduring, ongoing relations with other such unities.

If we recollect the essential characteristics of an organism sketched by Macmurray (see pp. 65–66), I believe it is fair to say that Whitehead's organic philosophy consistently exemplifies them. According to Macmurray, an organism (1) is alive and its parts contribute to the growth process by becoming differentiated and coordinated. This certainly happens within the actual entity's process of concrescence. (2) The differentiation does not impair the unity of the whole—the differences must be complementary and harmonious. The doctrine of prehension insures that this is the case. (3) The growth process combines reproduction with variation. The doctrine that each occasion reproduces what its data determine, but with variation through its subjective aim and the underlying principle of novelty, adequately represents this characteristic. (4) That the unity of differences within the organism will be represented in aesthetic terms is expressed by Whitehead on a number of occasions, especially when he suggests that the satisfaction or unity of the occasion is "felt" as one of the harmony of relations. The value of each occasion's experience is essentially a value of beauty, that is, a harmony achieved out of its constituent parts in and through the process of concrescence. Like a painting, the beauty achieved by the occasion is the work of bringing a felt unity out of a multitude of potentially discordant elements. The strength of beauty is composed of the complexity of elements brought into unity and the intensity of the contrast that has to be harmonized. (5) The notion of growth is conveyed by becoming or process. There is no question that "process" is the central category of Whitehead's philosophy of organism. (6) Organisms have a teleological dimension. Certainly, the notion of subjective aim and satisfaction conveys this element in the character of the organism as sketched by Macmurray.

The notion of a hierarchy within the organism is not part of Macmurray's description of it and is not really developed by Whitehead (though he has a place for it in his discussion of societies) because the basic elements of reality, the actual entities, are all generically identical. As we shall see, the notion of the hierarchy is really developed with respect to the *difference* between human and nonhuman organisms by some of Whitehead's followers within the biological community. In general, then, we can say that Whitehead's philosophy of organism represents for the most part the traits of the organism as Macmurray has outlined them. Given this conclusion, we can now pursue the questions raised earlier about how adequately the organic model as developed by Whitehead can handle our experience of ourselves as persons and as persons in relation.

If we go back to questions 1, 3, and 4 (p. 105), which we suggested need to be asked of Whitehead's scheme as it applies to persons, we come up with the following considerations. The occasion is ultimately able to focus only upon its own self-realization. It *is* its process of self-realization and ceases to exist subjectively once that process has been completed. Its effect on other occasions can occur only when it has perished. The relation of the present occasion to other occasions is the relation of a not yet fully developed subject to already completed and thus perished, or dead, objects. Relationship is, in this sense, a one-way street, between the living and the dead. The dead give up (obviously without intention) their parts to the living, and the living focus upon their own subjective becoming until they, too, perish and can be used functionally by subsequent occasions. This understanding of relationship is reinforced by the principle that no contemporary occasions can prehend (or causally affect) each other. Thus, the occasion can have no ongoing relations with or enjoyment of other occasions as they are experiencing their own subjectivity. Inasmuch as occasions are the basic units of reality, persons (being societies of occasions) exist only in and through the latest or present occasion in the train of occasions and thus persons suffer from the same inability to enjoy or relate to other persons in the present. The fact that persons endure over time (and occasions do not) does not affect the fact that there is no way for a living occasion (the locus of the life of the person at any given moment) to relate to the life of another living occasion. A society is, in a sense, an abstraction from the more basic unity of the occasion. And if the basic unities cannot relate contemporaneously, it is hard to see how an abstraction can be more successful in so relating.

Mutuality, as we understand it in everyday experience, is the ongoing relationship between two or more enduring persons who affect and are affected by each other. It is this sense of mutuality which seems to be missing from Whitehead's scheme. Part of a mutual relationship with another person means that the

"I" which acted upon the other is the same "I" which will be affected by the reciprocal action undertaken by the other. And in a mutual relationship, "I" have the freedom to concern myself with the needs of the other as the other is experiencing them subjectively. "I" have enough substantiality (and endurance through time as a self-identical being) to be able to care for the other without having to be preoccupied (as it were) with creating myself. My being is already, in some sense, given to me, freeing me to love the other, to transcend my own needs precisely because I am "complete" enough to move beyond a narrow focus on my own self-realization. In Whitehead's scheme, this kind of mutuality seems difficult to justify since the occasion (or society of occasions existing in the present occasion) must necessarily be involved solely in self-creation *before* it can "give" to others. Its "giving" is dependent upon its having been completed and its having been completed is tantamount to its perishing (ceasing to be a subject) and to its transition to being an object.

Nevertheless, Whitehead does, in his references to societies, and especially in his discussion of "peace," provide an indication of his concern for self-transcendence or living for more than oneself. He describes Peace as a "broadening of feeling due to the emergence of some deep metaphysical insight" whose first effect "is the removal of the stress of acquisitive feeling arising from the soul's preoccupation with itself. Thus Peace carries with it a surpassing of personality... It results in a wider sweep of conscious interest. It enlarges the field of attention. Thus Peace is self-control at its widest,—at the width where the 'self' has been lost, and interest has been transferred to coordinations wider than personality.... One of its fruits is the love of mankind as such."[25] This means, for Whitehead, that history will disclose instances of "the essential transcendence of each individual actuality beyond itself."[26] This stress upon self-transcendence is a corollary of Whitehead's notion that all reality is interconnected and that the self-realization of each individual "is bound up with a relativity which it issues from and issues into."[27] But the notions of self-transcendence, relativity, and interconnectedness should not be taken as qualifying in any ultimate way the primacy of self-realization, as distinct from living in and for another, in Whitehead's organic scheme. We need always to remember the centrality of Whitehead's claim that "self-realization is the ultimate fact of facts."[28]

With respect to the question of the intrinsic worth of a subject apart from its literal inclusion of other (perished) subjects, Whitehead's philosophy cannot justify any notion of a being which exists and has relations with other beings without literally ingressing or prehending them. We need to remember that in Whitehead's organic scheme, relationship really means "inclusion." The occasion's relationship with its past (it has none with those occasions co-present to it) is a relationship by prehension: an evaluative grasping of the past into itself since "it" is itself only through such a grasping. In one sense, it could be argued, Whitehead has gone beyond relationship "between" persons: prehension is not a relation between two different beings, but the ingression, indwelling, or literal inherence of one "in" the other. But this kind of inclusion is not what we normally mean by mutuality, which, as we have just suggested, seems in its ordinary sense to involve ongoing relations between two beings, each of whom retains some kind of irreducible, unchanging identity or completeness. Whether we can make a case for this kind of mutuality without falling into the obvious problems of dualism and incoherence (the very problems which drove Whitehead to his particular understanding of the actual entity) will depend upon a set of arguments to be developed in my last chapters.

Before we move to a discussion of the model of mutuality, however, we need to consider the work of a number of contemporary philosophers of biology and "systems" thinkers who have been deeply influenced by Whitehead's philosophy. Their importance to us is that they have, in various ways, tried to develop a notion of the person as an organism which has both a continuity with the rest of nature (panpsychism—the second question in our list of four which we have not yet discussed), and a place for those distinguishing traits of human persons, such as love and intentionality, which seem to separate them from lower level organisms.

One of the greatest strengths of Whitehead's philosophy is its repudiation of dualism through his principle that the character of reality is exemplified in each actual entity and that all parts of nature are composed of actual entities. What is true of entities in the human brain is equally true of God, of the most trivial puff of existence in far-off empty space, and of every occasion or society of occasions in between. Whether this kind of panpsychism can be interpreted in such a way as to justify our common-sense belief that persons possess traits which distinguish them from nonpersonal beings, is what needs to be examined. But regardless of the result of such an investigation, we have seen in

Whitehead's philosophy a highly sophisticated, challenging, and metaphysically powerful expression of one version of an organic model of community. It remains to be seen whether versions of his model can go further in providing a basis for the mutuality most of us take as characteristic of what it means to be in loving relation with other persons.

SYSTEMS THEORY AND THE PHILOSOPHY OF HIERARCHY

Panpsychism. In the last section we raised the question of whether Whitehead's metaphysical scheme was adequate to our experience of ourselves as persons who are somehow distinguishable from other, especially organic, levels of nature. We need to explore just a bit further the problem of how persons and nonpersons are both similar to and different from each other and whether, within what we have called a broad or open-ended use of the metaphor of "organism," we can find a place, or at least an opening, for the kind of "personal entity" which is capable of self-initiating action, long-range intentions, and other-directed love or mutuality.

One of the great strengths of Whitehead's philosophy is its development of a set of explanatory principles by which the *whole* of reality can be rendered coherent and unified. This means no appeal to any kind of metaphysical dualism or incoherence (what Whitehead calls the arbitrary disconnection of first principles).[29] The criticism that can be directed at Whitehead in this respect has been well expressed by Ian Barbour in an otherwise very sympathetic review of Whitehead's system.

> ... Whitehead's use of such a very general conceptual scheme does not allow adequately for *the diversity among levels of activity* in the world. He has taken categories most appropriate for a 'middle range' in the scale of being (biological organisms) and extended their use both 'up' and 'down' the scale; consequently his concepts seem to be insufficiently 'personal' to express the enduring unity of human selfhood, but too 'personal' to be applicable in the inorganic realm ... [As a result] Whitehead's concern for continuity, coherence, and generality led him to give too little attention to the contrasts between events at various

levels, or to the differences between distinctively human experience and the experience of other creatures.[30]

Whitehead's concern for continuity, coherence, and generality has seemed well justified to a number of biologists and philosophers of biology who have been influenced by him. They have, as a result, been willing to accept Whitehead's panpsychism, which attributes to all levels of reality the same essential characteristics. As we can recall from our discussion of Whitehead's philosophy, this means breaking reality down into its basic components, the actual entities, and describing them in generically identical terms. No actual entity will be fundamentally different from any other in terms of its basic structure, process, and character.

This means, in particular, that subjectivity (the experience of the actual entity undergoing its process of concrescence) must be attributed to every single entity in the universe. At first sight this seems very counterintuitive. We don't normally think of the occasions constituting the life of an atom or a stone as having subjective feelings, let alone subjective aims and the ability, no matter how minimal, to contribute something "novel" to the universe. And yet, on Whitehead's principles, if we are to avoid drawing a dualistic line between feeling and nonfeeling parts of reality, we have to insist that even atoms and stones "feel."

Charles Birch, a biologist, has said that

> there is no logical reason to restrict the subjective to organisms with a nervous system... Even an individual cell... "takes account of" other entities in its environment... It may move toward some things and move away from others. These are the sort of criteria we use to infer subjectivity in organisms like ourselves. But why limit subjectivity to just those complex organisms? If we do that, then we imply that subjectivity 'emerged' out of objectivity... This is to imply a discontinuity in the evolution of subjectivity; from no subjectivity came subjectivity... Since in the rest of the world besides ourselves, processes of "taking account of" are going on, be it in electrons or atoms or cells, then it is logical to suppose that this subject-object relationship involves subjectivity for these other entities. This is Whitehead's proposition that you have either got to have subjectivity everywhere or nowhere. Since it is obviously in us, then it must be everywhere.[31]

The problem with the traditional dualistic view, Birch suggests, is that it leaves us with the insoluble difficulty of "emergence." Emergence is the sudden appearance of some characteristic, especially mentality, or life, out of nonmentality or nonliving nature. That kind of emergence is a problem of the relation between living and nonliving parts of nature requiring a solution. Modern biology, Birch insists, "has demonstrated the continuity of the evolutionary process in the sense that what has evolved constitutes a continuum without any sharp dividing lines, even between non-living and living."[32] The geneticist Sewall Wright has said that the "emergence of mind from no mind at all is sheer magic... Mind... must be a universal aspect of existence... The arguments from continuity require the presence of mind in cells and, back of this, in molecules, atoms, and all that exists."[33]

Charles Hartshorne. There is no philosopher of process who has argued more strongly and perhaps more persuasively for panpsychism than the contemporary American philosopher Charles Hartshorne. The study of reality which he calls "psychics" must "generalize such ideas as feeling, perceiving, remembering, anticipating, intending, liking and disliking, so that they can apply not only to animals, but even to the real individual constituents of the vegetable and mineral portions of nature."[34] This does not mean for Hartshorne—and did not mean for Whitehead either—that all entities have "consciousness" as we experience it in ourselves. The experience of mentality has many grades of complexity or degree and consciousness proper occurs only in the most complex organisms. The kind of mentality in a bird may be, by comparison, only primitive, short-run, and naive, with little or no novelty or creativity.

The important point for Hartshorne is that the difference between so-called "lifeless" nature and living organisms must never be absolute, but instead only relative or a matter of degree. The only reason for denying mentality, intentionality, and feeling to some parts of nature is the lack of our ability to perceive their effects. But "since physics and chemistry have demonstrated how limited in penetration our mere sense perceptions are, how radically they fail to disclose what is really there in nature, it follows that the entire traditional foundation for materialism and dualism alike has been destroyed by the advance of knowledge."[35]

Hartshorne seems quite clear that his panpsychism is logically linked to an organic model of reality. Defining an organism as "a whole whose parts serve as 'organs' or instrument [sic] to purposes or end-values inherent in the whole,"[36] Hartshorne says that man knows himself as an organism and that all natural wholes are organisms. This "organic monism" asserts that all "well-unified wholes are organic... and... that all wholes whatever both involve and are involved in organic wholes."[37] But as a whole, the organism cannot be divided into radically different parts: the parts have to cohere or interpenetrate in such a way as to support the unity of the whole. Only a panpsychistic view of reality can avoid a dualistic division fatal to the notion of the organic whole.

According to Hartshorne, science has made ever clearer that such dualism can have no scientific support. "All individuals can be viewed as physical systems, and all, even atoms, can be viewed as responding to stimuli with their own internal feelings.... The whole gamut of levels from atoms to man is for science basically one system."[38] Science simply provides no support for a "dualistic materialism in which the sentient and intelligent arise out of mere bits of dead matter, human evaluations out of a nature devoid of values. *Human* values emerge, sure enough, but are there not simian values, amoebic values—and who dares to assign a first level of values?"[39]

I believe that Hartshorne is correct in assuming that an organic model of the sort Whitehead and he are committed to, does, when pressed to its logical conclusion, require some form of panpsychism. The question is whether it is possible to insert into a more general organic model a concept (the hierarchy) which can avoid the most troubling aspects of panpsychism, such as the attribution of mentality and even intentionality to atoms, without at the same time falling back into the very problem (namely, dualism or incoherence, the acceptance of radical discontinuity in nature) from which panpsychism promises to deliver us. There are philosophers who have suggested that if we open up the organic model in the direction of recognizing some fundamental differences between inorganic levels of reality and the level of persons, then we can escape both panpsychism and the dreaded dualism it is trying to avoid. If these philosophers are successful in defending a broader view of the organic model than that found in Whitehead, then the transition to a mutual/personal model of community will be made much smoother.

"Systems" or a Hierarchy of Levels. Nevertheless, there will still remain a significant metaphysical alternative to developing a more open-ended use of the organic model. That alternative will be to turn to what I believe is a metaphysically cleaner and more straightforward model which puts mutuality and intentionality (the two most important distinguishing characteristics of human persons) squarely at the center of its understanding of community. This model will have the advantage of starting its understanding of persons in relation with the *primacy* of persons and their relationships based on love. From this starting-point, the mutual/personal model will be able to include within itself the structures and dynamics of organic and mechanical levels of reality. Persons will not be treated simply as more complex, more highly organized entities whose essential characteristics must be defined in terms of organic functioning and structure. In addition, the mutual/personal model will be able to identify love as the single most important trait characterizing the relations of persons to each other. Even within a broadened organic model, the activity of love inevitably gets subsumed within organic categories more appropriate to (because they are originally derived from) nonintentional, symbiotic, stimulus-response relations between the entities of nature.

While the significance of the mutual/personal model will be demonstrated because of its ability to represent dimensions of community not as readily represented in the organic model, the relation between the two models is so close (given that both understand the irreducibly important fact of interrelatedness) that we need to see just how close they can be brought together and just how smooth the transition from one to the other can be. That, I think, is the significance of the work of some contemporary philosophers who have taken seriously the need for finding a place within a broad organic model for the uniqueness of persons.

The principle by which the organic model is being opened up is that of the multi-leveled nature of reality. Marjorie Grene, a philosopher deeply interested in the work of contemporary biologists, has insisted that there are conditions in nature which "can give rise to, or trigger, systems which once in existence are self-sustaining and hence not explicable entirely in terms of the conditions which produced them."[40] She applies this principle directly to persons and argues that we must recognize them as unique in the chain of nature "without violating our underlying belief in the continuity of nature."[41] Such recognition of personhood, she claims, "establishes a new level over and above the others.... In proceeding from the recognition of matter to life to persons to responsible persons, we are proceeding up a scale of complexities, each of which entails the earlier levels. Responsible persons are persons, persons are individuals, individuals are physical structures, yet each kind we recognize as also more, and other, than the preceding, or underlying, level."[42]

To reach an adequate understanding of persons, Grene is suggesting, we must get beyond the primitive reductionism which characterizes certain kinds of scientific thought. Reductionism, as Ian Barbour has defined it, is "the attributing of reality exclusively to the smallest constituents of the world, and the tendency to interpret higher levels of organization in terms of lower levels."[43] Grene believes, along with Barbour, that "to break the stranglehold of reductivism [sic], we must acknowledge *the multiplicity of forms of being*."[44] There are forms of being or levels of reality that transcend, but do not conflict with and are not radically discontinuous with, other forms of being and levels of reality. What we have to see, in order to accept this claim, is that some beings are *hierarchically* structured. That is, within the same being there are many levels of reality, not discontinuous with each other, but arranged in a hierarchical pattern such that the higher levels depend upon the lower for the conditions of existence and that the lower levels depend upon the higher for direction. "The higher level depends for its existence on the lower, but the laws of the lower level, though presupposed by, cannot explain the existence of the higher—although they may suffice to explain its failures."[45]

The notion of the hierarchy permits the biologist to focus upon the system as a whole and not exclusively upon the parts or organs of the system. Sometimes known as "organicism" or "systems philosophy," this approach to nature sees the organic whole as a unity subject to principles of explanation that are unique to the whole rather than reducible to principles that are drawn from and apply primarily at lower levels. As Ludwig von Bertalanffy, one of the first exponents of a systems philosophy in biology, has put it: "Every organism represents a system, by which term we mean a complex of elements in mutual interaction . . . [and] the organismic method is to find exactly formulated laws for the organic systems as a whole."[46]

The organism of Whitehead is replaced, according to Ervin Laszlo (who has developed systems philosophy perhaps further than most other contemporary philosophers), by the concept "of a dynamic, self-sustaining 'system' discriminated against the background of a changing natural environment."[47] The properties of such a "system" would include, according to von Bertalanffy, "hierarchic structure, stability, teleology, differentiation, approach to and maintenance of steady states, [and] goal-directedness."[48] The significance of this systems approach is that it can take all these elements and place them within a single whole which is itself an actuality capable, at certain high levels, of self-direction. And this notion of a self-directing actuality comes very close to what we normally believe a person to be.

This systems or hierarchy concept does not deny the reality of processes such as those which form the heart of Whitehead's organic scheme. But it places these processes within a larger organic whole which is not simply a "society" of basic actual entities but has its own basic unity and character which are, in important ways, other than or more than the unity and character of its component parts. Systems philosophy, as Laszlo has put it, apparently with reference to Whitehead, "reintegrates the concept of enduring universals [persons?] with transient processes [actual occasions?] within a non-bifurcated, hierarchically differentiated realm of invariant *systems*, as the ultimate actualities of self-structuring nature."[49]

The notion of the organism is one of unity attributed to the whole and the behavior of the whole determining its subordinate parts. In the rather complicated language of Laszlo, "Organisms of all kinds are built by the integration of systems into superordinate systems, and these again into still higher level systems, until we encounter the organism as a whole. Each subsystem finds constraints imposed on its behavior by the higher system, with the result that the total organism's functional behavior dominates the behavior of all its parts, through successive hierarchically organized steps."[50]

Paul Weiss, a biologist, has put it this way:

> An organism as a system reveals itself as encompassing and operating through the agency of subsystems, each of which, in turn, contains and operates through groups of systems of still lower order, and so on down through molecules into

the atomic and sub-atomic range. The fact that the top level operations of the organism thus are neither structurally nor functionally referable to direct liaison with the processes on the molecular level in a steady continuous gradation, but are relayed step-wise from higher levels of determinacy... through intermediate layers of greater freedom or variance... to next lower levels of again more rigorously ascertainable determinacy, constitutes the *principle of hierarchical organization*.[51]

This systems or hierarchy approach permits us to reject the notion of panpsychism because it is not necessary to attribute to each of the parts what may be true only of the basic organic whole. The whole possesses traits, such as self-direction, which lower levels within it may not possess. What is true of the system as a whole does not need to be true of the subsystems which constitute it. This fact would permit the "emergence" of something new, such as mentality or intentionality, at higher levels of organization without requiring us to postulate its presence at the lower levels as well. At the same time, however, the continuity of nature is preserved. Systems philosophy does not fall back into dualism. The higher level organisms include and depend upon the lower levels but within a single unified, not divided, whole. The presence of mentality or intentionality is not severed or bifurcated from dimensions lacking them, but emerges within the organically integrated whole when the hierarchical structure permits. The notion of the integrating yet basic whole prohibits the isolation of actualities from each other. As Ian Barbour has put it, "Recognition of both the diversity of activities at various levels and the continuity between levels enables us to avoid the ontological discontinuity of dualism as well as the one-level metaphysics to which reductionism usually leads."[52]

Now, the question to which this brief introduction to systems philosophy and the notion of hierarchy leads, is how such a new approach to the organic model can help us understand persons. What is suggested is that the person is "a many-leveled unity" who includes inorganic, organic, and what we might call supraorganic levels, hierarchically organized, but at the highest level expressing conscious, intentional self-direction. It is this last characteristic, in particular, that must not only be present in persons in order to justify our belief in their uniqueness, but must be distinguished from the kind of teleological behavior appropriate to organisms of a nonpersonal kind.

Teleology. In the narrower definition of the organism, teleological direction is generally used to cover any kind of movement or behavior which appears goal-oriented. Such movement can include the path of atoms, the turning of the plant to the sun, the growth of the acorn into an oak tree, the pursuit of the cat by the dog, the flight of the rocket to its target, the response of the robot to its employer's command, and the choice of a husband by a young woman.

Common sense tells us, of course, that there are some important differences between these various kinds of teleological movements. We do not normally believe that rockets "choose" their targets, or that acorns "intend" to become oak trees, or that the plant "desires" sunlight. There is something about the kind of conscious intentionality by which human persons make choices and determine their own behavior that sets their "teleology" apart from that appropriate to a plant, dog, or atom. Barbour has identified four basic meanings of teleology or purpose which help us to distinguish the various kinds of movements described above. One kind of movement is "functional behavior," which covers "the contribution that a part or process makes to the activity or maintenance of the whole."[53] This might cover the movement of the blood in the body. It does not require that the part or process have a goal in mind for its movement. A second kind of purpose is "self-regulating behavior." This applies to what are called servo-mechanisms, machines designed by human intelligence to respond in a regular way to certain changing conditions. A standard example is that of the furnace in one's basement. It "turns itself on and off" according to changes in temperature. The computer-guided rocket might also be seen as a servo-mechanism because it can change direction if certain conditions affect its onboard computer-guidance system. Still, we need to remember that the apparent goal-oriented nature of these machines is given to them by intelligent beings. The machines do not provide their own goals.

A third kind of teleology is goal-directed behavior, or "persistence toward a goal under varying conditions."[54] This would cover the dog's pursuit of the cat. The goal stays the same but there is a wide variation possible in the behavior of the pursuer. But there is no evidence that the dog is able to "decide" whether to pursue the cat. We are more likely to attribute the pursuit to a biological inclination or genetic predisposition. But there is a fourth kind of teleology, and that is intentional action proper, in which conscious intention and choice determine the action which is undertaken. It is the presence of this kind of unique conscious self-direction in persons which the notion of the hierarchy promises to preserve. Unless we can justify the distinction between purposes which an entity gives to itself and purposes given to it (by "nature" or by other purposive entities), then there will be nothing distinctive about persons and no way of explaining the fact that we certainly feel there is a difference between our intended action and the behavior of a plant, or even of most animals. In each case there is movement toward an end, but only in persons is that end consciously chosen. The "organicist," "systems," or "hierarchy" concept can give us a basis for attributing to an organic whole or totality that which "could not be meaningfully attributed to an entity or process to which the character of wholeness could not be ascribed. It is possible to refer to a process or part within the whole and to attribute to it a function as a part which is determined by and consonant with the goal orientation of the whole."[55]

One philosopher who has developed this idea, while remaining generally within an organic model of reality, with specific concern for a notion of the person as capable of conscious self-direction while at the same time nondualistically related to levels of nature which are not self-conscious, is Edward Pols. His work provides, I believe, an important transition from the organic model as such to a model of persons as agents whose conscious intentions create the bonds of community as a set of mutual/personal relations. Pols stretches the organic model to include the kind of nonreductive action unique to persons without falling into the dualism between persons and non-persons which the narrower organic model fears so much and which it avoids only by postulating panpsychism. In the process, Pols implicitly employs a notion of hierarchical inclusiveness which enables him to understand persons as including in their own organic unity those levels of nature which are nonintentional and inorganic. Some such notion of hierarchical inclusiveness, as we shall see, is central to the notion of the person in the mutual/personal model of community. If Pols is successful in defending a notion of the uniqueness of persons within a very broad organic model, he will have made possible a smooth and "metaphysically friendly" transition to a model of community based on the *primacy* in nature of persons in relation.

EDWARD POLS AND A HIERARCHICAL MODEL OF THE PERSON AS AGENT

Organisms and Persons. The contemporary American philosopher Edward Pols provides an excellent transition to the mutual/personal model because he makes an argument for the authenticity of persons as distinct from other entities in the universe (an authenticity which is crucial to the development of the mutual/personal model) and yet does so from within a broadened organic model. In fact, he is quite explicit about his acceptance of the organicist or systems notion of the biological hierarchy which seeks to find a place for the uniqueness of persons. There are five levels in the biological hierarchy, according to Pols: organism, organ, cell, organelle, and molecule. The topmost member is the organism, or "system."[56] The terms "system" and "organism" are used interchangeably by Pols with what he calls the Agent and what the mutual/personal model will also call the agent or person. The point is that within Pols' employment of "hierarchic science," the term "organism" includes all the necessary characteristics which the mutual/personal model wants to attribute to persons. Because this is so, Pols' argument slides nicely into the development of the mutual/personal model of community which is based on a notion of the person or agent as a unique entity, yet thoroughly continuous with lower levels of nature.

The significance and strength of Pols' argument is that it justifies an understanding of the agent as a basic unified whole making use of (by including within its unity) subwholes or infrastructures which are quite capable of being understood in themselves without reference to intention and self-direction. At the same time, however, hierarchic science demands that the agent's choices be treated as ultimate or basic, not potentially reducible, explanations of what the agent does. In speaking of Socrates' decisions and acts, Pols says that "an explanation that comes back to himself is final, satisfactory, and not to be set aside by any other. This means that it is also not to be set aside by scientific explanations that avoid the category of action entirely, and are couched instead in terms of entities, processes, functions, states, or events related under the laws of nature."[57] What this means is that the unity and action of agents are so basic, so authentic in their own right, that they cannot be reduced to more basic units without eliminating their own essential unity. When applied to personal agents, this means that when I choose to do something, the ultimate explanation for my act is "me" as a unified whole, not as a set or society of more basic parts which in the aggregate are "me." In particular, Pols wants to argue that the deterministic cause and effect form of explanation, which is clearly appropriate at levels of nature where conscious choice is not present, is not sufficient or adequate to explain the action of free agents.

Originative Acts. The act of an agent is, according to Pols, "originative." It originates and unifies a series of subacts. The originative act is not completely caused by prior acts nor by any set of acts within the series it unifies or controls. It extends over a period of time (of whatever duration) and cannot be broken down into shorter originative acts within that time period. "The simplicity, or unity, of an originative act means that it is exercised in a unit of action that requires a corresponding time-unit for its realization, and that it can not be identified as an exercise of power unless we take the whole time-unit into consideration. . . . It is of the nature of the power of an originative act that it reaches throughout a span distinct as to its limits and ordered within those limits both as to content and temporality."[58]

Pols is quite specific as to how this view of the unity of an agent's acts differs from the unity of the actual occasion in Whitehead's organic philosophy. It will be remembered that for Whitehead, the fundamental unities of nature were invariable in duration (lasting about 1/100th of a second) and, according to the ephocal theory of time, did not really admit of temporal sequence (that is, they were genetically divisible but not divisible into earlier and later phases, because Whitehead seemed to feel that temporal division would destroy their fundamental unity). Pols' originative act, however, occurs over a period of time and the length of that time will differ from one originative act to another.[59] In this sense, I believe, Pols' view of an act is much closer to a common-sense, intuitive understanding than is Whitehead's, and is to be preferred if it can avoid dualism and justify our understanding of persons as themselves fundamental unities. As we shall see, this is precisely what I think Pols succeeds in doing.

The significance of the notion of the originative act is that it includes but is not simply the aggregate of levels of nature which may not themselves be acts but are essential as the infrastructure by which acts are expressed. The originative act unifies a series of subacts but remains throughout the unification "an absolutely seamless unity."[60] This series of subacts is the infrastructure of the originative act. The concept of infrastructure "includes all the functions and processes that take place within the persistent physical structure of the body . . . "[61] These processes include the firing of a neural cell or a sequence of cells, the contraction of a muscle, the movement of a bone, circulation of blood, and all the other biological functions that are essential to the persistence of the biological body. The infrastructure consists of many levels, all appropriately subject, if taken by themselves, to explanation by scientific analysis and the laws of cause and effect.

The originative act, the act of the organism or agent, however, is more than simply the set or aggregation of the processes in the infrastructure. The act is "a power so permeating the spatiotemporal manifold of the infrastructure as to unify it—the unification being precisely the full concreteness of the act. This may be expressed in a number of other ways: the power of Socrates' act orders, disposes, uses, deploys, shapes, binds together, wields the multiplicity of the spatiotemporal elements that make up its infrastructure."[62]

The Infrastructure of an Act. There is a relationship of One and Many between the act and its infrastructure. Unlike Whitehead's understanding of the One and the Many (the Many being unified within the emerging actual occasion through concrescence and prehension), Pols' understanding is that the one act unifies the many processes within it. There is an asymmetrical identity between the act and its infrastructure. "The act 'is' its infrastructure by being 'in' it, by exercising its power on and by means of the infrastructure, by unifying the infrastructure in a power-unit. The infrastructure, on the other hand, 'is' the act by being the mutiplicity that is unified by it."[63] The difference between Pols' view and Whitehead's is that for Pols the act is the fundamental unit, no matter how long it takes to perform, and the processes within its infrastructure (which really correspond to Whitehead's actual occasions) are only "parts," though essential parts, of it. As long as we focus our attention upon a unity more basic than the act itself, we wind up losing the act, and in the process, the agent as well. "[W]ith the mode of attention characterized by event-ontology [Pols' word for Whitehead's view], linear time, and C—E [cause and effect] analysis we seem to be able to locate only 'causes without which the cause cannot be the cause'—causes, furthermore, that we must also take to be effects.... Looked for in this way, the act eludes us. If this is what we mean by 'somewhere', then the act, and hence the agent, must be nowhere."[64] But the act of the agent is "everywhere and at every time in the manifold of an infrastructure understood in other terms."[65] In other words, we can avoid reductionism and dualism only if we look for fundamental unity in the right place which, according to Pols, is in the agent and his originative acts.

This notion of an act and its infrastructure clearly is not dualistic because it affirms the fundamental unity of the act. It is "a unity-*in*-multiplicity that is quite at odds with dualisms of the kind that have so often been found to be logically objectionable."[66] Whitehead avoids dualism by containing everything within the actual occasion (leading him to the doctrine of panpsychism), whereas Pols avoids dualism by postulating a broader, more comprehensive unity originating in the act of an agent which can include within itself elements of reality which are less basic, nonoriginative, and dependent upon a more inclusive unifying power.

The upshot of this analysis of the unity of the act and its relation to its own infrastructure is that it leads to a strong affirmation of the fundamental unity of the agent without whom the act would not exist. The agent is the controlling unit of all the lower levels, or infrastructures within his system. Hierarchic science reminds us that each level within a system is controlled by the level above it and that the "laws" of cause and effect at one level do not determine or limit the freedom of the controlling unit at the higher levels.

There may be "laws" appropriate to each level but "though they are the laws *of* that level, the units of that level do not so much 'obey' them as they exemplify them. It is the units of the level beneath that 'obey' them or are determined, or controlled, by them."[67] It follows that the laws appropriate for the infrastructure level of cells, for example, would not be the same laws appropriate for the unifying level of the agent as a whole. Much of modern biology, including that which accepts the notion of hierarchy, has not been willing to grasp the significance of this notion of the relationship between laws and levels within the hierarchy when it comes to understanding the agent as a single unified whole. "It is a limitation ... of biology that it seems to be most at home when it studies any subsystem as a set of subsystems—that is, when it concentrates on the multiplicity and the interrelation of the elements and functions rather than on the unity that, though it might consist in the *relating* of them, might be inscrutable to a scientific method."[68] The strict application of such a method often winds up leaving out "the level of the individual organism—the unity at the top of a ramifying multiplicity of structural subsystems."[69] It is this unity, the individual agent, that Pols wants to rescue from reductive causal analysis but to keep continuous with those elements in nature (the infrastructure) which are subject to scientific explanation. The notion of the ontological authenticity of the agent and his originative acts succeeds in doing just that and, at the same time, points beyond narrower, traditional biological models (including many of those willing to affirm a multi-leveled nature and hierarchical structure) toward models that take the agent, or person, as the basic, primary unity from which other dimensions of nature are derived by abstraction.

The Agent. If we take seriously the hierarchical notion that "given any hierarchical system having levels some of which can not exist (in a natural state) independently of the uppermost level of that system, then the 'real causality' operative at any of those levels must be ascribed to the 'real causality' of the uppermost level."[70] This means that "any nonindependent unity exercising 'real causality' within the unity of the system we call Socrates— say an organelle over its molecule, a cell over its organelle, an organ over its cell—owes its 'real causality' to the unity of the Socrates himself."[71] This leads logically to the claim "that the category of agent is more fundamental than that of action..."[72] The agent is "an entity with an ontological status more fundamental than the acts themselves."[73] "The ontological feat of an originative act ramifying in sub-acts that are themselves originative acts is appropriately attributable to a subject-entity whom we appropriately call an agent."[74] This subject-unity is basic and authentic, that is, nonreducible, "even though analysis may find a variety of multiplicities" within it.[75] The unity of the agent is a power pervading the multiplicity of the infrastructure and is distinguishable "*as* a unity *from* that multiplicity to just the extent that its power *unifies* that multiplicity."[76]

On the basis of this notion of the unity of the agent, Pols can make the kind of claims about agents which Whitehead could not make and which need to be made if we are to justify the ongoing endurance of persons who enter into relations with others in community. If we accept the claim that agents are basic units, the agents "transcend" their individual acts. This means, specifically for Pols, that the category 'entity' is more fundamental than 'act'; that the entity "is continuous although his acts are distinct units"; that "his self-identity can not be adequately understood solely in terms of the inheritance by a given act of characteristics from earlier acts."[77] This last claim provides the basis for understanding the agent as able to act freely as an already unified being, and thus undercuts Whitehead's principle that the agent can not act on others until after its unity has been achieved, at which point it perishes. Pols' position also permits the agent to act with conscious intention. This is a form of the teleology so important to an organic model, but in Pols it is based upon the conscious self-direction of the agent and not simply upon programming provided by other entities or upon nonconscious response to stimuli.

It follows from this understanding of the agent that it has "fewer of the deficiencies he has in accounts that must construct him out of atomic units—memories, impressions, events, bodily states, or whatever—that are taken to be more patently authentic than the agent himself."[78] Pols is clearly thinking once again of Whitehead here, and supports the criticism we made of Whitehead in our section on him. Whitehead is compelled "to give entities like Socrates the derivative ontological status of 'societies' of . . . 'actual entities'," whereas Pols' position is that Socrates is "a fundamental entity, of the hierarchical kind that expresses itself in an infrastructure of discrete units some members of which are also fundamental entities."[79]

This notion of the fundamental unity of the agent is crucial to the mutual/personal understanding of persons and will be explored more fully in our discussion of Macmurray's notion of the self as agent. However, it should be noted at this point that Pols' position is now being given consideration by some philosophers who also take the scientific enterprise seriously. One of these is Hilde Hein, who has examined the scientific explanation of the origin of life in the universe. She points out that much traditional scientific thinking has "been indoctrinated with the geometric principle that complicated things are built out of simple ones, and that fruitful analysis is the result of careful separation of the simple elements which together produce a complex synthesis."[80] This way of approaching nature leads to reductionism and the inability to see unities any greater than the smallest entities.

However, she suggests that "there is nothing sacrosanct about the pattern of reductionism which is most ardently endorsed by contemporary reductionists."[81] There are modes of understanding, she claims, which start with the unity of a total context and understand other elements only within that unity. "Once we have a comprehension of a complex situation, individual features of it seem to fall into place with respect to it, but we could not have understood them apart from or prior to placing them within that total context."[82] It is this total context which I believe Pols is referring to when he talks about the unity of the agent being more basic than that of the acts which he performs or of the infrastructure through which the acts get expressed. Hein has even suggested that one day science may engage in a 'reverse reductionism', scrap its entire classification scheme, and "begin anew with a re-examination of phenomena according to a fresh set of categories."[83] It is this fresh set of categories which I believe Pols has begun to provide and which are necessary if the understanding of persons as abiding agents capable of entering into communal relation with each other over time, but as individual unities, not as organs within a larger organism, is to be justified. Pols has gone a long way toward establishing the metaphysical categories which must undergird such an understanding.

Pols' predilection for using the term 'organism' to refer to agents has the advantage of linking him with the concerns of those scientists and philosophers who are obsessed with the continuity of nature. The notion of the hierarchy of biological levels and the relation of the originative, basic act to its infrastructure enables Pols to accept the continuity of nature, but his focus upon the "transcendent" or unifying nature of the orginative act and its agent enables him to justify a notion of the uniqueness of the agent. In this way, Pols has provided an alternative to Whitehead's interpretation of the organism as reducible to the level of the actual occasion and of the need to resort to a panpsychism which must attribute essential personal characteristics to every level of reality. By having an ontological authenticity, the agent in Pols' scheme is not simply a complex relation between more basic units (such as a society of them in linear order). Pols also avoids the Whiteheadian problem of there being no enduring subject. As long as the unity of the agent is not limited to the unity of the occasion, the agent can endure for any length of time without his fundamental unity being thereby impaired. In this way, the agent is capable of entering into all kinds of relations while remaining the self-same, identical agent.

But what still seems to be missing, or at least not given sufficient attention, even by Pols, is any discussion of the *particular* intentions the agent might have for his activity. To what is it directed? How is the agent related to other agents? What place is there in that relation for love and mutual concern? Pols has, I think, provided the *grounds* for an understanding of the person as a fundamental unity able to enter into community with others. But what the model of the mutual/personal will provide is an emphasis on the primacy of community as the most important *intention* of persons. If we are to succeed in developing a full understanding of mutual love, we need to explore still one more model in which persons are intended for community by a Creator-Agent and intend community with each other, not simply as a functional cooperative endeavor or through inclusion as each seeks self-fulfillment, but as an end in itself which is constituted by seeking the fulfillment of others for their own sake. Pols' analysis is a necessary but not sufficient condition for the development of a mutual/personal model of community. But it takes us from the organic model into the mutual model without having to abandon or deny a broadened organic understanding of the continuity of nature and the interrelatedness of all things.

NOTES TO CHAPTER 4

1. There have appeared recently some works linking the thought of Whitehead to both Hegel and Marx. See especially George R. Lucas, Jr., *Two Views of Freedom in Process Thought: A Study of Hegel and Whitehead* (Missoula, Mont.: Scholars Press, 1979, American Academy of Religion) and Russell L. Kleinbach, *Marx via Process: Whitehead's Potential Contribution to Marxian Social Theory* (Washington, D.C.: University Press of America, 1982).

2. Alfred North Whitehead, *Process and Reality: An Essay in Cosmology*, corrected ed., ed. David Ray Griffin and Donald W. Sherburne (New York: Free Press, 1978), 18.

3. Ibid., 209.

4. Ibid., 21.

5. Victor Lowe, "Whitehead's Metaphysical System" (from *Understanding Whitehead*, in *Process Philosophy and Christian Thought*, ed. Delwin Brown, Ralph E. James, Jr., and Gene Reeves (Indianapolis: Bobbs-Merrill, 1971), 4.

6. Whitehead, *Process and Reality*, 18.
7. Ibid.
8. Ibid.
9. Ibid., 110.
10. Ibid., 211.
11. Ibid.
12. Ibid., 212.
13. Ibid., 22.
14. Ibid., 215.
15. Ibid., 214–15.
16. Ibid., 215.
17. Ibid., 23.
18. Ibid., 84.
19. Ibid., 88.
20. Ibid.
21. Ibid., 69.
22. John Cobb, *A Christian Natural Theology: Based on the Thought of Alfred North Whitehead* (Philadelphia: The Westminster Press, 1965), 96.
23. Whitehead, *Process and Reality*, 69.
24. Ibid., 109.
25. Alfred North Whitehead, *Adventures of Ideas* (New York: The Free Press, 1967), 285–86.
26. Ibid., 292.
27. Ibid.
28. Whitehead, *Process and Reality*, 222.
29. Ibid., 6.
30. Ian G. Barbour, *Issues in Science and Religion* (New York: Harper and Row, 1966), 347, 452.
31. L. Charles Birch, "Can Evolution Be Accounted For Solely in Terms of Mechanical Causation?" in *Mind in Nature: Essays on the Interface of Science and Philosophy*, ed. John B. Cobb, Jr. and David Ray Griffin (Washington, D.C.: University Press of American, 1977), 15.
32. Ibid., 14.
33. Sewall Wright, "Panpsychism and Science," in *Mind in Nature*, 82.
34. Charles Hartshorne, "Physics and Psychics: The Place of Mind in Nature," in *Mind in Nature*, 90.
35. Ibid., 95.
36. Charles Hartshorne, *The Logic of Perfection* (Lasalle, Ill.: Open Court, 1962), 191.
37. Ibid., 192.
38. Ibid., 309.
39. Ibid.
40. Marjorie Grene, *The Knower and the Known* (New York: Basic Books, 1966), 211.
41. Ibid., 212.

42. Ibid., 212, 217.
43. Barbour, *Issues in Science and Religion*, 52.
44. Grene, *The Knower and the Known*, 219.
45. Marjorie Grene, *The Understanding of Nature: Essays in the Philosophy of Biology*, Boston Studies in the Philosophy of Science, ed. Robert Cohen and Marx Wartofsky, vol. XXIII (Dordrecht, Holland: D. Reidel, 1974), 48.
46. Ludwig von Bertalanffy, *Problems of Life: An Evaluation of Modern Biological Thought* (New York: John Wiley and Sons, 1952), 11, 171.
47. Ervin Laszlo, *Introduction to Systems Philosophy: Toward a New Paradigm of Contemporary Thought*, with a foreword by Ludwig von Bertalanffy (New York: Gordon and Breach, Science Publishers, 1972), viii.
48. Ibid., xviii.
49. Ibid., 12.
50. Ibid., 97.
51. Paul Weiss, "The Living System: Determinism Stratified," in *Beyond Reductionism*, The Alpbach Symposium 1968. New Perspectives in the Life Sciences, ed. Arthur Koestler and J.R. Smythies (Boston: Beacon Press, 1969), 33.
52. Barbour, *Issues in Science and Religion*, 360.
53. Ibid., 337.
54. Ibid., 339.
55. Hilde Hein, *On the Nature and Origin of Life* (New York: McGraw-Hill, 1971), 60.
56. Edward Pols, *Meditation on a Prisoner: Towards Understanding Action and Mind* (Carbondale and Edwardsville: Southern Illinois University Press, 1975), 41–42.
57. Ibid., 11.
58. Ibid., 111, 112.
59. Ibid., 357–58.
60. Ibid., 99.
61. Ibid., 103.
62. Ibid., 105.
63. Ibid., 106.
64. Ibid., 110.
65. Ibid.
66. Ibid., 277.
67. Ibid., 48.
68. Ibid., 53.
69. Ibid.
70. Ibid., 65.
71. Ibid.
72. Ibid., 72.
73. Ibid., 309.
74. Ibid.
75. Ibid., 93.

76. Ibid.
77. Ibid., 310.
78. Ibid.
79. Ibid., 328.
80. Hein, *On the Nature and Origin of Life*, 172–73.
81. Ibid., 173.
82. Ibid., 172–73.
83. Ibid., 173.

5. The Mutual/Personal Model of Community: Metaphysical Foundations

COMMUNITY IN THE RELIGIOUS CONTEXT

The central problem of community for our age is how to reconcile our Western liberal insistence on the freedom of the individual with our desire to enter into interpersonal relations with others. As Stanley Hauerwas has said, "We have made 'freedom of the individual' an end in itself and have ignored the fact that most of us do not have the slightest idea of what we should do with our freedom. Indeed, the idealists among us are reduced to fighting for the 'freedom' or 'right' of others to realize their self-interests more fully." [1] The dominance of the atomistic-contractarian model of community (really, an anticommunity model) explains why there is so little discussion of the goal of freedom and so much struggle to establish the right of the individual to use his freedom in whatever ways he chooses. Because of the atomistic/contractarian model's asssumption that ultimately all individuals are isolated monads contracting for the terms of relationship, we accept our freedom and the primacy of self-interest as givens and then search desperately for some kind of bond with others that will transcend or mitigate the despair and loneliness which goalless freedom and self-interest have imposed upon us. We are trapped within an understanding of social relations in which others must be treated with distrust and fear because their self-interest may eventually conflict with ours. But this has a terribly destructive cyclical effect. As Hauerwas observes, "The more it becomes unthinkable to trust a stranger, the more we must depend on more exaggerated forms of protection. But the human costs of distrust are perhaps the most destructive. For we are increasingly forced to view one another as strangers rather than as friends, and as a result we become all the more lonely. We have learned to call our loneliness 'autonomy' and/or freedom, but the freer we become the more desperate our search for forms of 'community' or 'interpersonal relationship' that offer some contact with our fellows."[2]

While notions of community developed from within an organic model go a long way toward overcoming the isolation, separation, and loneliness of the atomistic model, they still seem curiously limited either by their emphasis on the functional subservience of the individual to a greater whole, on the primacy of self-realization, on the absence of an enduring individual capable of sustaining ongoing relations with others, and, most importantly, on the absence of any serious discussion of what the purpose or end of cooperative behavior should be. Even when cooperation and interdependence are stressed in opposition to the individualism and independence of the atomistic model, the organic models of community generally fail to concern themselves with what the individual who becomes free through cooperation with others should do with his freedom. The organic model has rightly justified the claim that only in relation can persons be truly free. But freedom is not an end in itself. Unless we have some better idea of what to do with our freedom for self-realization in the context of our interdependence, we will remain all the more desperate in our search for forms of community.

The Biblical View of Community. At the heart of the religious vision of community in the Western tradition, in both Judaism and Christianity, is the fundamental conviction that human freedom is ultimately meaningful and fulfilling only in a community of love, in which persons live primarily for others because of the power which God has given them for that purpose and because the conditions of their nature which he created can be fulfilled in no other way. Neither Judaism nor Christianity makes any sense unless it is rooted in the belief that through love God intends to achieve a universal community for and with his human creation. Only this understanding of the divine intention makes sense of history. "In the Christian faith love is disclosed as the centre and spirit of ... history. Love is not an idea which we add to our beliefs about God and his self-revelation. Love is what God's spirit is in his action in history, as he deals with human loves and lovelessness, and opens the way to a new community of life whose spirit is informed by love."[3] Jesus said to his disciples (the first Christian community), "As the Father has loved me, so I have loved you. Remain in my love ... Love one another, as I have loved you. A man can have no greater love than to lay down his life for his friends"(John 15:9-10, 12-13). And the earliest Christian communities, trying to live by this injunction to love following the death of Jesus, were said to be "united, heart and soul; no one claimed for his own use anything that he had, as everything they owned was held in common" (Acts 4:32).

According to the biblical tradition, the love which binds God's human creation together with him and with itself is the love known as agape, the community-creating force which God has released into the world and by which his intention for community will be realized. Community is the work of both God and human persons but its realization, or achievement, is sustained by the very conditions of reality itself because they are themselves God's creation and thus support God's intention. As Martin Luther King, Jr. put it, "All human efforts to establish community are supported by the laws of the universe because God created the universe that way."[4]

Judaism shares with Christianity (in fact, gave to its younger brother the imagery and understanding of) this deep commitment to community as God's intention for the world. As Martin Buber has said, "The primary aspiration of all history is a genuine community of human beings."[5] Such a community will arise through persons "first, taking their stand in living mutual relation with a living Centre, and, second, their being in living mutual relation with one another. The second has its source in the first, but is not given when the first alone is given ... The community is built up out of living mutual relation, but the builder is the living effective Centre."[6] This stress on the centrality of community in Judaism (perhaps seen initially as stronger in the elder brother than in Christianity, which has, erroneously, been interpreted as essentially individualistic) has even led one famous twelfth century Jewish philosopher, Maimonides, to say that "he who withdraws from the ways of the community ... such a one has no share in the World-to-Come."[7]

Most faithful Jews and Christians know that community is at the heart of their relationship with God and with each other. They also know that without God's creative work, both in the original setting of the conditions of reality and in His interventions within human history, community could not be realized. Unlike secular analyses of community, the people of God know that its realization requires the power of God, and not simply human power alone. They might also know that genuine community and other-directed love are correlative: that a primary concern for the well-being of the other person, a rejoicing in his or her otherness, is part of what makes the community authentic. But beyond these somewhat vague generalizations, it is not clear to many Jews and Christians, and certainly not to many philosophers, scientists, and sociologists, just what a community built upon the primacy of love and the power of God really can be. It has been all too easy to pass over a full, detailed, and often difficult analysis of the notion of community in the biblical tradition by vague appeals to the emotionally and rhetorically powerful language of love, trust, and fellowship.

The notion of a biblical community needs to be as grounded in an adequate metaphysical view of persons, God, and interpersonal relations as the other two models of community are grounded either implicitly or explicitly upon metaphysical assumptions. The biblical claims about community are intended to be claims not only about what is real, but about what is intended to become real through the power of human persons working in conjunction with God. If these claims are to be taken seriously, then some metaphysical grounding must be given to them. They must be subject to the same kind of metaphysical scrutiny to which, for example, Hobbes and Whitehead subjected their views. If claims about community are claims about reality, then it is incumbent upon those who make them to ensure that they cohere with and are supported by the best assessment we can make of the world in which we live.

BUBER'S I-THOU AND VISION OF INTERRELATIONSHIP

"The other is my *thou*—the relation being reciprocal—my *alter ego*, man objective to me, the revelation of my own nature. In another I first have the consciousness of humanity; through him I first learn, I first feel, that I am a man: in my love for him it is first clear to me that he belongs to me and I to him, that we two cannot be without each other, that only community constitutes humanity."[8]

Most contemporary readers of religious philosophy would probably identify this quote as Martin Buber's. But in fact, it is from Ludwig Feuerbach, the "river of fire" separating Hegel from Marx. The notion of the "I-Thou" relation goes back in modern philosophy at least as far as Feuerbach and indicates a stream of thinking which takes the relation between persons as the clue to human nature and the creation of community. In the past half-century, that stream of thought has found no more poetic or well-known exponent than the Jewish philosopher, Martin Buber. At the beginning of the second decade of this century a small book, *Ich und Du*, appeared in German and a decade and a half later appeared in English as *I and Thou*. Buber admitted the decisive influence on his work of Feuerbach's *Essence of Christianity*, from which the opening quotation was taken. But Buber has done more than anyone else to give the notion of the "I-Thou" relation a permanent place in the lexicon of religious philosophy. Although I believe Macmurray's philosophy (which was itself influenced by Buber to some degree) provides a more thorough and metaphysically comprehensive system, Buber's work must be included in any discussion of the mutual/personal model of community.

Buber's "I-Thou" notion is important for a number of reasons. First, it places a stress on the primacy of relationship (not the primacy of individuals), which clearly has little place in the atomistic/contractarian understanding of community. "The one primary word is the combination *I-Thou*."[9] Like the organicists, Buber believes that the isolated individual of the atomistic/contractarian model is a fiction, or at the very least, an incomplete person. Even the I who enters into "It" relations with the world is a connected"I." "There is no I taken in itself, but only the 'I' of the primary word *I-Thou* and the 'I' of the primary word *I-It*."[10] I and Thou by its nature precedes I taken alone.[11]

A second reason for the importance of the I-Thou concept is its claim that only in the I-Thou relation is the self fulfilled. "The primary word *I-Thou* can only be spoken with the whole being."[12] To meet the Thou is to meet directly and in love. The I does not possess the Thou but allows the Thou to meet, love, and be loved. "Love does not cling to the 'I' in such a way as to have the *Thou* only for its 'content,' its object; but love is *between I* and *Thou*."[13] The relation is mutual. "My *Thou* affects me, as I affect it."[14] It is only "through the *Thou* a man becomes 'I'."[15] Only in that relationship does the true person emerge. The "I" of the I-It relation is only an individual, capable of using others for its own self-interest. But the "I" of the I-Thou relation "makes its appearance as person ... by entering into relation with other persons."[16] And the fuller its relationship with other Thous is, "the more real it becomes."[17] "For the inmost growth of the self is not accomplished ... in man's relation to himself, but in the relation between the one and the other, between men, that is, pre-eminently in the mutuality of the making present—in the making present of another self and in the knowledge that one is made present in his own self by the other—together with the mutuality of acceptance, of affirmation and confirmation."[18]

A third aspect of Buber's thought which contributes to a model of community is his belief that only in a community of mutuality is the I-Thou relation fulfilled. "Structures of man's communal life draw their living quality from the riches of the power to enter into relation..."[19] And he believes that the human race is given by creation "the task of becoming a community."[20] Community, for Buber, is the concrete expression in the real world of the ideal relation of the I-Thou. Community is "a connection of men who are so joined in their life with something apportioned to them in common or something which they have apportioned to themselves in common that they are, just thereby, joined with one another in their life."[21] As Bernard Susser puts it, "*I-Thou* captures the unalloyed ideal while community is its translation—as in most translations something is lost—into immanent, worldly terms. From one perspective, community is the *I-Thou* relation as seen through the prism of the 'reality principle'."[22] Buber, I think, can be extremely helpful to the mutual/personal model of community just at this point because of his "realistic" understanding of how the struggle for community can be carried on in a world which is always seducing the I-Thou relation back into the I-It relation. We will return to this point later.

Fourth, Buber's importance resides in his stress upon the indispensable role of God as the Centre of community, the creator of its conditions, and the agent who calls it into being through his relations with his creatures. The context for the world of Thou is "in the Centre, where the extended lines of relations meet—in the eternal *Thou*."[23] Achieving community cannot occur "otherwise than out of a common relation to the divine center... Unity with God and community among the creatures belong together."[24]

Fifth, I think Buber's insight that genuine human community must be intentionally inclusive is important to a full working out of the notion of community. Too often communities are understood to be limited by just those persons who can be in direct communion with each other. While direct communion is the essence of communion, its absence should not be an excuse to draw a boundary of exclusion around the community. The real community, Buber believes, is one that is open to relationship even when relationship has not yet been realized in each and every case. "A real community need not consist of people who are perpetually together; but it must consist of people who, precisely because they are comrades, have mutual access to one another and are ready for one another. A real community is one which in every point of its being possesses, potentially at least, the whole character of community."[25]

Finally, we must note the significance of Buber's belief that the establishment of community is a cooperative endeavor. Man and God work together. "I believe that man is created as a partner of God; which means that I believe in a co-working of the deed of mortal man and the grace of eternity incomprehensible to the human mind."[26] "Do you not know too that God needs you—in the fulness of His eternity needs you? . . . You need God, in order to be—and God needs you, for the very meaning of your life."[27]

These six points—the primacy of the relationship between persons, the fulfillment of the person in relationship, the development of community as the way to that fulfillment, the essential role of God as creator of the conditions for community and as Agent working toward its completion, the importance of human activity in partnership with God, and intentional inclusiveness of the community—will all be taken up in Macmurray's philosophy and put into a coherent, systematic relationship with each other. Buber was not himself that interested in developing a descriptive metaphysics, and thus he provides us primarily with indispensable insights into, and not with a full metaphysics of, community.

But it is also significant, I think, that despite all of Buber's valuable contributions to the study of community along the lines of personal, I-Thou relations, he often relied upon essentially organic imagery to express his ideas. And in the end, this reliance often blunts the full force of what he intends to say because it implicitly suggests a less than fully personal understanding of persons-in-relation. I agree with Peter Bertocci, who has said of Buber that "his thinking at all explanatory levels seems to be closer to the unity of an organic whole."[28] Bertocci's criticism is based upon those passages in Buber's writings in which he seems to suggest that in some sense relationship is an inclusion of two partners into a greater whole. In speaking of the relation with God, for example, Buber says that he who enters into that relationship "is concerned with nothing isolated any more, neither things nor beings, neither earth nor heaven; but everything is gathered up in the relation ... to include the whole world in the *Thou* ... to include nothing beside God but everything in him—this is full and complete relation."[29] This seems to suggest a kind of Hegelian organic inclusion in which the parts become less significant than the whole which includes them within itself.

I think Bertocci's claim is refuted by Buber at a number of points, perhaps nowhere more strongly than in the latter's constant reference to "setting-at-a-distance" as a prerequisite for relationship. This "distancing" of selves from each other sets the conditions for their relating to each other. They must be "over-against" and "independent" before they can meet and enter into relationship.[30] Nevertheless, because of Buber's often highly poetic language, and because of his deep faithfulness to the Hasidic or mystical traditions of Judaism (which clearly stress the overcoming of distance and the inclusion of reality in a single Whole), he often falls into forms of expression which suggest an organic inclusion or a part/whole relationship much like that in Hegel.

Even in his detailed and informative discussion of building community in *Paths in Utopia*, Buber continually talks about both society and community in organic imagery. (Susser has even said that "Buber is at one with Aristotle in accepting community as organic."[31] When he criticizes the state and the political sphere, he does so by contrasting it with "the organic, functionally organized society as such, a great society built up of various societies, the great society in which men lived and worked, competed with one another and helped one another; and in each of the big and little societies composing it, in each of these communes and communities the individual human being ... felt himself at home ... approved and affirmed in his functional independence and responsibility."[32] And Buber's vision of many communities coming together "to form a shapely and articulated race of men" is summarized under the term "organic commonwealth,"[33] which is also described favorably as a "new organic whole."[34]

By themselves, these organic metaphors are not particularly troubling since I think one can see through them to the interpersonal relationships Buber wanted to foster and articulate. I think that like Marx, who had a deep influence on his thought, Buber was caught by the organic language because it came so much closer to expressing the intimacy and interdependence of persons than the language of atoms, machines, and contracts which dominated social philosophy at that time. But as I have tried to argue in the sections on the organic model of community, the language of organism is potentially misleading insofar as it suggests, in its narrow form, that persons are simply organisms and nothing more; and insofar as it tends to reduce personal relationships to the kind of interdependence appropriate to the lower levels of nature. I believe that Buber was genuinely inconsistent or ambivalent about the language and symbols he relied upon for his philosophy of persons. This does not undercut the extraordinary significance of many of his insights, but it does suggest that there is room for a philosophy of persons which more consistently and comprehensively works out a language which preserves the uniqueness of persons and expresses the special relationships they have with each other.

I believe that the philosophy of John Macmurray goes a long way toward providing a strong, adequate metaphysical foundation for biblical claims about community so poetically expressed by Martin Buber. It is a philosophy which can match Whitehead's for its comprehensiveness, coherence, and adequacy. But because it centers itself upon the primacy of persons, and especially persons in relation to each other and to God, it provides the basis for a third, distinct model of community (despite having many things in common with some versions of the organic model) which is not only metaphysically satisfying but is religiously consistent with the biblical view of community.

I certainly do not want to suggest that Macmurray alone among philosophers has focused on the importance of community in a religious context. The work of the personalists and of many others has taken up the task of understanding persons in relation within the framework of Jewish and Christian thinking. But Macmurray, among contemporary philosophers, has, I believe, one of the clearest and most comprehensive (though not always fully worked out) philosophical systems which *starts from and returns to the ontological primacy* of persons in relation.

It is precisely because of his starting-point in the primacy of persons and their ultimate fulfillment in loving relationship that Macmurray provides the categories and principles of a third, distinct model of community, which I am calling the mutual/personal. His starting-point is dialectically related to a major revision in modern philosophy's understanding of knowledge. By starting (as does Edward Pols) with the primacy of action (and the self as agent), Macmurray develops an argument that persons know themselves and others first as agents in relation, and only second as thinkers withdrawn from action when they are engaged in reflection. This epistemological conviction forms the foundation for all of Macmurray's claims about the centrality of love as the active form of relationship with other persons and about the role of God in the building up of a universal community of love.

THE METAPHYSICAL FOUNDATIONS OF THE MODEL: JOHN MACMURRAY

It is interesting, though misleading if pressed too far, to note that Macmurray's philosophy in its essentials did not evolve much after his first formulation of it in the late 1920s. This is significant because of his general rejection of what we have called the organic model of community, which stresses the importance of growth or evolution. Although Macmurray later deepened his thought, applied it to a broad range of subjects, and gave it systematic expression in the Gifford Lectures in the mid-fifties, its basic metaphysical principles were already in place by the time he began publishing in 1925.

One of the persistent and basic themes of his work is a distinction between three ways of conceiving the world. He calls these three ways "unity-patterns" or symbolic representations of reality. The first two patterns, or models, were fairly traditional in Macmurray's time. They are the mechanical and the organic. It is his claim that there is a third model (which he calls the personal), and his subsequent development of it in his later work, which set Macmurray off from his contemporaries and which justifies our analysis of his work as providing a more satisfactory basis for community than either the atomistic/contractarian or the organic/functional models.

We will examine the general characteristics of the three models or unity-patterns of reality as a way of getting into Macmurray's major revision of Western philosophical assumptions about understanding persons. This revision consists in thinking of persons primarily as agents, not as thinkers. Macmurray reverses the traditional epistemological assumption that knowledge is primarily what one can *think* correctly. He argues instead that knowledge is primarily what one *does* correctly in relation to other agents. This leads him into an analysis of what it means to be in active relation to other persons, which in turn leads to a discussion of community and society, love and cooperation.

As part of his analysis, Macmurray makes some important claims about the continuity of his position with that of the Hebraic and Christian understanding of God's role as divine Agent who intends community among and with his human creation. He places these religious claims alongside of and in continuity with his basic metaphysical principles and thus preserves the biblical understanding of community better than the atomistic and organic models do. However, along the way, Macmurray addresses explicitly the major concerns of Karl Marx (whom he studied deeply and with whom he shared a number of convictions), and implicitly the work of Whitehead and other organic thinkers. He was particularly concerned, as they were, with the issues of dualism and the relation of philosophy to science. But it is my conviction that Macmurray, through his own metaphysical system, more adequately comprehends the nature of human community within his personal unity-pattern than do the atomistic and organic models with which he compares his own.

The Representation of Immediate Experience. In his first book, *Interpreting the Universe*, published in 1933, Macmurray argued that reality is known primarily through "immediate experience," that experience which has not yet been thought about but which is the "effortless result of living in [the world] and working with it and struggling against it . . . We are immersed in it, . . . we are living it, and not setting ourselves over against it, as something other than us which we can contemplate and study."[35] This "living" is truly a kind of knowledge and is most obvious in our living with other persons. We know persons in a deep and real way through the dynamics of an active relationship with them even before we are able to think about or reflect on them.

From this starting-point (whose epistemological consequences we will examine shortly), Macmurray moves to the claim that all philosophy is a reflection on the knowledge of immediate experience. Philosophy is an activity in which the person withdraws temporarily from the full immediacy of experience in order to try to re-present it in and through conceptual symbols. One does this primarily to be able to reenter the immediacy of lived experience more fully and satisfactorily. A philosophy of reality, a metaphysics, like a map for a traveller, helps the one who is thinking about experience to get back into life on the right path, that is, on the path which can lead to the greatest possible satisfaction or to the most successful fulfillment of one's intentions. The map of reality developed in reflection is thus both drawn from experience and is ultimately to be verified by its success in returning the person to the fullness of his or her experience. The purpose of the symbolic map is to enable one to act within the context of immediate experience in a way that most satisfactorily accords with his or her intentions.

This means that the map must symbolically represent reality in the most accurate and faithful way possible. Now the immediacy of experience from which thought arises is characterized by "unity and completeness. Nothing in it is really separate from anything else. Its parts are not 'cut off with a hatchet'; they flow into one another and belong together. Its aspect as knowledge, for instance, is not a separable part of it. It is unified with and co-extensive with feeling and action... Cognition, conation and feeling—are fused into a single whole in the living experience."[36] Because of this unity and completeness in immediate experience, its conceptual map must also be unified and complete. In philosophical terms this means it must be coherent and comprehensive. Any principle of thinking which would destroy "any essential characteristic of reality as we know it, would destroy the basis for any conclusion about the nature of reality so far as we do not know it."[37] Throughout the process of thinking, therefore, thought must be controlled by a "conception of unity.... The absence of contradiction, the maintenance of consistency, [and] the securing of strict implication in the relation of consecutive stages in the thought-process are all aspects of this effort to maintain the unity of structure in a system of ideas from which we start, through the whole process of activity until the conclusion is reached."[38]

This unity of structure, this symbolic thought form, or set of relations between ideas, is what Macmurray calls a "unity-pattern." It is a

> formal conception of the way in which different symbols can be united so as to constitute a whole... The unity of immediate experience, when it is broken by reflection and by the analysis of description, results in a set of symbolic images or ideas which are isolated from one another in the

sense that it is in our power to arrange them as we please. Before they can be used for the purpose for which they are designed, they must be arranged in a way that is determined by the reality which they are to represent. This, obviously, is only possible through some representation in imagination of the unity which is given in immediate experience itself... The unity-pattern is, thus, the conception of a unity constructed by the imagination.[39]

What I have been calling the atomistic and organic models of community are unity-patterns in Macmurray's sense of the term. They are models which are developed by reflection as representations of reality. We have seen that in most cases the defenders of the atomistic and organic models of community implicitly assume that these models also apply to reality as a whole, the community of persons being simply one aspect of that whole. What Macmurray wants to argue is that these two models do, in fact, accurately represent unity-patterns as they occur in reality, but that these patterns are not *exhaustive* of reality and, in particular, that they do not fully capture the kind of unity which persons are, both individually and in communion with each other. To capture that kind of personal and communal unity, a third model, inclusive of the first two but going beyond them in ways that cannot be reduced to their levels of explanation, is required. And that model is what Macmurray calls the personal model, and what I have been calling the mutual/personal model.

The Mechanical Unity-Pattern. The first unity-pattern, which Macmurray calls interchangeably the mechanical or mathematical, is essentially what I have called the atomistic/contractarian model. "It arises from the necessity of manipulating physical objects and is, therefore, adapted to the representation of reality so far as reality is stuff to be used ... so far as reality is material."[40] Historically, this way of viewing reality was prominent in those philosophers who accepted the atomic nature of reality. Everything real was essentially an atomic individual, materially identical with every other individual. The relation between these atomic bits was a causal one; that is, the strict laws of cause and effect could be exhaustively applied to the relationship between bits of matter. Each 'thing' is a "bearer of causal properties."[41] This is the characteristic that it has in common with all other 'things.' The symbol for such a thing is "the unit. Every thing is one thing. From this completely abstract point of view reality as material appears as an infinite assemblage of units, and therefore, any finite part of it, as a definite number of units ... [A]ny material whole can be represented symbolically as a unity produced by the repetition of identities."[42] Anything other than a single unit must be represented as a sum or aggregate of units. Anything complex can be broken down, ultimately, into its atomic units. "The differences between objects must be represented as differences either in the number of unit-elements in each or in the order in which the unit-elements are arranged in each."[43]

In a world represented by this mechanical unity-pattern, relationships must be conceived as causal interconnections in which one unit causes or is caused by others in some ordered pattern. Anything other than the bare unit itself (however small that unit is to be conceived) is a mechanism: a machine or aggregate of parts in some kind of causal relationship to each other. The movement of a part is always determined, not by the part itself but by some part external to it causing it to move. "The symbolism of mathematical thought forces us to represent all change as determined by an external cause and, therefore, all action as mechanical action ... Mechanical action is action in which all change is the effect of a cause external to that which is changed and in which, therefore, the changes of an object and so all its activities are determined not by its own nature but by a force acting upon it from outside."[44] This leads necessarily to determinism. "Determinism and mechanism are, in fact, the same thing,"[45] as Thomas Hobbes was one of the first modern philosophers to demonstrate.

The mechanical unity-pattern has important implications for human relationships. If it is the model for community, then it must view all personal relations as mechanical, deterministic, material complexes of essentially independent, individual units. This can have the advantage of justifying a claim that all such units are equal, but if there are intrinsic differences between persons then each person can be expected to accept his place within the mechanism of the state. Macmurray argues that in such a mechanical view of the community of persons, their value "depends not on their intrinsic differences (for none are allowed), but upon their position. Hence the social duty of the eighteenth-century individual is to maintain the dignity of his position, or to be content with his appointed lot and not look above his station."[46]

But if all persons are atomically equal, how does it happen that some have greater station than others? The only answer is essentially the one that Hobbes gave. Some have greater rank because they exercise greater power. Each unit, being essentially identical, seeks its own interests. Eventually, these units choose one of their own to whom to cede their power in return for the promise of individual security. "Then the monarch finds himself with all the power, and the people who have sold themselves into slavery, with their children, can't get it back again. No wonder that Hobbes spent his leisure time as an amateur mathematician in discovering how to square the circle!"[47]

The contract relationship between atomic units is the clearest symbolic representation I can think of for this understanding of reality. The contract is an impersonal, mechanical form of relationship between identical units (or between units who through the contract try to establish in that context a particular kind of equality). The connections between contracting units can be explained in geometrical, scientific terms, as again Hobbes so clearly demonstrates. Force, or power, is the glue which holds the contractual connections together. The contracting parties, or persons, conceived mechanically, are like mutually repellent particles. "To hold them together an 'impressed force' is required, strong enough to overcome their centrifugal tendencies."[48] Since the components of the contract "are atomic units, inherently isolated or unrelated ... there is nothing in them to hold them together. They are united in a whole by an external force which counteracts the tendency of their individual energies to repel one another. But as rational individuals who need one another, they themselves establish the power which unites them."[49] Such a view "yields a mechanical concept of society ... society is maintained by power.... [This concept] identifies society with the State, since the power of government is a necessary condition for the existence of such a society. It conceives the structure of society in terms of law—whether moral or civil law—and its maintenance as achieved by power.... Law, backed by force, is the technical solution to the problem of a society of persons, and the creation of the State is the highest achievement of technological reason, of our human capacity to devise efficient means to achieve our natural ends."[50]

Macmurray shares with philosophers in the organic tradition the rejection of this eighteenth century mechanical, atomistic model of community. While that model is perfectly adequate for understanding the material, lifeless dimension of reality, it simply cannot account satisfactorily for "the element of spontaneous construction, of self-determining and self-directed development which is present in the activity of the Self, but which is excluded from the conception of the material."[51] And yet immediate experience is clearly evidence of self-determination, spontaneous growth, in short, of living as opposed to dead, mechanical matter. To represent this dimension of reality it was necessary, Macmurray argues, for philosophy to develop another unity-pattern, based on the dynamics of the living organism. "For it is in the phenomena of life, and particularly in the processes of growth, that this spontaneity of inner self-determination and directed development seems, at least, to be characteristically manifest."[52]

The Organic Unity-Pattern. In our discussion of the organic model of community, we had occasion to list a number of its traits as Macmurray had identified them. At that time, we found his characterization of the organic model (as it is exemplified in Hegel, Marx, and Whitehead, in particular) to be generally accurate, although he did not give sufficient attention to the notion of the hierarchy or to its potential as a concept which might link the organic model to the mutual/personal model. In general, the organic unity-pattern assumes that in the biological organism the philosopher has a model of the complexity, dynamics, and interconnections central to the life-process, all of which have to be symbolically represented if the unity-pattern is to be faithful to the experience of the vitality of life.

In this representation, "the organism is conceived as a harmonious balancing of differences, and in its pure form, a tension of opposites; and since the time factor—as growth, development or becoming—is of the essence of life, the full form of the organic is represented as a dynamic equilibrium of functions maintained through a progressive differentiation of elements within the whole."[53] We have already observed that this description of the organic whole corresponds very nicely to Hegel's notion of the Whole, whether it be State or Absolute Spirit, which takes up into itself as moments its individual organic parts. It also corresponds, I believe, to Whitehead's notion of the actual occasion in which, through a progressive differentiation of elements (through the process of prehension and concrescence), a harmonious balancing is achieved (in the satisfaction or unity of the occasion), all of which depends on the functioning of the various elements that make up that process of becoming.

In the organic whole, there must be a differentiation of functions in order to maintain the unity of the whole. The unity of the whole is a unity of differences, not of identical units. The organic whole is not the sum of its parts. Like a painting, the organic whole is a balancing or unity of differences. In addition, the organism is alive: it grows and develops. Each of the organs within the whole is itself alive and in process "and these processes of the different elements as themselves harmoniously combined... form a unity of processes which is the life of the organism as a whole."[54]

Macmurray places a great deal of stress on the functionality of the organs within the organic whole. "[Each] different element in the living creature has a function to perform in the whole, for the whole.... [T]he differences of the material elements in the organism are determined by and relative to the differences in the function which each has to perform in the life of the organism ... [T]he unity of the organism is a unity of functions."[55] In a sense, the organic unity-pattern gives up the bare identity of atomic units (as found in the mechanical or atomistic unity-pattern) and replaces it with functional differences between the units within a larger whole.

> Each organ contributes something unique, something it alone is adapted to contribute to the life of the whole. The organ can only live in the organism, and only by performing its proper function, which is complementary to the functions of other organs. Separate it from the organism, and it is no longer alive, because it is deprived of the only position in which it can function.... Thus we may define the schema of Organism as the conception of a unity which is a unique harmony of complementary functions, expressing itself in a structural harmony of different organs.[56]

This fact has the important consequence that the relations between the parts within the organism are "determined internally, by the nature of the parts themselves, that is to say, by their differences.... all relations are internal to their terms... the differences of the elements determine their harmonious relations in an organic complex."[57] This notion of internal relations determined by their functional differences is precisely what I think Ollman means when he ascribes to Marx a philosophy of internal relations, and it justifies our inclusion of Marx within our study of the organic model of community. For Marx, the important differences between the parts of the whole are the differences of function within that whole. When the functions change, the individuals' "identities" also change. That is why Marx can both identify and distinguish various elements, depending on the functional context he is considering.

Macmurray also singles out the characteristic of teleology within the organism. To understand an organism, it is necessary to understand the final stage, the telos, toward which it has been developing. "An organism can be defined only in terms of its maturity, and its growth only as the series of forms which it takes on its progress to maturity. For this reason the representation of life can only be described and understood by reference to the final state of its natural development."[58] For Macmurray, this teleological dimension is merely a way of *describing*, not explaining, growth. "It does not involve any conception of conscious purpose, or, indeed of consciousness in any form."[59] The organism does not need to know or be aware of its final stage in order to grow toward it. Certainly, an acorn does not seem to know that it is going to become an oak tree. As we have seen, Whitehead thinks that denying any kind of mentality to the acorn bifurcates reality and makes it incoherent, leading him to resort to panpsychism.

Nevertheless, it is an indispensable part of Macmurray's description of the organic unity-pattern that it does not imply conscious purpose in the organism. It only has to ascribe movement or growth toward an end which will necessarily be reached as long as the organism fulfills its potentialities stage by stage. By reserving conscious purpose or intention for the personal unity-pattern, Macmurray intends to make a clear distinction between the two ways of representing reality. This clear demarcation may, if we pursue the line of argument set forth by Edward Pols and the systems or hierarchical organicists, become much less obvious. By appealing to a series of levels within the organism, the top one of which may be purposive but the lower of which need not be, provided they are included as infrastructures within the higher level, Pols and the organicists have laid the foundation for a model of the person as unique (having conscious purpose) but also in nondualistic continuity with nonpurposive levels of nature (the infrastructure). We will see later how this might be developed in continuity with Macmurray's own position.

Macmurray believes that each unity-pattern has social consequences. That is, a particular form of society corresponds to each unity-pattern. The organic unity-pattern overcomes the isolation and individualism of the mechanical model, but only, Macmurray warns, by depriving "the individual elements of their uniquenesss . . . it destroys their individuality."[60] By stressing so strongly the functional nature of each organ within the whole, the organic model makes each individual "essentially complementary, each relative to all the others. Only in functional connection with the other elements has each any being in the whole. Thus the whole value of each element depends upon its subordination, as it were, to the whole complex; none of the organs of the body have any value except in so far as they subserve the function of the whole."[61]

One can see this functional subordination of the part to the whole especially clearly in Hegel, in which the Whole (State or Spirit) takes precedence over its "moments" who have value only insofar as they serve it. In political terms, the only value a citizen has is through his functional incorporation into the whole which is greater than he, that is, through his subservience to the state. The seeds of totalitarianism are clearly present here, although they have not necessarily grown to maturity in Hegel as such. But as long as the organic unity-pattern puts its emphasis on the organic whole and subordinates its parts to it as organs functioning to maintain its unity, the whole will become virtually the only significant individual and the parts will have value only to the degree that they can make a valuable contribution to the whole. There seems no basis on which to erect a notion of the intrinsic worth of the functional organs.

Nevertheless, the discovery of the functionality of each person within the organic whole had important and valuable consequences. Instead of simply looking to each individual as a bare identical unit, the organic notion of society could appreciate the differences between persons and could assign each one to his or her appropriate place within the whole. Each person has an important and irreplaceable role to play. This image of the whole body needing the work of each of its parts can be found from St. Paul to the present. No part can claim that it is independent of all the others, and no part can be denied the value of its own contribution, however small, to the totality. This understanding of the importance of each part within the whole can lead to a strong sense of patriotism and a willingness to sacrifice oneself for the state.

But with its stress upon the functional contribution and interdependence of the parts to and within the whole, the organic unity-pattern necessarily has to turn its attention away from the humanity of each person and focus instead upon his or her ability to function productively with respect to the society as a whole. "[W]hen we ... ask what is the function of the individual in the State, we find that the important thing about him is not that he is a human being, but that he is a bricklayer or an engineer, a doctor or a member of Parliament. ... Only as a function has the individual any value for the State. The more organic, in fact, society becomes, the more the organic whole absorbs him, willing or unwilling, and sucks the life out of him for its own purpose, until he can only save his soul by revolting against this slavery to his job."[62]

The state or the society determines the functionality of its citizens and when they can no longer function as it decides (the state itself having become a kind of person), then there is nothing in the organic unity-pattern to tell us what value they still have or whether they have any value at all. As long as value is based on function, then the whole must determine that value, since the parts have value only insofar as they functionally serve the whole. But there is nothing said here about the value of the whole itself. If value is based on function, then how can the whole have value since it is the unity of its functions and, presumably, does not itself serve as a functional part for some greater whole? But the organic unity-pattern, as Macmurray interprets it, leaves the whole, as a whole and in terms of itself, functionless. It stands, in a sense, outside its own unity-pattern.

There is no "good" or "value" to the organic whole unless one wants to claim the organic whole, or the state, is good in itself. Hegel, of course, could fit this claim into a grand metaphysics and tie it to the self-development of Spirit and the realization of freedom. But in ordinary political terms, it seems to mean that serving the state is a good thing because the growth of the state (the organic whole) is a good thing in and of itself. When we ask, what is the purpose of the state, the answer is, "it is its own purpose." "The organism has a life of its own—its growth and development; the modification, training, and increase of its organic structure so that it may reach its full stature and maturity.

The real life of the State is in its self-development, in progress, in evolution."[63]

When we have reached this point in our development of the idea of society, then we have abandoned any notion of society as the fulfillment of individuals. The society has taken on a life and a value of its own which is superior to, though dependent upon, the life of its members. It is not difficult to understand why regimes which have adopted this unity-pattern as the basis of their ideal community, have so easily been led to place the functional organization of the state ahead of the intentions and values of its individual citizens, and why individual dissent has so often been suppressed on the grounds that it does not serve the needs of the whole.

The only way to escape from these consequences of the organic model of community, according to Macmurray, is to recognize that in fact persons are not primarily functions in a greater whole, but that organic wholes are functions for persons. That is, persons can belong to and use organic wholes but their capacity to do so presupposes the essential and revolutionary fact that persons must be more than and inclusive of organisms. Consider the simple fact that a person can decide which of a number of states or organic wholes to belong to. She might decide to become a citizen of the United States and belong to an international society of anthropologists. The very fact that she can consider this kind of relationship to organic wholes indicates that she is not a function of either one (at least not wholly or exhaustively, though she may play a functional part in each).

In the transition from the organic unity-pattern to the personal one, as Macmurray puts it,

> a person who can enter at once into two competing organic unities is not a function of either. They rather are functions of him.... He is no function for their uses. They rather are for his use, and subservient to his purposes. But this is a refutation of the organic schema. The Self is not an organism... It is something higher than [organic] life; something that subordinates to itself and uses for its purposes the structures and functional harmonies that life, in its passage, builds up and maintains... The Self turns out to be super-organic."[64]

There is here a hint, but no development, of the clue found in Pols, systems theory, and organicism that the self, or person, uses "the structures and functional harmonies" of the organic level, which Pols called the infrastructure. In this sense, the person is intimately tied to the organic dimension of reality. But he or she, by virtue of self-consciousness and the ability to form and enact intentions, is able to give to the organism a purpose from outside itself. And that purpose will be one in which persons find fulfillment, not primarily in contracting with others for self-interested ends, or in serving the needs of a greater whole, but in loving one another and living in the love which communion with others brings. In 1929, when Macmurray wrote the essay "The Unity of Modern Problems," from which we have taken much of his analysis of the political consequences of adopting a particular unity-pattern, he proclaimed that the problem of his age was going to be the development of "a new schema of the Self, which shall transcend both the mechanical and the organic schema; and which will enable us to construct, consciously and deliberately, a civilization whose mechanical and organic structures will be at the service of a personal life, whose meaning and essence is friendship."[65] It is to his subsequent development of that schema of the person, and its implications for community, that we now turn.

THE PERSONAL UNITY-PATTERN

"All meaningful knowledge is for the sake of action, and all meaningful action for the sake of friendship."[66]

It is Macmurray's fundamental conviction that if a unity-pattern of the person (which by the Gifford Lectures of 1953-54 he calls "the form of the personal") is to be developed, it must first overcome the traditional philosophical dualism which separates the person into thinker and agent. If we are to understand the person as a superorganic unity, in whom we find mechanical and organic dimensions but who is a basic, primary, and irreducible unity, we must first understand that the person is essentially a doer, an agent, only one of whose activities is thinking. Only if we can establish the primacy of the self as agent, claims Macmurray, can we justify the inclusion within the self of the mechanical and organic levels of reality, and ground the belief that "the unity of the personal cannot be thought as the form of an individual self, but only through the mutuality of personal relationship."[67] If we try to conceive of the person as primarily or essentially a thinker, then we will not have a sufficient basis for claiming that persons are fulfilled not in their thinking about other persons but only in their active, mutual relations with them. In our metaphysical endeavor, Macmurray announces, "we must introduce the second person as the necessary correlative of the first, and do our thinking not from the standpoint of the 'I' alone, but of the 'you and I'."[68] Macmurray, in other words, wants to take the I-Thou relationship first articulated in contemporary philosophy by Martin Buber, and give it a metaphysical grounding.

Thinking the Self as Agent. One of the most persistent obstacles in philosophy to creating a metaphysics of mutuality has been the assumption that persons are primarily thinkers, characterized essentially by rationality or mentality. On the basis of this assumption, persons have been distinguished from the rest of nature by their capacity to think or reason. René Descartes' "cogito, ergo sum," "I think, therefore I am," summarizes this rational, reflective starting-point in philosophy.

It is Macmurray's conviction that as long as this assumption remains unchallenged, philosophy will be unable to develop a true understanding of community because community is never primarily the work of reflection or theory. As Macmurray suggests in the title of the first book in the Gifford Lectures, *The Self as Agent*, community can be adequately conceived only if the self is held to be primarily an agent, and only secondarily or derivatively a thinker. Only by establishing the primacy of the self as agent is it possible to lay the foundation for a philosophy of community in which persons fulfill their natures through action intended to embrace others in mutuality and love.

To start one's understanding of persons with the assumption that they are essentially thinkers is to start with the person in practical isolation from other persons, as Descartes himself did when he began by doubting everything with which he was immediately in relation. The result of beginning with the person in isolation from others can be seen by the persistence of one of the questions that haunts modern philosophy, namely, "How does the thinker know that other persons really exist?" Only if one begins thinking about the world with the assumption that nothing can be known initially except the workings of one's own mind, and that any further knowledge must first pass the test of theory, does the question of the existence of something other than one's own mind become urgent.

From this starting-point, philosophy must be regarded as essentially egocentric. That is, it "takes the Self as its starting-point, and not God, or the world or community . . . ."[69] And the Self with which it starts is essentially an isolated self, turned in upon itself, sure only of the fact that it thinks and knows that it exists because it thinks. It does not know from the outset that it is a "thou" in relation to other selves because its starting-point does not permit it to accept anything as a given other than its own thinking withdrawn from relation to others.

And so modern philosophy develops as the endeavor to justify the practical, working hypotheses and beliefs (which all persons necessarily live by) that there is a world filled with things and other persons exterior to the thinking self. But no matter how successfully one can justify these beliefs and hypotheses in thought, they remain theoretical. They can give, at best, theoretical knowledge of things and persons exterior to the thinking self but they cannot, in and of themselves, give practical knowledge of them. Any immediate or direct experience of other persons cannot be called knowledge because, from the standpoint of thinking, only what is thought is knowledge. And yet when theoretical knowledge is ostensibly achieved, it cannot *create* an experience with another person because thought is what goes on within one's mind, not between oneself and another person. Thought is essentially private and yet, if it is the essence of what it means to be a person, then it cannot explain those experiences of mutuality in which the self is not private but related to others.

The result of thinking of the self essentially as a thinker is a series of dualisms between theory and practice, reason and emotion, mind and body, appearance and reality. At the same time, action, the practical bond between persons, becomes a philosophical mystery.

> Any philosophy which takes the 'Cogito' as its starting point and centre of reference institutes a formal dualism of theory and practice; and . . . this dualism makes it formally impossible to give any account, and indeed to conceive the possibility of persons in relation, whether the relations be theoretical—as knowledge, or practical—as co-operation . . . If we make the 'I think' the primary postulate of philosophy, then not merely do we institute a dualism between the-

oretical and practical experience, but we make action logically inconceivable ... However far we carry the process of thought it can never *become* an action or spontaneously *generate* an action.... Consequently I can never know another person, since thinking about another person can never amount to personal knowledge of him, nor even to personal acquaintance.[70]

There is, Macmurray contends, a certain air of unreality about this conclusion, for I do in fact know other persons every day in my lived relations with them. If I doubt that I truly know them, then my doubt is a kind of pretense: my activity is still informed by my "practical" knowledge of them. Knowing that I am in relation to other persons should be "the starting-point of all knowledge."[71] "If we did not know that there are other persons we could know literally nothing, not even that we ourselves existed. To be a person is to be in communication with the Other. The knowledge of the Other is the absolute presupposition of all knowledge, and as such is necessarily indemonstrable."[72]

But surely one could reply to these claims that there are times when what I took to be "practical knowledge" of another person turned out to be false or misleading. I thought I "knew" Martha but discovered that I had misread her in a particular situation. Surely this means that practical knowledge is not true knowledge? But how can I correct my erroneous beliefs and why should I bother? It is precisely here, Macmurray suggests, in our answer to these questions, that we get the essential clue to our understanding of the self as agent.

For when, in my immediate experience, I find my practical knowledge of the world going askew, I need to withdraw temporarily from the fullness of that particular experience in order to figure out what has gone wrong. This withdrawal takes the form of thinking. I step back in order to reflect so that I might be able to see a better, more successful way to act in relation to the particular portion of the world in which I am temporarily experiencing failure or frustration. Like a traveler following a trail through the woods, I need, when I find myself lost or off the trail, to stop walking and consult my map.

If we remember Macmurray's discussion of unity-patterns, we remember that they are conceptual maps of the reality which is first experienced in the immediate mode, that is, experienced through our full (emotional, active) involvement in it. In thinking, we withdraw from that full experience in order to determine whether the map we have been following is wrong or whether we have been following the map wrongly. During that time of reflective withdrawal, we need to focus our attention upon the map, not upon walking. But once we have examined the map and thought about its relation to what we have been actively doing up to the time of examination, we have to start walking again in order to test the adequacy of our reflections.

This whole process of reflective withdrawal, following some kind of frustration in our active involvement with the world, and succeeded by a return to that involvement (with a clearer sense, one hopes, of what we should do), is a process in which thinking occurs within the context of action. Acting, that is, engaging ourselves with a world exterior to us, both precedes and follows the temporary withdrawal into thinking. And the time of reflection is taken, as it were, in the service of acting: it is a time in which the self can figure out how to make its action more congruent with the exterior world in which it is making its way, not by thinking about walking but by walking. It is also true to say that the time of reflection is a time of action, though of a particular kind. For during reflection, the self is acting: reflection is what it is doing. This simple fact underlies all of what Macmurray intends to say when he insists that the clue to the understanding of persons is that they are primarily agents, one of whose actions is thinking.

Macmurray is, to be sure, still thinking about the person. His is a metaphysics of persons, and in that sense it is still philosophy and still assumes the indispensability of thinking. But it does not assume that the person is primarily a thinker. Instead it thinks, in reflection, of the person as primarily an agent. And it refers us to action, not to thinking, as the locus for determining whether our conceptual "map" of the person is correct or not. "Philosophy is necessarily theoretical, and must aim at theoretical strictness. It does not follow that we must theorize from the standpoint of theory."[73] To be sure, the thinking one does about the self as agent must be coherent, consistent, and clear, just as any map must be as faithful to the reality it intends to represent as it can be. But the ultimate test of one's thinking must be in its ability to return one to the fullness of immediate experience without frustration or repeated failure, just as the ultimate test of a map is to return one successfully to the trail upon which one was walking.

Macmurray insists that one of the most important consequences of adopting the standpoint of the self as agent is that it removes the dualisms which have characterized modern philosophy. If the self is primarily agent, then no dualism between thought and practice need arise since thinking becomes a form of practice. Mind and body are not two metaphysically distinct entities—they become, instead, two dimensions of a single unified agent, neither of which in isolation is *the* distinguishing characteristic of the person. The self is never simply engaged in theory divorced from the other dimensions of immediate experience. To become completely isolated in thought

> is impossible in practice, and in conception self-contradictory. If we could so isolate our theoretical activities from practical influences—from the emotional motives, for example, and the intentional valuations which determine our behavior, we should have destroyed our own integrity. We should need to become two selves, neither of which would be a complete self. There would be a 'practical' or 'bodily' self which acts without thinking, and a 'theoretical', 'spiritual' or 'mental' self, which thinks without acting. This is the genesis of the 'mind-body' problem.[74]

But the mind-body problem is not a problem if the self is agent because, in acting, the self both thinks and moves bodily, and is, in both cases, acting. If action, not reflection, is the essential trait of the self, then the self can be understood as a basic unified whole since within the action of immediate experience one necessarily has to include emotion, thinking, and bodily movement. Action, for Macmurray, is an inclusive concept. It is "a full concrete activity of the self in which all our capacities are employed; while thought is constituted by the exclusion of some of our powers and a withdrawal into an activity which is less concrete and less complete . . . The concept of 'action' is *inclusive*. As an ideal limit of personal being, it is the concept of an unlimited rational being, in which all the capacities of the Self are in full and unrestricted employment."[75] Action, therefore, includes thinking in a way that the traditional notion of thinking does not include acting.

If we want the most adequate, the most comprehensive concept of the person possible, one that does justice to the fullness of the person without tearing him or her into dualistic parts, then the concept of the self as agent seems to meet our needs. There is no dimension of the person which cannot be conceived either as an action, a constituent of action, or as part of the infrastructure necessary for action. The unity of the person is affirmed by conceiving of him or her as an agent since within agency can be included all that goes to make up the person, i.e., "all the capacities of the Self in full and unrestricted employment."[76]

This has the interesting implication that only if the person is essentially an agent can we understand how a person might, on occasion, choose to be less than what he or she might be. As agent, the person can choose to act, as far as possible, only as a thinker. As agent, the person can choose to cut himself off as much as possible from other persons. As agent, the person can choose to allow some of his capacities to lie fallow and undeveloped. He can, for example, choose (or be influenced) to act toward other persons as if they were alien or hostile toward him, or as if they and he were only functional parts in a greater whole. But only if the person is truly agent can he ever hope to act toward others as if they were intrinsically worthwhile and capable of entering into loving relationship with him. For action is the bond that unites persons in the reality of immediate experience. Within action, thought necessarily plays an important role, by helping steer the course of intention correctly and in accord with what the realities of the situation demand. "Ideas are the eyes of action."[77] But without action, intention can only dream of the other person: it can never succeed in reaching out to embrace him. It can see but not touch the other in love. And if the embrace of the other, in fact, is not possible, if the fullness of the I-Thou relation can only be thought, not experienced, then the full and unrestricted employment of the capacities of the person can never be achieved, and the person can never be complete or fulfilled.

But if the person is primarily agent, then fulfillment requires an other. Action is incomplete unless it is action in relation to something other than the agent taken in isolation. In action the person encounters, or engages, something exterior to himself. And it is through this practical encounter that the agent knows that something other exists. The person experiences something 'there' against which his action is pushing. "For without resistance no action is possible. To act at all is to act *upon something*. Consequently, the Other is discovered ... both as the resistance to, and the support of action."[78]

Eventually, the self has to determine what kind of Other it has encountered if it is to "negotiate" or deal with it successfully in subsequent and ongoing action. The conceptual map has to be filled in correctly so that its employer knows whether he is dealing with trees, rocks, or other persons. Initially, Macmurray claims, we conceptualize the Other as a person like ourselves. "The Other is given as a resistance to my action; I must therefore characterize the Other as an agent like myself, acting against me ... I must attribute to the Other, if I am to understand it, the form of activity that I attribute to myself."[79] But, of course, I soon discover, through trying to act according to the conceptual map, that not all "others" respond to my action as I would expect intentional agents to do. When that turns out to be the case, I "drop" from my characterization of the Other those traits that are not appropriate. Traditional peoples may have originally populated all of nature with beings similar to themselves. But over time, they eliminated the 'personal' traits assigned to the wind or water because these things could be more successfully dealt with without assuming that they possessed intentionality or will.

The important point, for Macmurray, is that we arrive at our ideas (on our conceptual maps) of other things, if they are not persons, by eliminating or abstracting elements from a full, inclusive idea of what persons are, which is itself based on what we know ourselves as persons to be. "We do not necessarily characterize every particular other, by crediting it with *all* the characteristics of the Self, particularly with its rational characteristics ... [W]hatever characteristics we attribute to the Other must be included within the full characterization of ourselves. When we distinguish between persons and material things, the characteristics we attribute to things are a selection from the characteristics we attribute to a person."[80]

The concept of a person will include the ideas of materiality and of organism, for example, because the person *is* material and organic even though he is also more. "The concept of 'a person' is inclusive of the concept of 'an organism', as the concept of 'an organism' is inclusive of that of 'a material body'. The included concepts can be derived from the concept of 'a person' by abstractions; by excluding from attention those characters which belong to the higher category alone."[81] We learn to characterize something as nonpersonal "only by a *reduction of the concept of the Other which excludes part of its definition*; only, that is to say, by a partial negation: only by down-grading the 'You' in the 'You and I' to the status of 'It' ... The non-personal Other is that which is active without intention."[82] And the reason why we need to exclude some traits from the concept of the person is ultimately a practical one. We simply cannot act in relation to some other things successfully if we persist in treating them as persons when they are not. "We cannot deal with organisms successfully in the same way that we can with material objects, or with persons. The form of their resistance—in opposition or in support—necessitates a difference in our own behaviour."[83]

Ultimately, we can know the success of our characterization of others only by acting upon our conceptual map in relation to them. We must return to the fullness of the practical experience from which we have chosen to withdraw temporarily in thinking. And it is only in this return that we can know (in the fullest practical sense) that we exist and are fulfilled only in relation to other persons. "In reflection we isolate ourselves from dynamic relations with the Other; we withdraw into ourselves, adopting the attitude of spectators, not participants."[84] But the given from which our reflective isolation took its departure is the world of participation. And in our immediate experience of this world we know the existence of other persons. "We know existence by participating in existence. This participation is action... Existence then is the primary datum. But this existence is not my own existence as an isolated self... What is given is the existence of a world in which we participate—which sustains and in sustaining limits our wills."[85]

It is only through active participation in a world of other persons that we originally and after reflection know that other persons exist. And it is this knowledge that leads Macmurray to the most important conviction of his entire metaphysics: namely, that the person "is constituted by its relation to the Other; that it has its being in its relationship; and that this relationship is necessarily personal [i.e., communal]."[86]

THE CHARACTERISTICS OF PERSONS

We are now about to enter into the world of persons in relation. But before we do, we need to understand what, in Macmurray's personal unity-pattern, distinguishes persons from nonpersonal entities. What is the 'more' in persons that requires that they be represented in a unity-pattern that includes but goes beyond the representations of the mechanical and organic dimensions of reality? The ultimate 'more' is that persons can be persons only in the consciousness of mutual relationship with other persons. But that characteristic is supported and grounded in other aspects unique to beings who are agents. These include a consciousness of being in relation to that which is not oneself and an ability to initiate actions in accord with consciously chosen intentions which seek to develop that relationship. In other words, the person is a free agent capable of intentional action in relation to that which is over-against or objective to him. The consciousness, freedom, and agency necessary for relationship with that which is not oneself are all distinguishing characteristics of persons.

In his development of these characteristics, Macmurray notes the importance of the capacity of persons to be rational. By this he does not mean primarily the ability to think. Thinking can often be irrational. Rather, he means the capacity "for objectivity."[87] This is the capacity "to stand in conscious relation to that which is recognized as not ourselves ... it is the very essence of our experience as persons."[88] Consciousness is clearly implied here but it is a consciousness of the 'otherness' of the Other, not primarily a self-consciousness. Self-consciousness is a correlate of other-consciousness, which is the awareness that one exists in relation to something outside oneself. Now this awareness, insists Macmurray, is not just attributable to the cognitive faculties. It can be equally attributable to the emotions. Emotions also refer to things which are outside the person. When I fear the wild bear coming toward me, my emotion is 'rational' and objective since it correctly recognizes my relationship to what is not myself and energizes my action for the appropriate response. Sometimes, of course, my feelings can be as erroneous as my beliefs. I might feel anger toward someone when none is appropriate (if I have completely misread the situation). In this sense, emotions, like ideas, can be rational or irrational, depending upon their appropriateness in representing the objective world with which I am engaged. "My emotions are capable of exhibiting the quality of reason, ... they may or may not fit the objective world to which they consciously refer."[89]

Action and Causality. In addition to the capacity for rationality or objectivity, which implies the necessity of consciousness, persons are distinguished from nonpersons by the capacity for free, or intentional, action. Action, Macmurray insists, is more than behavior or movement. Action is movement initiated and intended by an agent. Movement is change which occurs without being intended. Action involves objectivity or rationality: it requires knowledge or an "awareness of the Other and the Self in relation."[90] Knowledge in this sense enables the agent to plan his act before he enacts it: it gives him a freedom which is denied to mere movement.

Macmurray nowhere gives an extensive definition of either freedom or intention. He writes as if their commonsense definitions are sufficient for his purposes and he ties the concepts of intention and freedom into a virtually unbreakable bond. Freedom is, for Macmurray, "simply our capacity to act—not to behave or to react, but to form an intention and seek to realize it. To act is to be free."[91] This is what Macmurray calls the absolute character of freedom: the capacity for oneself to determine the future (to some extent) as an agent (as opposed to having it determined entirely by forces outside of one's conscious choice and purpose).

One's intention is one's conscious decision or choice as to what one proposes to do in and through one's action. It is one's purpose or goal in acting. It is distinguished from motives in that it is within one's conscious control. One chooses one's intention, whereas one does not choose one's motives, which are essentially organic or biological. But an action must be intentional: if it lacks an intention and is driven by motive alone, then it is not an action but a piece of behavior, a movement. In this sense, according to Macmurray, action, intention, and freedom are indissolubly linked: to understand one, you must necessarily understand the other two. There must be at least a minimal degree of freedom both to form an intention and to act upon it. This said, we must certainly acknowledge that Macmurray does not examine intention with the same care and precision that recent philosophers of action and intention have given the concept. Macmurray's analysis of intention, freedom, and action is, I believe, essentially correct, but only in its essential insights. His level of analysis on these points is indicative of the level of analysis of much of his thought. It remains highly suggestive but not nearly as carefully or thoroughly worked out as the philosophy of someone like Whitehead, for example. Nevertheless, I believe the basic claims and the essential interconnections and implications of his philosophical scheme are profoundly right and provide the ground on which someday a fuller philosophy of persons in relation can be more exhaustively and completely erected.

Despite the lack of full exploration of these basic concepts of intention, freedom, and action, it is important to note that Macmurray does develop his understanding of freedom somewhat by distinguishing between its relative and its absolute character, and using that distinction to suggest that freedom can be fully experienced only in relation to other persons and for the purpose of self-realization. The relative character of freedom is the experience of intending that which is not yet accomplished. The most important goal which we can intend in this regard is the goal of being ourselves. "Our human nature eludes us. There is a gap between the reality of our being and its empirical expression, which teases us perpetually.... We are and yet we are not ourselves: and in this is our freedom. Our own human nature lies always beyond us as a goal to be aimed at, an objective to be fought for... So freedom is at once absolute and relative: absolute, because if we were not free we should not be human at all; relative, because this freedom lies always beyond our present achievement as the goal of our existence. It is at once the Alpha and the Omega of our humanity."[92] And, as we shall see, the goal of freedom can ultimately be realized only in and through fellowship or community. This is the great paradox of human life: that the realization of the self can only be accomplished through a fundamental caring for the not-self. Only in relation to another person can "the self-transcendence of every aspect and element of our nature [be] expressed and fulfilled. This is the implicit intention of all fellowship—the complete realization of the self through a complete self-transcendence."[93] The relative character of freedom is the ability to intend fellowship; the absolute character of freedom is that we can only be ourselves if we consciously choose, i.e., intend, to realize our human nature. As Macmurray says, "human nature is not merely matter of fact. It is also matter of intention. What makes us human is the intention to realize our humanity."[94] We will discuss the paradox of self-realization by intending the welfare of others (and its attendant difficulties) later. At this point, we need to follow a bit further Macmurray's development of the notion of freedom.

One of the most important implications of his understanding of the free act of an agent is that he believes that he can harmonize it with the scientific explanation of cause and effect, and by so doing, undercuts any charge that he is reintroducing a dualism between the free and unfree parts of nature. His argument revolves around the distinction between events which are caused by other events and acts which are caused by the agents who initiate them. If the event or occurrence in question is the act of an agent, then the agent is its cause and one cannot go back behind the agent in order to discover a more basic or ultimate cause. On the other hand, if the occurrence is not the result of an agent's decision, then in principle an entire nexus of causes, stretching indefinitely backward in time, can be found to explain it, or more accurately, to describe it.

The laws of cause and effect, the hallmark of scientific understanding, actually describe the world of events which are not caused by the decisions of free agents. These laws are perfectly appropriate as long as they are confined to the world of nonagents. But as long as there are acts which are caused by the freedom of the agent, these acts cannot be fully explained (though perhaps their infrastructures can be) by the laws of cause and effect. A causal law covers those events in nature which occur with a regularity not disturbed by the freedom of agents. An act is an occurrence in nature which originates in the free decision of an agent, not completely predetermined by causes beyond the agent's conscious control.

This understanding of the act is similar, we may recall, to what Edward Pols has called the "originative" character of the agent's action. As originative, the act can extend over any time span necessary for the agent to carry it out. This avoids, as we have seen, the Whiteheadian conviction that each act must be as short in duration as possible, and it provides a foundation for accepting the duration of the self-same agent, his identity as a basic unity through time. Without this duration, as we saw, no agent could act (and be acted upon) in ongoing, reciprocal relation to other agents.

But an agent includes within himself those levels of nature which are appropriately described under the laws of nature. His acts include within themselves dimensions or levels which are not themselves free and are accordingly subject to the laws of nature. Thus, a full explanation of the act of an agent includes reference both to the free origin of the act, in the free decision of the agent, and to the causal network by which the act is carried out. The explanation is not split into dualistic halves but is integrated into a comprehensive unity by the overarching, inclusive, and yet basic unity of the agent who acts.

For example, when the agent decides to raise his arm from the table (perhaps because he wants to look at it more closely), the act is freely initiated. But once the agent has chosen to raise his arm, the causal nexus of neurons, cells, organs, organelles, etc. which make up the physical infrastructure of the brain, nervous system, and arm must be utilized to carry the choice into effect. At that level of occurrence, all that takes place from brain to arm can be appropriately described in causal terms, provided only that the origin of the occurrence is not itself reduced (that is, without remainder, or exhaustively) to the effect of a prior cause without any place for the agent's free decision initiating that particular act.

While he does not use the term in this context, Macmurray could have appealed to what we called earlier the 'systems' or 'hierarchy' concept for integrating various levels of reality in a single, overarching unity. This is not the place to pursue the full implications of the idea, but it is important to register the fact that Macmurray's understanding of the person, while it transcends the levels of the mechanical and the organic, does not fly off into a realm irrationally separated from the world to which the laws of science apply. As long as one remains within a mechanical or organic (in the restricted sense) framework, any occurrence which seems to violate or escape from strict and exhaustive explanation according to the laws of cause and effect is unintelligible.

But if we adopt the notion of the hierarchy, especially as developed by Edward Pols, it becomes possible to suggest that the freedom of action, the intentionality peculiar to personal agents, is intelligible (as the act of a basic unified being) without being incoherently related to predetermined movement at lower levels within the hierarchy of the agent. As long as no agent chooses to interfere, the laws of nature will thoroughly and adequately describe what takes place at the nonintentional levels of nature. And when the agent does choose to act, his interference into the laws of nature simply permits a new sequence of movements to begin, even though the course of that sequence, once freely initiated, can be plotted according to the laws of nature. In this sense, causality falls *within* action and is perfectly representative of a large portion of the world, provided only that it does not stretch itself so far as to eliminate the very act which utilizes its structures and regularities.

Macmurray gives as an example the scientist who sets up an experiment to determine the causal laws governing the swing of a pendulum. The scientist chooses the experiment and freely sets it up. Then she withdraws from the subsequent sequence of events as far as possible. What she measures within that sequence is the kind of movement which is strictly subject to the laws of cause and effect. Then, when the experiment is over, she closes it up and writes her report. But the experiment is contained *within* her intentional activity. She thinks:

> The whole experiment is an action of mine: I *do* the experiment. But the pattern of movement I observe and the

law that I elicit, refer only to what happens *within* my action. I leave out of account my starting the pendulum when I begin and my stopping it when I have finished. The law of the particular instance refers to what happens between these points; to that aspect of my doing the experiment which I do not *do*; that is to say, the negative aspect of my action. If now we call this a causal process, we realize in another way that causality is the negative aspect of agency, and falls within action.[95]

By falling within action, therefore, causality or the world of nature subject to the laws of cause and effect, is perfectly harmonious with free action and there need be no dualism between them. The hierarchy of the agent including and utilizing levels of nature which are not themselves free agents permits us to accept both causal determinism, where appropriate, and freedom of action, without having to set them in opposition to each other. The importance of this conclusion is that Macmurray's notion of the person as a free agent can be justified without having to abandon the insights and truths of the mechanical and organic unity-patterns. One does not have to choose *between* freedom and determinism. The solution is to accept the inclusive hierarchical nature of the person and then to determine with respect to what levels of reality one should apply explanations which appeal to causality or freedom.

In this way, Macmurray's view of the person, with the help of insights from the organismic, hierarchical studies of contemporary biology and philosophy, can be synthesized (without reduction) with the scientific understanding of nature. Unlike the mechanists and the more restricted organic thinkers, however, the view of the person in the personal unity-pattern does not have to eliminate consciousness, freedom, or intentionality, or, conversely, to postulate their existence at all levels of nature. The personal unity-pattern subsumes the levels of nature appropriate to scientific analysis within a more inclusive hierarchy transcended and governed by those levels which are unique to persons.

This returns us to our basic question, one that we raised originally at the conclusion of our discussion of Edward Pols. Once we understand what distinguishes persons from the nonpersonal levels of nature, we have to ask, what intentions do persons seek to enact? What do they want to do with their freedom of action? By answering this question primarily with reference to the mutuality of love or friendship, Macmurray demonstrates the essential contribution of the personal unity-pattern to our understanding of community.

PERSONS IN RELATION

As I have indicated, the thesis Macmurray has been building toward is "that the Self is constituted by its relation to the Other; that it has its being in its relationship; and that this relationship is necessarily personal."[96] By establishing that the self is primarily agent, he has shown that relationship with an Other of some kind is essential to the Self since agency requires an Other against whom or in relation to whom it expresses itself. "The idea of an isolated agent is self-contradictory. Any agent is necessarily in relation to the Other."[97] But what requires that this Other be itself personal for a person to "have his being" in the relationship?

If we are to understand the nature of personal relationship we must begin, Macmurray contends, with the most basic form of that relationship: the bond between parent and child. (Macmurray uses the mother as the symbol of the parent in relation to the child but does so more out of convention than a conviction that only mothers can truly nurture. He notes in passing that "a man can do all the mothering that is necessary . . . ")[98] His point is that in the parent-child relation we can learn the essential ingredients in any fully personal relationship. First, he contends, we discover that the intention for relationship with other persons is learned. Nevertheless, the conditions for its development are provided by the physical, biological, and psychological infrastructures inherited by the infant.

Macmurray argues that while the first responses of the child are "biologically random," he has needs which are not "simply biological but personal. . . . He is made to be cared for. He is born into a love-relationship which is inherently personal."[99] This love relationship is necessary for the survival and development of the child and is over and above the satisfaction of his biological needs. In fact, if he depended entirely upon the biological instincts of his parents, he would probably not survive (unlike an organism or lower-level animal). His needs must be met, at least in part, by the *intentional action* of his parents. If the child were nothing more than an organism, "he could live by the satisfaction of organic impulse, by reaction to stimulus, by instinctive adaptation to his natural environment. But this is totally untrue. He cannot live at all by an initiative, whether personal or organic, of his own. He can live only through other people and in dynamic relation with them. In virtue of this fact he is a person, for the personal is constituted by the relation of persons."[100] Later, with the proper intentional nurturing by his parents, the child will learn to form his own intentions and to acquire "the skill to execute them and the knowledge and foresight which will enable him to act responsibly as a member of a personal community."[101]

The development of the child's skills is the building up of levels of support for his intentional action as he grows into a full person. This development takes advantage of all the processes, structures, dynamics, and forces of the mechanical and organic levels of reality within the child. But development only achieves a unity when it is "taken over," as it were, by the governing decisions of the maturing person at the stage of self-conscious intentionality. One of the most important skills which the child develops is that of communication with the personal other (the parent) who is teaching it.

"The impulse to communication is his sole adaptation to the world into which he is born."[102] Even in its implicit and unconscious stage, this impulse "is sufficient to constitute the mother-child relation as the basic form of human existence, as a personal mutuality, as a 'You and I' with a common life. For this reason, the infant is born a person and not an animal. All his subsequent experience, all the habits he forms and the skills he acquires fall within this framework, and are fitted to it."[103] And this is the clue to the development of community and mutuality. For if the child learns only within the framework of the personal relationship intended by the parent and desires, instinctively at first, to communicate with the parent, then it is apparent that "the unit of personal existence is not the individual, but two persons in personal relation; and that we are persons not by individual right, but in virtue of our relation to one another. The personal is constituted by personal relatedness. The unit of the personal is not the 'I', but the 'You and I'."[104] If this fact had been understood by such thinkers as Hobbes and Locke, perhaps the notion of the isolated individual who only enters into relationship with others out of fear and through calculation would never have gained the dominance it has had during the past 200 years.

There is another element in the relationship of child to parents which is crucial to the development of community. In addition to meeting the child's biological needs within their intentional concern for him, the parents, and later the child, find that "there is from the beginning an element of symbolic activity involved which has no organic or utilitarian purpose, and which makes the relationship, as it were, an end in itself. The relationship is *enjoyed*, both by mother and child, *for its own sake*. [emphasis mine] ... [There is] a mutual delight in the relation which unites them in a common life."[105]

Here we have the germ of community. Love of the other person for his or her own sake is a love which is intrinsically delightful. It has no purpose beyond itself. It can be intended solely for its own sake. It is not a function of or condition for some higher goal. Simply being in loving relation to another person is fulfillment enough and can itself be the telos of human activity. That this is at least a possibility is established for the maturing person in the most intimate of relationships: between parent and child. We should not, Macmurray warns, read into this relationship solely organic meaning, as has so often been done by organic thinkers. We must not attempt "to understand the field of the personal on a biological analogy, and so through organic categories."[106] "We are not organisms, but persons. The nexus of relations which unites us in a human society is not organic but personal."[107] It is the personal nature of the parent-child relationship which Macmurray has attempted to demonstrate by the development of his claim that that relationship presupposes that the parents enfold the child's biological needs within the inclusive, intentional activity of their love for him.

Love and Fear. As the child grows, he moves from a total dependence upon the nurturing activity of the parents, not toward a total independence of them, but toward a "mutual interdependence of equals."[108] But this interdependence is characterized by two possible orientations toward other persons. One of these is Love, the other is Fear. These orientations are not the same as conscious intentions. Macmurray sometimes calls them motivations in order to bring out their character as drives which are more organic and innate than they are intentional and purposive. They are genetically prior to the formation of conscious intention and they set the conditions for and often determine action in the absence of reflective knowledge, more as a reaction to stimuli than as deliberate choice. But within the hierarchy of the self as agent, these motivations are the organic infrastructure necessary for the carrying out of any higher-level purposes. No activity "is possible in the absence of a motive... they function in behaviour to determine the direction in which we expend our energy."[109] But when we focus our analysis upon motives alone, we produce a pseudo-science which presumes to explain the self reductively and exhaustively through its infrastructures without ever recognizing the governing and irreducible level of intentionality and freedom of choice.

Normally, we are not fully conscious of these motives, "because our attention is focused upon the intention which determines them. It is only when action is thwarted or inhibited, when the motive is prevented from functioning in bodily movement, that it is reflected back upon itself, as it were, and so thrust into explicit consciousness as an emotion."[110] But when they have come into consciousness we discover that these basic "personal motives" are directed to a personal Other. Both fear and love are ways of communicating with an Other.

> The need which they express is one which can only be satisfied by another person's action. The behaviour which they motivate is therefore incomplete until it meets with a response from the other, and the character of the response—or indeed its occurrence—depends upon the other person. This primary and distinctive character of personal behaviour we shall refer to hereafter as the *mutuality* of the personal. It is what we mean when we say that the personal is constituted by the relation of persons. The reference to the personal Other is constitutive for all personal existence.[111]

Fear is a fear that the Other will not respond to my need "and that in consequence my personal existence will be frustrated. Fear... is at once fear of the other and fear for oneself."[112] It leads to the inhibition of action, to a continual fear of making a mistake in relation to the Other, of doing the wrong thing. It is the awareness that 'You' have as much to do with my fulfillment as I do and that, therefore, I must fear making you angry at me. "'My' success depends upon 'your' motive and 'your' intention."[113] But through fear, I will act defensively and egocentrically. I become the center of reference for my action since I am fearful of you and for myself. It is my need which determines the course of my action in relation to you.

An important motivation which is derived from fear is that of hate. It originates when the Other does not respond to my need as I would like him to. I become resentful of the Other and resentment leads to hatred, not as a persistent or dominant feeling but as an inevitable element in my relation to the Other "because it is impossible that you should always be able to respond to me in the way that my action expects."[114] That is why, according to Macmurray, any fully personal relationship must include forbearance and forgiveness as parts of itself.

Now fear and hatred cannot in and of themselves sustain a personal relationship because they inherently contradict its very conditions. They are built upon the necessity of a relationship to the Other and yet in themselves they seek to break it.

> [A] negative relation of persons is a practical contradiction. It is a relation which is at once maintained and refused, and which is therefore inherently self-stultifying ... Hatred, therefore, is a motive of self-frustration. Since the 'You and I' relation constitutes both the 'You' and the 'I' persons, the relation to the 'You' is necessary for my personal existence. If, through fear of the 'You', I reject this relation, I frustrate my own being. It follows that hatred cannot, as a motive of action, be universalized. It presupposes both love and fear, and if it could be total it would destroy the possibility of personal existence.[115]

This fundamental contradiction runs throughout the atomistic/contractarian model of community. Its understanding of personal relationships assumes the primacy of fear and yet tries to construct a society by means of contracts which domesticate and regularize the expressions of fear. It assumes that persons do not intend relationship as part of their essential nature and yet it also assumes that they *must* intend relationship if their very being is to survive.

The other basic motive, love, is heterocentric. It is for the Other. It takes delight in the Other for the sake of the Other. It reaches out to rather than withdrawing from the Other. But it also looks for a response from the Other and is as fully mutual as fear. "Love is fulfilled only when it is reciprocated."[116] But one does not love the Other simply as a means to self-fulfillment. To do so would be to treat the Other as simply an extension of oneself and is tantamount to denying the Other as Other. In love, however, one is willing to sacrifice one's own interests and needs for the Other. We will have more to say about the dynamics of this relationship later. What we need to recognize at this point is simply that a positive relation to the Other based on love should not be explained either as total altruism or as exploitation based on one's own needs. The love relationship presupposes both the individuality of the lovers and the necessity for their mutuality. I and You are constituted by relationship and the relationship is neither an extension of essentially egocentric needs nor a dissolution through incorporation of each partner into the other.

Entering Community. On the basis of the two primary motivations, fear and love, the individual proceeds to build his relationships to others. In the process he learns to discriminate in his perceptions of and subsequent action in relation to the Other. Ideally, he will try to establish a relation with the other that is positively oriented, that is to say, motivated by love and able to control the negative motivations accordingly. The agent can to some degree choose the kind of response he will make to the Other even though he cannot choose whether he will act in relation to him or her since any relation to the Other demands action.

Macmurray contends that the choice of action is essentially a moral choice. "Since action is choice, the distinction between 'right' and 'wrong' is inherent in the nature of action ... To act is to be active in terms of a distinction between right and wrong, and what is done rightly and wrongly."[117] But without an Other there is no possibility of action. Therefore, action involves moral choice in relation to the Other. When I act, I necessarily enter into relation with the Other and since I act by intention, I necessarily intend that relationship.

But if the Other is also personal, then his intention and mine must somehow be brought into conformity with each other if we each wish to realize our intentions successfully. As long as our intentions clash and our actions are interconnected, our intentions must frustrate each other. We have a conflict of wills and morality is the effort to resolve this conflict. "The moral rightness of an action ... rises from the fact that the actions of one person affect, either by way of help or hindrance, the actions of others."[118] If as individuals we are constituted by our relation to each other, then "the intention of one particular agent is therefore inherently related to the intention of the Other."[119]

The Mutual/Personal Model of Community

As long as agents make up a common world, then the condition for their successful action is "a unity of intentions."[120] If two agents or groups of agents "have incompatible intentions, both intentions cannot be realized."[121] Either one agent will freely yield to the others or one must impose his will on the others. "In the first case one of the agents loses his freedom, and cannot realize his nature as an agent; in the second, both lose their freedom until one has mastered the other and forced him to abandon his intention."[122] This is just as true of indirect relations in an interdependent world as it is of direct relations. "The success of an operator on the New York Stock Exchange may ruin a number of people in Germany or China."[123]

This leads to the conclusion that the interdependence of all agents in a worldwide community "makes the freedom of all... depend upon the intentions of each"[124] and this is the ground of morality. "It provides a reference beyond themselves for all possible intentions in virtue of which they can be either right or wrong, and this rightness or wrongness is neither technical nor aesthetic, but moral."[125] In other words, no intention can be right if its enactment would destroy the very conditions of its fulfillment. But these conditions presuppose the unity of intentions in a single, interdependent world, and therefore a morally right action "is an action which intends community"[126] if by community in this context we simply mean "the harmonious interrelation of agents."[127] Whatever an agent does is morally right "if the particular intention of his action is controlled by a general intention to maintain the community of agents, and wrong if it is not so controlled."[128]

Such a general intention is "a unifying intention. Not only is it the intention which maintains the personal unity of any group of agents; but it also unifies the actions of an individual agent in a single life. For it is the intention which remains the same for all his actions, and to which they all have reference."[129] But it must also be the intention of all the agents who stand in relation to each other "since the relation of persons is constitutive for their existence as persons. They can only be themselves and realize their freedom as agents through their relation to one another."[130] In the absence of this intention to maintain community, no ground for morality is possible since the conditions for morality are themselves absent. "It is this that enables us to define morality by reference to maintaining community in action."[131] It is not enough that persons are interdependent and in relation to each other. They must *intend* to maintain and sustain that relationship as long as they are conscious, acting beings.

But this fact does not tell us much about the various modes of "being in relation to others" which can comprise the interconnectedness of the social world. One of the most significant aspects of Macmurray's understanding of community is his distinction between cooperative, contemplative, and communal modes of relationship. In the contemplative mode (one of two negative modes) the person conforms his practical life to the demands of the social order but in his private life withdraws into what he regards as his 'true' self. If the real world does not meet his needs, he creates an ideal or spiritual world where they can be met. Real life is enjoyed at the level of contemplation, meditation, or simply privacy. A person who withdraws into the world of thought or imagination in this way does not, of course, cease living in the practical world. But he does try to avoid concerning himself with that world as much as possible. He makes his activity in the practical world as automatic as he can. This can occur if there is a form of morality in which the individual is asked to contribute to the practical world as little that is unique or different as possible. He adjusts his behavior to a "common form which is unchanging, within which the activity of each member is adjusted to that of the others automatically."[132] And this form is what Macmurray calls the organic mode of relationship.

It is a morality of social habit, "in which the activity of each member is functionally related to the activity of the others, so that the practical life of the society is a balanced and harmonious unity, a system of social habit. To maintain this each member must have his function in the common life; he must be trained from childhood to recognize the social pattern and his own function in it, and to develop the system of habits which makes conformity to it a second nature."[133] The morality of the organic society is that of "good form,"[134] doing that which is seemly or fitting. "It is a kind of beauty or grace in social relations, a matter of style, of balance, of tact and poise."[135]

The other negative mode of social relationships is what Macmurray calls the 'pragmatic' or cooperative mode. It takes the practical life with utmost seriousness, regards it as essentially a clash of wills, and resolves the conflict by the individual appropriation of power. The relation of agents in this mode is essentially one of competition for power. "The problematic of action becomes the effort to achieve my own purpose in the face of resistance from the other. But because of the interdependence of agents, this must be limited by the necessity to maintain the unity of society, that is, the systematic co-operation of agents."[136] The form of morality appropriate for this mode of social relationship is that of obedience to the Law, including a moral law which the individual imposes upon himself. It will be a morality of self-control with external sanctions in the form of social punishment by legislated norms of conduct. These norms will limit social behavior and the uses of power by each individual. It is, in effect, the morality of the atomistic/contractarian community.

It should be obvious that these first two negative modes of social relationship are motivated essentially by fear and occasionally hatred. The contemplative mode is based on fear of relationship with the actual other: a fear that in practice the other can disturb the center of my being. Hence, my retreat into contemplation. The pragmatic or cooperative mode, as we saw so clearly in Hobbes, Locke, and other atomistic/contractarian thinkers, arises out of fear of the power of the other person to limit my freedom to do what I want. I appeal to the morality of law as a way of keeping the other at bay. It is only when we enter the communal mode of relationship that we discover a motivation for community which is based on love, a genuine desire to be with and for the other person.

We should not immediately assume that the third model of relationship, which Macmurray calls the communal and we have called the mutual/personal, is utterly distinct from the contemplative and cooperative. In fact, it should not surprise us that ultimately these two other models fall within the inclusive nature of the communal model as necessary conditions or infrastructures for mutuality. In the final section I will discuss in more detail the important implications of considering the cooperative, pragmatic, and political dimensions of a mutual/personal community. But taken by themselves they do not capture the essence of what it means to relate to others communally by intending, in a direct and positive way, the welfare of others for their own sakes.

NOTES TO CHAPTER 5

1. Stanley Hauerwas, *A Community of Character: Toward a Constructive Christian Social Ethic* (Notre Dame, Ind.: University of Notre Dame Press, 1981), 80.

2. Ibid., 81.

3. Daniel Day Williams, *The Spirit and the Forms of Love* (New York: Harper and Row, 1968), 11.

4. Kennth L. Smith and Ira G. Zepp, Jr., *Search for the Beloved Community: The Thinking of Martin Luther King, Jr.* (Valley Forge, Pa.: Judson Press, 1974), 131.

5. Buber, *Paths in Utopia*, 133.

6. Martin Buber, *I and Thou*, second ed., with a postscript by the author. Trans. Ronald Gregor Smith (New York: Charles Scribner's Sons, 1958), 45.

7. Quoted in Jakob J. Petuchowski, "Toward a Modern Brotherhood," in *Contemporary Judaic Fellowship in Theory and in Practice*, ed. Jacob Neusner (New York: KTAV Publishing House, 1972), 35.

8. Ludwig Feuerbach, *The Essence of Christianity* (New York: C. Blanchard, 1855), 208.

9. Buber, *I and Thou*, 3.

10. Ibid., 4.

11. Ibid., 22.

12. Ibid., 3.

13. Ibid., 14–15.

14. Ibid., 15.

15. Ibid., 28.

16. Ibid., 62.

17. Ibid., 63.

18. Martin Buber, "Distance and Relation," in *The Knowledge of Man: Selected Essays*, edited with an introductory essay by Maurice Friedman, trans. Maurice Friedman and Ronald Gregor Smith (New York: Harper and Row, 1965), 71.

19. Buber, *I and Thou*, 49.

20. Buber, *Philosophical Interrogations*, 20.

21. Ibid.

22. Bernard Susser, *Existence and Utopia: The Social and Political Thought of Martin Buber* (Rutherford, N.J.: Fairleigh Dickinson University Press, 1981), 47.

23. Buber, *I and Thou*, 100.

24. Martin Buber, *The Way of Response: Martin Buber. Selections from His Writings*, ed. N.N. Glatzer (New York: Schocken Books, 1966), 158.

25. Buber, *Paths in Utopia*, 145.

26. Buber, *Philosophical Interrogations*, 74.

27. Buber, *I and Thou*, 82.

28. Peter Bertocci, *Philosophical Interrogations*, 42.

29. Buber, *I and Thou*, 78–79.

30. See especially Buber's "Distance and Relation," in *The Knowledge of Man*.

31. Susser, *Existence and Utopia: The Social and Political Thought of Martin Buber*, 184, n. 12.

32. Buber, *Paths in Utopia*, 131.
33. Ibid., 136.
34. Ibid., 79.
35. John Macmurray, *Interpreting the Universe* (London: Faber and Faber, 1933), 16, 21. The notion of immediate experience in Macmurray is best understood, I think, as a limiting concept, not as a phenomenological description of what actually takes place. It is probably impossible to imagine any kind of experience which does not involve at least a minimal amount of interpretation. In using the notion of immediate experience, Macmurray is attempting to place thought into a broader and more basic context.
36. Ibid., 22.
37. Ibid., 59.
38. Ibid., 60.
39. Ibid., 61.
40. Ibid., 85.
41. Ibid., 89.
42. Ibid., 89–90.
43. Ibid., 94.
44. Ibid., 96.
45. Ibid., 97.
46. John Macmurray, "The Unity of Modern Problems," *Journal of Philosophical Studies*, 4 (1929): 167.
47. Ibid., 168.
48. John Macmurray, *Persons in Relation* (New York: Harper and Brothers, 1961), 137.
49. Ibid.
50. Ibid.
51. Macmurray, *The Self as Agent*, 33.
52. Ibid.
53. Ibid.
54. Macmurray, *Interpreting the Universe*, 111.
55. Ibid.
56. Macmurray, "The Unity of Modern Problems," 171.
57. Ibid., 170–71.
58. Macmurray, *Interpreting the Universe*, 112.
59. Ibid., 113.
60. Macmurray, "The Unity of Modern Problems," 172, 171.
61. Ibid., 172.
62. Ibid., 174.
63. Ibid., 175.
64. Ibid., 177.
65. Ibid., 179.
66. Macmurray, *The Self as Agent*, 15.
67. Ibid., 38.
68. Ibid.
69. Ibid., 31.

70. Ibid., 73.
71. Macmurray, *Persons in Relation*, 76.
72. Ibid., 77.
73. Macmurray, *The Self as Agent*, 85.
74. Ibid., 79.
75. Ibid., 87.
76. Ibid.
77. John Macmurray, *Creative Society: A Study of the Relation of Christianity to Communism* (London: Student Christian Movement Press, 1935), 151.
78. Macmurray, *The Self as Agent*, 110.
79. Ibid., 116.
80. Ibid., 117.
81. Ibid.
82. Macmurray, *Persons in Relation*, 80.
83. Macmurray, *The Self as Agent*, 118.
84. Macmurray, *Persons in Relation*, 16.
85. Ibid., 17.
86. Ibid.
87. Macmurray, *Interpreting the Universe*, 128.
88. Ibid.
89. Ibid., 132.
90. Macmurray, *The Self as Agent*, 129.
91. John Macmurray, *Conditions of Freedom* (London: Faber and Faber, 1950), 16.
92. Ibid., 17–18.
93. Ibid., 82.
94. Ibid., 76.
95. Ibid., 159–60.
96. Macmurray, *Persons in Relation*, 17.
97. Ibid., 24.
98. Ibid., 50.
99. Ibid., 49, 48.
100. Ibid., 51.
101. Ibid., 53.
102. Ibid., 60.
103. Ibid., 61.
104. Ibid.
105. Ibid., 63.
106. Ibid., 45.
107. Ibid., 46.
108. Ibid., 66.
109. Ibid., 68.
110. Ibid.
111. Ibid., 69.
112. Ibid., 70.
113. Ibid.

114. Ibid., 74.
115. Ibid., 74–75.
116. Ibid., 73.
117. Ibid., 112–13.
118. Ibid., 116.
119. Ibid., 117.
120. Ibid., 118.
121. Ibid.
122. Ibid.
123. Ibid.
124. Ibid.
125. Ibid., 119.
126. Ibid.
127. Ibid.
128. Ibid.
129. Ibid.
130. Ibid.
131. Ibid., 120.
132. Ibid., 124.
133. Ibid.
134. Ibid.
135. Ibid.
136. Ibid., 125.

6. Religion and the Nature of the Loving Community

THE COMMUNAL MODE OF RELATIONSHIP

The third mode of relationship, the communal, is, for Macmurray, the only positively motivated form of relation with the personal Other and is the only form within which the person can be fully personal. It is positively motivated in the sense that the person's orientation toward the Other is heterocentric, concerned for the Other as Other. And it is only in such an other-oriented mode of relationship that the person's full potential can be exercised and enjoyed.

The communal mode of relationship is "a unity of persons as persons.... It is constituted and maintained by a mutual affection."[1] Each member of the community is in "positive personal relation to each of the others taken severally. The structure of a community is the nexus or network of the active relations of friendship between all possible pairs of its members."[2] Friendship, fellowship, love, and mutuality all serve as synonyms describing this communal mode of relationship.

As heterocentric, each person is positively motivated toward the other as other. "For each ... it is the other who is important, not himself. The other is the centre of value. For himself he has no value in himself, but only for the other; consequently he cares for himself only for the sake of the other."[3] This seems to suggest a completely self-sacrificial orientation which if consistently carried through would entirely negate the person's integrity and intrinsic worth. How can love be built upon the intentional self-destruction of each partner? These questions are legitimate if we think about relationship from the point of view of the individual alone: if the single individual determines what is worthwhile, then obviously his desire to concern himself solely with the other is tantamount to his own negation. But Macmurray reminds us that in the communal mode of relationship we are not to think exclusively from the point of view of the isolated individual. His relationship to the other is by definition "mutual; the other cares for him disinterestedly in return. Each, that is to say, acts, and therefore thinks and feels for the other, and not for himself."[4]

It is only in the crossing of other-concern, in the mutuality or reciprocity of reaching out for the other as other that the worth, integrity, and dignity of each is affirmed. As long as we try to erect self-worth on the basis of what I alone can do, even it it is to sacrifice myself for another, then we fall back into an essentially individualistic or egocentric way of thinking. The only way to avoid individualism, even when it is self-negating, is to accept the mutuality inherent in communal relationship. If each self is heterocentrically oriented, and if all selves are in relation, then no self stands alone because each one is affirmed and loved by the others. The miracle of mutuality is that while loving the other, one discovers that one is being loved by the other in the same way. Without intending one's own affirmation, one finds oneself affirmed because that is the meaning of mutuality: two persons loving each other create through the mutuality of their love the worth and dignity of each.

If we first try to give ourselves worth, then we will be engaged in a futile quest because self-worth is mutual, not individual. We are, in fact, fully interdependent. "This complete and unlimited dependence of each of us upon the others is the central and crucial fact of personal existence. Individual independence is an illusion; and the independent individual, the isolated self, is a nonentity. In ourselves we are nothing; and when we turn our eyes inward in search of ourselves we find a vacuum. Being nothing in ourselves, we have no value in ourselves, and are of no importance whatever, wholly without meaning or significance."[5] Unless we understand that relationship is the very ground of meaning or significance for persons, we will misunderstand Macmurray's point. We are so much under the sway of the individualistic assumptions of the atomistic/contractarian view that it is almost impossible to think of the person as person only in and through relationship, rather than thinking of the person as an individual who only derivatively and coincidentally enters into relationship. But Macmurray argues that it is only in relation to others that we exist as persons; we are invested with significance by others who have need of us; and borrow our reality from those who care for us. We live and move and have our being not in ourselves but in one another; and what rights or powers or freedom we possess are ours by the grace and favour of our fellows. Here is the basic fact of our human condition; which all of us can know if we stop pretending, and do know in moments when the veil of self-deception is stripped from us and we are forced to look upon our own nakedness.[6]

(If this language sounds suspiciously religious, it is for a good reason. We will examine shortly why Macmurray feels that the task of building community is a uniquely religious task and how he understands its relation to the Christian faith.)

We mentioned earlier the paradox of intending to live for others as a condition for self-realization. In addition to acknowledging interdependence as a fact which all attempts at self-realization must accept, we must also, according to Macmurray, acknowledge that it is part of the condition of human nature that we cannot be fully ourselves until and unless we live self-transcendently. Interdependence is a matter of fact: community is a matter of intention. It is constituted paradoxically by a motivation of complete self-realization through an intention of complete self-transcendence. Using typically extreme language, Macmurray says, "If this intention could be realized in an actual instance, the self would 'care for' the other totally ... 'I' would think, feel and act *for* 'you', in terms of 'your' nature and being. In this way, and only in this way, could a personal being achieve and experience a complete objectivity, a complete rationality, a complete self-realization. The ground of friendship is, therefore, the inevitable need we have to be ourselves. It is our nature, as persons, to ... have the centre of intention and realization outside ourselves, in that which is other than ourselves.'"[7]

This notion of heterocentricity, despite the extreme way in which it is stated and Macmurray's reluctance to acknowledge explicitly the paradox it creates, does not introduce a dichotomy or dualism between self-concern and other-concern into his thought, nor does it necessarily suggest an unrealizable and therefore unrealistic ideal. Dualism is, in fact, automatically avoided because selves are not set in relation against their essential human nature. Nor is self-realization as a motive denied. The central point for Macmurray is that the conditions of reality are such that self-love or self-realization becomes possible essentially because another has first chosen to affirm 'me' and I have chosen to affirm him or her. In the absence of that affirmation, no effort on my part can give me self-worth, or self-fulfillment, at least in the fullest sense. This claim of Macmurray's is implicitly supported by the religious conviction that in the final analysis God provides the affirmation for every human self which gives it the basic worth on which it is then freed to go out and give worth to others and receive it from them reciprocally. Only if the self had to somehow manufacture its own worth independently of others would dualism emerge, because once having given itself worth it would not be clear what, if any, essential bond it had with other equally self-constituted selves.

Macmurray explicitly acknowledges that self-realization is always a part of one's motivation in entering into relationship. He does not intend to deny a concern for self-realization but merely to argue that it can be achieved, paradoxically, only by *intending* primarily the realization of the other. The paradox of heterocentricity is not a dualism between self-regard and regard for the other, but a reversal of the traditional ordering of their priority. It is no more, but no less, paradoxical than such claims as "he who would save his life must lose it." The paradox is "resolved" only within the context of a philosophy of persons which claims that persons can be fully self-realized only when they first seek the realization of others and when others reciprocally seek their realization as well. "The essential condition for *realizing* fellowship is a mutual reciprocity. The individual cannot achieve freedom in fellowship unless the other person does so too ... Without reciprocity no common life can be established ... "[8] When Macmurray says that in ourselves we are nothing or that we live and move only in others, he is simply affirming that we cannot create by ourselves our fundamental sense of self nor can we achieve the fullest possible experience of being a self: but in a relationship, a community, of essentially heterocentrically oriented selves, each will be given, as a kind of grace, the conditions for self-realization. The self always has worth but this is the gift of another's love, not the product of self-concern.

Macmurray is implicitly suggesting, I believe, that we need to adopt a view closer to the dialectic of the organic model than the strict cause and effect pattern of the atomistic model. We should not try first to establish the meaning and worth of the individual in isolation before he or she enters into relationship.

The relationship is the condition or context for the establishment of meaning and worth. But the whole point of the relationship is to establish that each partner is to be treated in and for himself, not subordinated to the other or to some mystical or abstract "whole" within which both partners function as parts. Thinking from the point of view of mutuality requires, in a sense, a logic which departs from strict sequential cause and effect as well as from organic functionalism. It requires us to think of persons as distinct individuals, but whose individuality is achieved only in the mutuality of relationship in which each lives for the other. Ultimately, Macmurray implicitly suggests, we can discover this "logic of mutuality" only in the full experience of living it.

One of the moments when we are most aware of the mutuality of relation is in the intimacy of friendship, one of Macmurray's synonyms for community. If we can think of two friends together and "completely at home with one another," then we have a paradigm of mutuality and a revelation of the fullest possible expression of human nature. These friends "know each other and love each other. So they can think and feel for one another. Each is the object of the other's thought and affection. They each think and feel in terms of the other. And they behave in terms of one another. They make plans together and cooperate and share their enjoyments and their thoughts."[9] They trust each other and do not fear each other. They enjoy being with each other solely for its own sake, as an end in itself. They are, in Macmurray's terms, objective to each other. That is, they live toward each other on the basis of what the other is objectively, in and for himself. When this kind of love is experienced, then the two persons are completely real, completely free, and fully personal.

If one of the distinguishing traits of being persons is the ability to live in terms of what is not ourselves, then a fully personal life is one that is fully objective.

> It is our nature to apprehend and enjoy a world that is outside ourselves, to live in communion with a world which is independent of us. We have the capacity to know other things and other people and to enjoy them. And when we are completely ourselves we live by that knowledge and appreciation of what is not ourselves, and so in communion with other beings... The capacity to live in terms of the other, and so of what is not ourselves, to live in others and

through others and for others, is the unique property of human beings.[10]

But the only way by which we live fully objective lives is to live them in relation to the kind of Other that can bring the fullness of our being into expression. "Complete objectivity depends upon our being objectively related, in action as well as in reflection, to that in the world which is capable of calling into play all the capacities of our consciousness at once. It is only the personal aspect of the world that can do this, and, therefore, it is only the objectivity of our conscious relation to other persons which can express our rationality fully and so reveal its essential character."[11] It is only in a fully personal relationship that I "find a response at my own level. My own objectivity meets an objectivity which corresponds to it, so that for the first time I can achieve self-consciousness."[12]

In other words, I can be conscious of myself as a person only in relation to another person. Self-consciousness is only the "inner aspect" of our consciousness of other persons. Personality is mutual "in its very being. The self is one term in a relation between two selves. It cannot be prior to that relation and equally, of course, the relation cannot be prior to it. 'I' exist only as one member of the '*you and I*'. The self only exists in the communion of selves."[13] We must be careful here not to understand Macmurray to be saying that the self is only an organic part of or function for something greater and more basic, namely, the relationship itself. The relationship is not a thing or substance. It is not a more inclusive person or personality.

Macmurray is quite clear that although the person is fully a person only in relation to other persons, the relation presupposes that each person in it is a unique individual. The unity of persons in community "is no fusion of selves, neither is it a functional unity of differences—neither an organic nor a mechanical unity—it is a unity of persons. Each remains a distinct individual; the other remains really other. Each realizes himself in and through the other."[14] "Two persons in personal relation are not complementary. They do not lose their individuality to become functional elements in an individuality which includes them both. In fact, in the personal field the only real individuals are individual persons. Groups of persons are not individuals. Nevertheless, the individuality of a person exists only in and through his relationship to other persons and the more objective his relations become with other persons, the more his individuality is enhanced."[15]

For example, only in the relationship does the individual person experience full equality, an equality which assumes that each person is unique. (This notion of equality is Macmurray's implicit tribute to the fundamental insight of the atomistic/contractarian view. Macmurray does not draw from this notion of equality, however, either the conclusion that all persons have equal talent, function, or rights, or that each one is fundamentally an atomic unit similar in all essential respects to all the others.) The equality which "is an aspect of the mutuality of the relation"[16] is an intentional equality. It is a way of regarding the other so as not to exploit him as a means to one's own end. In a mutual relationship the partners cannot use each other or subordinate each other simply because they have different abilities and personalities.

While it is perfectly appropriate to speak of persons fulfilling themselves, or realizing their personal natures in the relationship of mutuality, this should not be taken to mean that relationship is simply a means to the egocentric end of self-fulfillment. Again the "logic of mutuality" demands that we think of personal relationship as involving both heterocentric orientation and the experience of fulfillment. But the mystery of mutuality is that if we aim solely at fulfillment, we will miss it. The mystery of the created order, Macmurray suggests, is that only by loving another person not for our own sake but for his do we find fulfillment for ourselves. Again, as we shall see, Macmurray is not unselfconsciously trying to state in metaphysical language what Jesus may have been saying when he proclaimed that it was only by losing one's life that one can save it.

It is in this understanding of mutuality that I believe Macmurray goes beyond both Marx and Whitehead. Both of these earlier thinkers, as we saw, seem to understand and emphasize the interdependence of the parts of reality as the condition for self-realization. Unlike the atomistic thinkers, both Marx and Whitehead know that interdependence is a fact which cannot be wished away by dreams of individualism or independence. But neither one seems to have much to say about the kind of interpersonal relationship in which one person lives for another without consciously aiming at self-fulfillment. The purposive goal of self-fulfillment seems to be the remaining legacy of the atomistic view in the organic model of Marx and Whitehead, despite the priority they give to interdependence rather than independence. For Macmurray, interdependence is also a fact but it is experienced most fully when the person does not aim at his own fulfillment but lives, instead, objectively and heterocentrically for the other person.

Another aspect of experiencing one's full personal nature only in relationship is the realization of freedom. If each is heterocentrically oriented toward the other, then there is no fear for the self and thus no constraint on either partner. Each "can be himself fully; neither is under obligation to act a part. Thus equality and freedom are constitutive of community; and the democratic slogan, 'Liberty, equality, fraternity', is an adequate definition of community—of the self-realization of persons in relation."[17] If freedom is the freedom to realize one's nature "to the full, without constraint or hindrance,"[18] then only when two persons can be fully themselves, which can happen only in the communal mode of mutuality, can they be truly free. "Because . . . the freedom of anything is its ability to express its own nature to the full without constraint, human freedom is the ability to express this peculiar property which belongs to human beings—the ability to live spontaneously (that is, from themselves) in terms of the other (that is, for and in and by what is not themselves). Only when we live in this way can we be free; for only then do we express our own nature in action."[19]

Religion and Universal Community. I have already alluded to the fact that Macmurray self-consciously utilizes religious, especially Christian, symbols and ideas in the elaboration of his metaphysics. This fact is significant if the full import of his model of community is to be appreciated. Today there are many religious writers who have mined the work of Marx and Whitehead for insights and arguments which they believe can be made congruent with Christian interpretations of reality. A Christian-Marxist dialogue has been going on for at least twenty years and has had a major influence on what is called "liberation theology." There is also a growing literature on the contributions of Whiteheadian and process philosophy to Christian theology.

In the cases of both Marx and Whitehead, however, the links with Christian theology have to be forged for the most part by their contemporary interpreters because neither Marx nor Whitehead was particularly interested in Christian thought. Marx, of course, explicitly repudiated Christianity and religion in general (though his reasons for doing so were not always well substantiated). Whitehead, while clearly interested in God, did not feel any particular attachment to defending or interpreting the Christian understanding of deity by means of his process or organic categories. What makes Macmurray's work stand out in this regard is that he did take seriously both religion in general and Christianity in particular. In fact, his metaphysics of community was intended by him to reflect the essence of the Christian, or biblical, understanding of God's intention for humanity. If Macmurray's model of community can be distinguished from the organic model implicit in both Marx and Whitehead, and if he intended his model to be congruent with Christian thought, then his understanding of religion and of Christianity should be of particular significance to Christian theologians seeking a model of community which is metaphysically sound, empirically viable, and faithful to fundamental Christian convictions.

Religion, according to Macmurray, is a universal human experience. It is also unique to human beings and thus has its root in the personal dimension of human life. "Religion is bound up with that in our experience which makes us persons and not mere organisms."[20] And, most importantly of all, religion intends to be inclusive or universal, that is, to include all persons within its life. These characteristics of religion signify that it is ultimately concerned "with the original and basic formal problem of human existence, and this is the relation of persons.... Religion has its ground and origin in the problematic of the relation of persons, and [when it is theoretical] reflects that problem... Religion is about the community of persons."[21] Or, to put it somewhat differently, the field of religion is the field of personal relationships. Everything is seen, in religion, "in its relation to personality. The personal is the fact of central importance. All other facts are valued in relation to this central value... The field of religion is the field of personal relations, and the datum from which religious reflection starts is the reciprocity or mutuality of these. Its problem is the problem of communion or community. Religion is about fellowship and community, which are facts of direct, universal human experience."[22]

This means that the task of religion, in reflection and in action, is the achievement of fellowship, or communion with the Other. Ultimately, this means a universal human community must be intended (even though it may never be reached in fact). The ideal of the personal is "a universal community of persons in which each cares for all the others and no one for himself.... Short of this there is unintegrated, and therefore suppressed, negative motivation; there is unresolved fear; and fear inhibits and destroys freedom."[23] Macmurray is aware that this ideal of the universal community "is just what all the universal religions have always said in simpler and more comprehensive terms,"[24] but that is precisely why he thinks his understanding of religion is correct. It captures the fundamental conviction of the major world religions.

Macmurray's ideal for universal community is, of course, an extension of his notion of heterocentricity. In its bald statement it can appear to be extreme and bordering on the unrealistic. How can one not love oneself, at least to some degree? Is it really possible to love others without any degree of consideration for oneself? Didn't Jesus say that you should love your neighbor *as yourself*?

In his more carefully nuanced treatment of heterocentricity, Macmurray does acknowledge that it is an ideal and that in practice it will be realized only in rare instances. "Friendship," he admits, "is a very personal and intimate thing, and no man can have more than a few real and lasting friends."[25] Nevertheless, community is constituted not solely by its degree of achievement but by the intention which sustains it. This means that in any meeting of persons there is the *potential* for friendship. To love others in community is to recognize and explicitly affirm "the intention which constitutes our own personal nature ... It is to maintain the disposition and the purpose to care for *any* human being with whom we are brought into relation, in whatever fashion circumstances make possible, and simply on the ground of our common humanity."[26] And religion is simply the activity which intends to create the conditions for the extension and expression of the consciousness of fellowship. The paradox of heterocentricity includes, as we have seen, the acknowledgment of the motivation for self-realization and the conviction that this motivation can be achieved only through the intention to care primarily for the realization of others. In this sense, I think Macmurray's ideal of community conforms to the basic intention of Christianity as well as of many of the other major world religions. That intention does not deny the presence of the concern for the self: but it sets that concern into the context of a more basic other-regarding intention for community and at the same time contends that only in this way can the concern for self be fully realized.

Nevertheless, Macmurray is quite clear that he is not describing the actual practice of the world's religions. He is referring to the *intention* which lies behind and is often perverted by the actual behavior of religious groups. Simply having an intention does not guarantee that it will be realized. This is what Macmurray calls the "problematic" of life. We intend communion and experience division and hostility.

> [A]ll personal consciousness is problematic; ... the consciousness of the common life is *ipso facto* a consciousness that it may or may not be realized in action. It is the consciousness that hostility may take the place of fellowship, and the unity be broken. This will happen if personal relations become negatively motivated, if fear of the other replaces love for the others. Thus the problem of community is the problem of overcoming fear and subordinating the negative to the positive in the motivation of persons in relation.[27]

Religion in its reflective mode is the representation in thought of this problem and the symbolic celebration of its resolution. Religion tries to understand how community gets broken and how it can be restored. Symbolically, it celebrates communion, that is, it expresses in symbols a consciousness of community and a joy in being conscious of it. It is a celebration of the experience of mutuality which is delightful for its own sake, which is joyful and pleasing as an end in itself. But this symbolic activity must be itself communal since what it is celebrating is communal. Historically, this kind of symbolism manifests itself in ritual. But what is being celebrated is not always actually attained. "The continuous possibility that hostility and enmity may break out between the members of the community and destroy the fellowship is inseparable from any consciousness of it. For community is matter of intention and therefore problematical ... In face of this problem, religion is itself intentional. Its celebration of communion is also a means of strengthening the will to community."[28]

This means that religion has the task of strengthening the positive, heterocentric motivations in its members and subordinating the motivations of fear and hatred. "We may define the function of religion as being to create, maintain and deepen the community of persons and to extend it without limit, by the transformation of negative motives and by eliminating the dominance of fear in human relations. To achieve this would be to create a universal community in which all personal relations were positively motivated, all its members were free and equal in relation. Such a community would be the full self-realization of the personal."²⁹

To intend anything less inclusive than a universal human community would be to intend to exclude some persons from relationship. But to intend to exclude some requires us not to love them. You cannot love someone for his own sake and at the same time consciously intend to exclude him from relationship with you. Therefore if you intend to exclude some from your community you can only do so by constricting your capacity to love and when that happens, your full personhood is constricted accordingly. As long as the fullness of my personal being is only brought to expression by a fully positive, loving relation to another person, then when I deliberately shut off part of that relationship to another, I automatically restrict part of my being from its realization or expression. Therefore, if the fullness of personal being is to be achieved, its condition must be the intention for a universal community of persons in which no one is intentionally excluded.

Macmurrray does not mean to suggest that no community can exist until a universal community exists. That would be naive utopianism. His point is that no small or restricted community can be fully personal unless it *intends* to include all others within it. There will, in practice, be all sorts of practical obstacles to such universal inclusion. But as long as the community does not deliberately and consciously exclude others as a matter of policy, then it is positively motivated and thus characterized by the essential religious intention. There is a kind of "religious irrationality" in the limitation of community to a restricted group. The development of religion, Macmurray contends, eventually reaches the point

> at which this potential inclusiveness is realized, and the universal religions appear. They represent the discovery of the implication of all religious reflection, that the basis of human community is common humanity. With this, religion takes on a new task—the realization of the unlimited community, the brotherhood of mankind. So religion becomes prophetic, and its reference is not to an actual community merely, but to the community that ought to be and is to be ... The function of a universal religion is to create the conditions for its realization.³⁰

God as Personal Agent. At the heart of a universal religion which intends community (in its reflective mode) must be "the idea of a personal Other who stands in the same mutual relation to every member of the community, . . . a universal Agent, whose action unifies the actions of every member of the community, and whose continuing intention is the unity of their several intentions . . . a representative of the unity of the community as a personal reality, so that each member can think his membership of the community through his relation to this person, who represents and embodies the intention which constitutes the general fellowship."[31] This is, of course, the idea of God as a personal Agent. It is the idea of an Agent who creates the conditions for and acts intentionally in order to realize community.

Macmurray believes that this idea of God as creative Agent is to be found in its clearest form in the religions of the Bible—Judaism and Christianity. He is a Christian because he also believes that in Jesus God made manifest His intention for community in the most decisive way possible. But Macmurray's Christianity is not, in the strictest sense, orthodox. It is not defined by the Christological affirmations of the creeds or early Christian theology. It is much more Hebraic or Judaic in tone and substance. Macmurray claims that Jesus is to be understood in Hebraic terms, not in the categories of Greek (i.e. Platonic or Aristotelian) philosophy.

At the heart of the Hebraic monotheism of the Hebrew Bible is the conviction that the union of mankind into one community is "the intention of God, and so the necessary end of the historic process."[32] The Hebrew people saw themselves as the instrument through which this intention would be realized universally as they realized it within their own community. Macmurray understands Christianity to be a religion which took over from Judaism the task of preparing the universal community, even while in practice it betrayed the task many times over.

The essential condition for realizing the universal community is that the world be conceived as "the act of God, the Creator of the world, and ourselves as created agents, with a limited and dependent freedom to determine the future, which can be realized only on the condition that our intentions are in harmony with His intention, and which must frustrate itself if they are not."[33] It is this notion of the ultimate frustration of human intentions if they are not in conformity with God's intention for community that underlies all that Macmurray says about Judaism, Christianity, and, especially, Jesus.

When human beings act against the intention of God (the intention for a universal community of mutual love), then they act against their own nature and must ultimately frustrate themselves since they are acting against the conditions for successful action. "Human intentions which are opposed to the intention of God for man are necessarily self-frustrating."[34] God has created human beings so that they can be fulfilled only when they act in conformity with him. Given the power of God, both in setting the conditions for action and in acting in history to further his intention, to try to frustrate God is inevitably to frustrate only ourselves. "Thus whether our intention conforms to the purpose of God or opposes it, we cannot *achieve* anything but the purpose of God."[35] "When we defy the will of God we defy our own nature. People have this curious capacity for not being themselves."[36]

In a way reminiscent of Marx, Macmurray suggests that history is the story of man's alienation from his true nature because of his repeated attempts to act against the fulfillment of himself in community with others. Only by returning to himself, by accepting his created intention toward mutuality, can the human being discover the path toward fulfillment. Echoing many of Martin Buber's points about the relation between God ("the living centre") and human beings, Macmurray believes that the person must cease to be alienated from himself, and this means from others as well, since the realization of human nature can occur only in the relationship of 'I and You', not in isolation or through the assertion of individualism.

He continues to reaffirm Buber's position when he claims that history is the action of both God and human beings. "History has to be thought both as the act of God in the world, and as the act of Man in the world ... The intentions of men are manifold. The problem for thought is to think the manifold realizations of human intentions as the realization of the one intention of the supreme and universal Agent."[37] That divine intention, working now under the conditions of a fallen creation in which human beings act in opposition to God, is for "a universal community of persons, with freedom and equality as its structural principles of relationship."[38] But since human beings are co-agents of history, God cannot impose his intention upon them (beyond creating their natures such that their fulfillment consists in adopting it). The creation of such a universal community "is not possible unless Man wills it, because the structure of human relationships is the expression of human intentions ... [therefore] God's action in history must be the creation in Man of the effective intention to realize freedom and equality."[39]

The way in which God tries to make His intention an effective part of human intentionality is by continual prophetic activity. He inspires prophets, and ultimately Jesus himself, to preach the message "that man's rejection of freedom and God's intention for him is necessarily self-frustrating. In rejecting freedom man rejects himself, and negates himself."[40] In Jesus, God made manifest the self-consciousness of his purpose as the purpose already inherent in human nature. He had begun the activity of revealing this fact in the Hebrew prophets, "and it culminates in Jesus."[41]

At the heart of God's revelation is the proclamation that "the determination of all that happens in the world lies in the hands of a power that is irresistible and yet friendly."[42] Only love can experience the fullness of this friendly power. But this means that human beings must be released from the fear which keeps them from each other and from the world itself. When fear is removed, persons can begin to accept and to trust their created nature. And when they can trust the nature God has given them, they can begin to love. Love, as we have seen, is heterocentric. "Love is the affirmation of the being of another person . . . Where it is mutual, it integrates human beings in a way which is positive and absolute. For in its very nature it is unconditional, since love is in its essence the mutual affirmation by a community of human beings of one another's existence. It is thus the positive and absolute condition of community."[43] In Jesus, this kind of love and its meaning were both taught and embodied.

What keeps the meaning of love from being appropriated by human beings is fear: fear that one cannot eat, clothe, or shelter oneself unless one has the power to subdue others. Fear can lead persons to cooperate in mastering the material conditions of nature in order to provide the essentials of food, clothing, and shelter. The fullness of human life requires that these needs be met. But as long as "the defence of the human organism against death" is the predominant motivation for acting in relation to others, then "the self-realization of the essence of human life in its positive creativeness" will be denied.[44]

Religion is the activity intended to remove fear as the dominating motive in human action and to replace it with love. Ultimately, this means removing the fear of death since the ultimate threat to the organic needs of the self is death. When the fear of death is removed, the freedom to love others is released from its prison and energizes the activity of persons in relation. In the resurrection of Jesus death is given its own death sentence and love is freed to become a realistic basis for relationship rather than a naive fantasy.

Overcoming Dualism. One of the most important aspects of the embodiment of love in Jesus was his repudiation of the dualism of thought and practice. To be real, love has to be manifest in the fullness of human life. But human life is an inclusive whole in which material, organic, and spiritual dimensions are unified in the primary unity of the whole person. This means that there is no fundamental dualism between the reflective and active parts of the person, just as there is no dualism between this world and another. Macmurray frequently noted the absence in Judaism of any kind of dualism between the spiritual world and the world of matter or empirical experience. God has created a single, unified world and it is in this world that human fulfillment, the creation of universal community, is to be found.

Life in community manifests the fullness of human nature. It does not split it into two antithetical parts, one spiritual and one material. Jesus did not teach or embody a dualist understanding, despite the many interpretations which have claimed for him a spiritual dimension alone. The kingdom which he came to announce and to inaugurate was, according to Macmurray, a fully earthly kingdom within history, "the unification of God's intention in history and man's."[45] "So long as we are dualists, we cannot understand Jesus . . . A religion which was not concerned with the re-creation of society, or an effort to reform society which was not the expression of a religious purpose, would have been equally meaningless to him . . . . The distinction made by the dualist between Heaven and earth could not occur to Jesus."[46] As a good Jew, Jesus would "feel no need to look beyond this world, for a meaning and a significance which is not contained, at least potentially, in it . . . For Jesus, the realization of the Kingdom of God in this world, and in a thoroughly 'this-worldly' sense, is what is looked for."[47]

This means that the achievement of community will require praxis as well as reflection. Christians must become concerned with the actual, material conditions (political and economic) which presently block the integrity of life which is at the heart of true community. We can achieve "an understanding of the religious thought of Jesus provided that we *intend* the disappearance of dualism in practice; if we will the end of our claims to superiority and the achievement of equality and freedom. This is the meaning of [Jesus'] statement that 'If any man will do his will, he shall know of the doctrine'."[48]

True to his epistemological principles, Macmurray reminds us that we cannot know whether his interpretation of reality, even in its Christian form, is true until and unless we are willing to commit our action to it. If we think the unity of the world as a unity of action under the guidance of a supreme Agent, then we must allow this understanding to influence our action. "Any thought, however formal, requires verification, and the possibility of verification is grounded on the differential effect it has upon intention. If we act as if the world, in its unity, is intentional . . . we shall act differently from anyone who does not believe this. We shall act as though our own actions were our contributions to the one inclusive action which is the history of the world . . . Our conception of the unity of the world determines a way of life; and the satisfactoriness or unsatisfactoriness of that way of life is its verification."[49]

But "the heart of this verification must lie in the effect of the belief upon the relations of persons."[50] If we act upon the belief that we are in relation to a loving God and through his intention to other persons, then we will discover a ground for the hope that the meaning of human life is an "ultimate unity of persons in fellowship."[51] This means that we must act religiously, that is, with the intention of creating the conditions for fellowship. When we act with the intention for community, we will discover in practice, in the immediacy of living experience, how to celebrate communion—"the fellowship of all things in God."[52]

Certainly, Macmurray's interpretation of Jesus as the embodiment and teacher of this understanding of community is far more empirical and this-worldly than most traditional, orthodox interpretations. This is not the place to defend Macmurray's reading of the Bible or his understanding of Jesus. What is significant about his view is that it places the notion of God as Agent at its center. By means of this placement, Macmurray can make sense, in a straightforward, nonreductionist way, of the biblical language in which God is clearly referred to as a loving, personal being who acts continually in history. Macmurray has a set of metaphysical categories in which theological doctrines which assume the importance of divine agency, history, and the divine intention to create a community of mutuality and love can be given philosophical grounding and legitimacy without having to resort to paradox and irrational mystery. At the same time, Macmurray's metaphysics comes much closer than do the philosophies of atomism and organism to representing the fundamental convictions of the biblical and Christian story. If a model of community consistent with Christian belief is to be developed, it would seem to fit far more comfortably into the language and thought forms of Macmurray's form of the personal than into the categories of organism and atomism. That fact, in itself, justifies the attention I have paid to Macmurray's understanding of community and mutuality in the context of his philosophy of persons in relation.

I have already indicated that Macmurray's philosophy, as he himself presents it, is not fully worked out. This, I think, is one of its basic weaknesses. Its strengths lie in highlighting a number of basic principles and concepts, in relating them to each other in a coherent way, and in suggesting some of their essential implications for persons in relation. The weakness in his written work is the lack of precision and the incompleteness of his analysis of some of his more basic principles, especially those of intention, action, and freedom. He relies primarily upon a commonsense understanding of these notions which, while essentially correct, does not speak directly to the more subtle, intricate kinds of issues which have been the concern of more recent analysts of language and philosophers of action. Macmurray paints his picture of persons in relation with very broad strokes. I believe that his painting is much closer to the truth of relationship than alternative philosophies of community. But a more practical artist will eventually have to complete his work by deepening and refining his analyses. This would be true, for example, about his assumption that we *do* have enough freedom to choose what we intend to do. Macmurray needs to defend this claim against those materialists and determinists who, through intricate studies of the brain, physiology, and the mind/body relation, have concluded that our assumptions about freedom of action are usually naive and that freedom is much more circumscribed than Macmurray and many others would believe.

Macmurray also has an unfortunate tendency to state some of his most important claims in language that is stark, grandiose, or extreme. The most obvious example is his proclamation that in community no self cares for itself but only for others. A more careful reading of Macmurray, as we have seen, reveals that he does in fact acknowledge either that this is an ideal rarely achieved or that there is always the presence in human action of self-concern; but he is so preoccupied with making the point that self-realization can only be *achieved* by intending the welfare of others that he often lapses into unnecessarily extreme and unqualified assertions.

Macmurray is also so focused upon outlining an ideal of community that he fails to provide a completely convincing demonstration that the ideal is achievable, given present reality. While he acknowledges the difficulty we have in being ourselves (and even attributes this to what theologians have called original sin), the thrust of his philosophy is to highlight the conditions and principles by which we *can* be ourselves. Certainly, in this post-Holocaust age we are far less inclined to accede to Macmurray's thought is his assumption that until a conviction more solid argument by him that his view of human nature really does take account of the more tragic elements in the historical experience of the human race.

Essentially, it is the *realism* and *thoroughness* of Macmurray's claims that can be most easily questioned. His lack of thoroughness is readily conceded. But on the ground of realism, I think the case has yet to be made that his principles do not ultimately conform to the structure of the universe. It is not *obviously* the case that they do so conform, but neither is it obvious that they do not. It must be remembered that one of the keys to Macmurray's thought in his assumption that until a conviction about the nature of human beings is acted upon, we cannot know conclusively whether it is true or false. Given Macmurray's own epistemological principle that the validity of ideas, especially about agents in relation, cannot be established in the absence of the very same agents acting upon them, it is not possible to reject his claims conclusively until we have tried to act as if they are true. The ultimate test of his superficially naive belief that we can achieve self-realization only by acting primarily for the realization of others can only be our actual decision to act precisely in this way. Macmurray refuses to permit us the option of determining the final validity of his basic principles in isolation from the action which they encourage.

TOWARD AN INCLUSIVE COMMUNITY: RECONCILING THE MODELS

We have now examined the essential elements in the three models of community. It remains to explore some of the ways in which these three models can be brought into relation with each other. From the outset, we have assumed that while each model is distinct and has characteristics which set it off from the others (especially with respect to differing metaphysical assumptions about persons in relation), the models are in fact interrelated in diverse and complex ways in everyday experience. What we need to examine here are the principles by which that interrelationship can be understood. There are clearly areas of human life in which the individualism and power relations of contract, the functional subordination within an organic whole, and the intimacy of heterocentric love all have a place.

The guiding principle by which the reconciliation of these models of community can be effected must be that of inclusion within a comprehensive and overarching intention. This is essentially the logical conclusion of adopting Macmurray's claim that the primary metaphysical unity is the intentional agent. It is only within the unity of the agent's intentions that we can find a coherent place for the other dimensions of his individual reality, such as the mechanical and the organic. It follows, logically, that the unified reality of many agents in relation, the community, must also be an inclusive unity within which we find the other dimensions of social reality, such as those represented in the atomistic and organic models of association.

We can appeal, once again, to the hierarchical concept of the organicists, the systems theorists, and philosophers of biology such as Edward Pols. Within the most comprehensive, unified, and inclusive community of persons, there will be a hierarchy of levels of relationship, the lower ones serving the overarching and controlling higher ones. These lower levels will serve as the infrastructure of the community. They will make possible the effective functioning of the purposes initiated by the higher levels. They will be the material support, as it were, for the intentional goals originating in the higher levels. In the individual human person, the physiological, molecular, and biological structures of the body are the necessary instruments, the essential material substrata, by and through which the person enacts his or her intentions. These intentions cannot be formed without due consideration of (and with partial determination by) these infrastructures with which they are intimately linked. I cannot intend to type the keys which print the letters on the page unless the infrastructure of my nervous system, and all its collateral physiological systems, have prepared the ground for that intention and are able to carry it into action.

There is no reason to think that this notion of the hierarchically ordered infrastructure of the individual person would not apply equally well to the community of persons taken as a whole. If the members of the mutual/personal community have as their overarching intention to enjoy fellowship with each other, then there must be material conditions which both prepare for the possibility of that intention and enable it to be carried out in practice. In other words, a mutual intentionality for community requires material conditions and infrastructures which are subordinate to but essential aspects of the full realization of that intentionality. These infrastructures will find their place and meaning within the unified, inclusive whole which is the comprehensive community characterized by the dominance of the intention for mutuality. It is only the fundamental and controlling intention for mutuality which can order, structure, and determine the place and value of different forms of relationship which are subordinate to and instruments of its realization. Only intentions are inclusive of those dimensions of reality which are nonintentional and can use them for their enactment.

Too often, discussions of mutual community have assumed that power, politics, and economics are either irrelevant or antithetical to the dynamics of love. As a result, descriptions of a community of love have been dismissed by "realists" as naive, utopian, and out of touch with the realities of social life. But the alternative to what Martin Luther King, Jr. called "the beloved community" has then been delineated in terms which tend to reduce it solely to the level of power, politics, and economics, with the result that the experience of mutuality is relegated to a peripheral sphere and glossed over with sentimental rhetoric and pious irrelevancies.

Only a hierarchical notion of community, which includes within a single unified, comprehensive whole all the dimensions of human association (the individualistic, the organic, and the mutual), governed by the intention for mutuality, can avoid the implicit dualism between the so-called "realist" and "utopian" visions of community. We need an understanding of community which can find an appropriate place for the various but related kinds of associations we experience every day in the multitudinous contacts we have with others. To dismiss or explain away any of these is to be ultimately unfaithful to experience. But at the same time, we need to have a governing principle, an ultimate standard of judgment, by which to determine and order the intentions and actions which constitute each of these forms of association. Only a hierarchical notion of community can provide such a principle.

It should not surprise us that John Macmurray's metaphysics of community has such a principle or that Macmurray developed it with respect to those other forms of association which are subordinate to and infrastructures for the mutual/personal community. While he did not himself employ the hierarchy notion explicitly, I believe his discussion of the mechanical and organic dimensions (as expressed through power, politics, and economics) of the comprehensive community implicitly assumes such a notion. In the course of that discussion, Macmurray gives us the essential ingredients for a reconciliation of the models of community. At the same time, however, he forces us to consider some crucial, final questions about the "realism" of personal community in the world today. In particular, we need to consider, in addition to the role of power in the political and economic spheres, the place of cooperation (as distinct from love), individual freedom, justice, and the relation between smaller groups and the inclusive community. And to put the discussion into the context of some basic Christian theological doctrines, we need to examine briefly how such notions as agape, koinonia, and the prophetic hope for the kingdom of God on earth relate to the metaphysical principles of the mutual/personal community.

Power, Justice, and Law. All forms of human association are unities of persons. The distinguishing characteristic of each is its mode of unity. As we have seen, the three basic modes are (1) essentially individualistic atoms contracting with other atoms on the basis of power and out of fear for their own security; (2) essentially interdependent organs functionally and internally related to other organs, serving the organic whole; and (3) individual persons mutually related in and through intentional love for each other for the sake of the other. Now it seems clear that the third mode of relationship must be inclusive of the other two inasmuch as an intentional relationship cannot be solely organic (since the organic mode does not require intention) and a love relationship cannot be based on fear or contract.

The community of mutuality is also intentionally universal: that is, it intends to include all persons within a single community. As we have seen, Macmurray regards this intention both as crucial to community (because its alternative is to exclude some persons intentionally, which is tantamount to living in relation to them out of fear, thus denying to ourselves the fullest possible experience of mutuality), and as problematic, because the larger the community becomes, the harder the intimacy and fellowship of direct relation become. Therefore, even while a mutual community *intends* universality, in practice it will include within itself forms of relationship which are indirect and not yet fully mutual.

The existence of indirect or impersonal relations necessitates the emergence of social structures determined by power and law. "The necessity for the State and for politics arises with the breakdown of the customary community of direct personal relations."[53] Historically, the organization of society (and the state which is one of its dimensions) took form either in what Macmurray calls the pragmatic or the organic mode. The pragmatic mode is what we have called the atomistic/contract form of community. Essentially developed by Hobbes, it is based on the fear individuals have of each other and, accordingly, on the necessity of establishing some kind of order in the power relationships of these individuals. What saves individuals from mutual destruction is the fact that in addition to being "aggressively egocentric" they are also rational; that is, they have the capacity to devise a system of law (the contract) by which anarchy and the domination of some at the expense of others is kept within bounds. Within this mode of relationship, enlightened self-interest produces a state with the power to govern the terms of relationship. "It conceives the structure of society in terms of law . . . and its maintenance as achieved by power. This yields a mechanical concept of society. Its components are atomic units, inherently isolated or unrelated, and ideally equal . . . . There is nothing to hold them together. They are united in a whole by an external force which counteracts the tendency of their individual energies to repel one another."[54]

The alternative mode of social organization is the organic, which Macmurray associates with Rousseau. Society is an organic whole in which each individual is exhorted to play his appointed role, a role which is inherently social and not individual. The society has priority over the individual and the appropriate behavior is that of submission to the whole. This is best done by accepting one's function within the whole. The individual "must identify himself with his role—his station and its duties—and suppress his impulse to be himself."[55]

Both of these forms of relationship can be characterized, in Macmurray's terms, as negative. That is, they arise out of a fundamental fear of the other and are essentially forms of association designed to make living with that fear as beneficial as possible to the individuals whose self-interest is, in the end, paramount. Now Macmurray does not deny that in the "problematic" of community, that is, in community as it actually is experienced in everyday life, there must be provision made for such self-interest and the fear which nurtures and sustains it. Macmurray has no illusions about the reality of what the Bible calls "sin" ("the modern abolition of sin is only one form of the idealistic illusion that we can abolish facts by refusing to take account of them").[56]

As long as persons have indirect or impersonal relations with other persons, as will happen in large societies, then there will be negative forms of relationship. But these negative forms can be controlled by the positive forms if they are *intentionally* controlled. One of the most important of these negative forms of relationship is the economic. It is a relationship of cooperation in work, "action directed upon the world-as-means, to the corporate production and distribution of the means of personal life in society."[57] The economic dimension of human life is an essential ingredient in its fullness. It is the most extreme form of dualism to deny that persons can experience fulfillment without a material substructure. Persons are the unity of body and soul, and economics is the social instrument for the production of the goods needed for the sustenance and nurture of the body. Much of Macmurray's life was spent in dialogue and agreement with Marxism on the importance of meeting the material needs of persons.

Materiality and the Economic Dimension. Macmurray, in fact, claimed an essential continuity between the materialism of Marxian thought and the materialism of the Bible. As we have seen, he repudiates any dualism between matter and spirit in Hebraic thought and in the religion of Jesus. The "materialism" of some of Jesus' promises to his disciples is "all of a piece with the general attitude" of his teaching. He felt that the "possession of wealth in society which was not a true community was itself necessarily accompanied by a spirit which isolated its possessors from true community."[58] Macmurray could even go so far as to say that "Jesus was essentially class-conscious and His interpretation of the social problem was an economic interpretation in precisely the sense that the Communist means, and also He was a materialist in the sense that the Communist is a materialist."⁵⁹ The audacity and exaggeration of this claim should not obscure the basic point Macmurray is trying to make. Materialism is simply the belief that human life has a material dimension, that it is embedded in the material conditions of the world, though it is clearly not reducible to them.

The economic dimension is the provision of these material needs. Macmurray believes that these needs are quite specific: "there are certain fundamental necessities of human life which are inherent in our relation to the world, such as the need for food, clothing, shelter, and so on, which cannot go unprovided for in any society of men without making life intolerable. There must, therefore, be a relation in any society between the material necessities of life, and the beliefs that it holds about the proper ordering of life ... No society can exist except in a form which provides for the basic, material needs of human life."⁶⁰ The forms of economic life are the essential foundation for mutuality. They do not determine the content of mutuality but they do determine its possibility. This means that an intentional mutual community must include within itself appropriate political and economic structures, and if the present ones are not appropriate, part of the realization of true community will require their transformation. "The economic and political relations of men are not merely the basis of personal life, they are an inherent part of it and the criterion of its reality. In our day the economic integration of humanity determines in large measure what forms of personal life are possible. As a result it is no longer possible to maintain or extend the personal life that Christianity demands of us without a transformation of the existing political and economic structure of human life as a whole."⁶¹

Now in order to carry out the economic task, it is necessary for persons to cooperate with each other in indirect relationships. "This co-operation in work establishes a nexus of indirect relations between all the members of the co-operating group, irrespective of their personal relations ... Such relations are not relations of persons as persons, but only as workers; they are relations of the functions which each performs in the co-operative association; and if this aspect of the personal is abstracted, and considered in isolation, every person is identified with his function. He *is* a miner, or a tinsmith, or a doctor, or a teacher."⁶² But, as we have seen, the abstraction of the functionality of persons in indirect relation from the fullness of their mutual relation is the organic mode of relationship. And so, we have within the mutual model of community an instrumental and indispensable place for organic relationship. But that place is determined by the overarching intentionality of the fully personal life. The "economic aspect of the personal—the working life—is both intentional and for the sake of the personal life ... It must be produced, maintained and developed by deliberate effort. As negative—being for the sake of the personal life to which it is the means—it requires to be justified by reference to the personal life which makes it possible."[63]

Cooperation is clearly an interdependent mode of relationship and as such stands in contrast to the ideal of individual independence. Nevertheless, cooperation is not the same as mutuality even though it is often confused with it. Only if we have a metaphysics of community in which mutuality is the dominant intention can we locate and give appropriate meaning to those forms of relationship in which persons come together but not primarily for the sake of being with and for each other. Cooperation may, in fact, prove to be a catalyst for the discovery of the joy of fellowship but it is not, in and of itself, a substitute for it. For example, workers may cooperate so closely in a common economic task that they begin to experience a commonality of interests. Out of that interest they might form a union whose primary objective is to secure the practical realization of their common economic concern. But derivatively, out of the union experience may eventually come the experience of delight simply in being together. Now this latter experience is not the original function of the union nor its primary purpose, but it may arise out of the conditions of association provided by its function.

While the relations between the workers in providing the economic sustenance of community are organic and functional, the determination of the success of economic work is essentially pragmatic, and thus falls within the atomistic/contractarian mode of relationship.

By calling the criterion of economic work pragmatic, Macmurray means that it is to be judged internally by its efficiency in the production and distribution of goods. "Its standard is efficiency, and its problematic is in terms of efficiency and inefficiency. Its aim is to deliver the goods, in the maximum quantity, quality and variety for a given expenditure of labour. From the economic point of view, every person is a potential source of energy and skill to be used with the maximum of efficiency in the mechanism of production."[64]

There is a sense in which the economic field of activity is like a machine (and thus subject to the mechanical unity-pattern) in which each worker is forced to perform a specific task. Within current capitalist systems, there is for most workers no freedom not to work, but to the extent that workers can bargain for the conditions and compensation for their labor, there is a basis for rational contract. At the most basic level, the worker enters the economic order under the necessity to provide for himself, and what can be provided is itself determined by the material conditions of that time and place. However, in a society which permits workers to choose, within limits, the form of their labor, the basis for a rational contract is established. Through the contract, the worker negotiates with his employer the kind, conditions, and remuneration of his work. Once he has met those conditions, he has no further contractual obligation or tie to the person or group for which he has worked.

Macmurray suggests, implicitly, that this kind of contract relation (which presumes many of the principles of the atomistic/contract model of community) is perfectly appropriate within the context of the pragmatic mode of relationship which prevails in the economic order. When I take my car to the garage to be serviced, I expect (in effect) to establish a contract relationship with the mechanic. Our relationship is not fully organic since we are not interdependent organs within a greater whole, and it is certainly not mutual since I need him, not for himself as a person, but for his particular skills. As a rational agent, he presumably (in the ideal situation) enters freely into contract with me. I will evaluate his work solely on the basis of his ability to meet the terms of the contract and he will evaluate me solely on my ability to pay his wages.

Now it can be argued that while our relationship is indirect and impersonal (being mediated by the primary consideration of efficient work), this is not necessarily a bad thing. I need the car to work well and he needs the money in order to survive financially. (I am not assuming or defending the goodness of an economic order such as capitalism which depends on wage labour for survival—I'm simply drawing an example from the present economic order with which we are all familiar.) In the particular situation I have described, neither of us may be interested in or ready for a mutual relationship. We both may be fully involved in our own separate communities of intimacy and have more than we can do to be faithful to them without initiating relations of intimacy with each person we come in contact with.

The point is that as long as we are dependent on the production of economic goods, it will be necessary for some relationships associated with that production to be either organic, contractual, or both, without being mutual. "[T]he economic field is, for all workers, a field of necessity, not of freedom. The work must go on, irrespective of the particular intentions and motives of the workers ... Economic activity is in principle a routine of action which has to be maintained; which has to be adapted to the resources available, both material and technical; which has to be made as efficient as possible ... "[65]

However, all this being said, if the overarching community within which economic activity takes place is a mutual/personal one, then the field of economics "has to be subordinated and adjusted to the personal life of society as a whole, and to the personal lives of all its members. Necessity is for the sake of freedom: the economic is for the sake of the personal."[66] Taking my car to be fixed cannot be an end in itself, nor can the entire nexus of contract relationships with others. Ultimately, economic activity must be a means to a greater end. It must serve the life of mutuality by providing the material necessities on which that life is built but which is not fulfilled by such provision. "An economic efficiency which is achieved at the expense of the personal life is self-condemned, and in the end frustrating,"[67] because it has destroyed the very end for which it should be only a means. Those systems which have made economic efficiency the only standard for determining the value of economic activity as a whole have reversed the true relation in which economics and mutuality should stand to each other. For example, if economic efficiency requires that workers be forced by market conditions to break up their families or be constantly mobile, then it has destroyed some of the essential conditions for the realization of mutuality and family life, and for that reason stands condemned.

But we have said that economic efficiency is, within the economic field itself, the standard of value. So it is, provided that the standards of the economic field are not the standards of value for life as a whole. If I discover that the mechanic with whom I have contracted for work to be done on my car suddenly falls ill or is called away by a family crisis and does not finish the work on time, I should be prepared to abrogate some of the terms of the contract in order to respond to the unexpected, but far more important, needs he is suddenly experiencing. This is what it means to intend community to be universal (i.e., I do not intentionally exclude him from a mutual relation with me, even though in the specific context of our contract I do not expect to relate to him primarily on the basis of mutuality). However, when his human need touches me over and above the contract relationship, I must respond to it if the intention for inclusive mutuality is my overarching and governing intention. This does not mean that I abandon the contract I have established with him, but rather that I place its terms into the context of a larger, more important intention, and that is to foster mutuality when conditions make that possible. When the crisis has passed, I can still expect his work on my car to be judged by the standard of efficiency. But unless we have established the proper priority between our economic expectations and our intention for the development of the personal life, we are likely to confuse economic efficiency or the fulfillment of mechanical services with the personal fulfillment that occurs only in relations of mutuality.

Justice. One of the most important ways in which the overarching value of mutuality affects the indirect relations of the economic order is through the establishment of justice. In its most basic sense, justice is that set of principles "by reference to which each of us can determine what would or would not be fair to the other person if we did it,"[68] or in the words of the contemporary moral philosopher, John Rawls, justice is fairness. (See Chapter 2, on the atomistic/contract model of community, in which I criticize Rawls' treatment of community. Despite that criticism, I believe that Macmurray would agree with his definition of justice, provided that it is subordinated to the governing principles of the mutual/personal community.) We cannot go into detail as to exactly what fairness means, except to observe that justice "expresses the minimum of reciprocity and interest in the other in the personal relation—what can rightly be exacted from him if it is refused."[69] Justice is also "a restriction which I impose on my own power for the sake of others. To be fair in my dealings with others means that I do not exploit their weakness to my own advantage. To intend justice is to intend that my own claim shall not take precedence of the claims of others. Justice is an obligation that each of us has to other people."[70] The claim to justice is a claim "to have my interests considered equally with those of all the others, and this can only be settled by a general rule which is external to the particular claim I make. My case must be subsumed under a general principle which is the same for all like cases."[71]

The intention to establish and maintain justice presupposes a society of cooperation. It "concerns the relations of individuals who co-operate without being in direct personal relation to one another."[72] There must be enough common consent within the society that the basic principles of what is fair are not in dispute, even though the application of those principles to specific situations may well be. Justice is clearly not love since I can demand justice of myself and others but I certainly cannot demand love. Justice is the negative element in love. It "safeguards the inclusiveness of the moral reference, and so the unity of the Other."[73] It provides the conditions necessary for the experience of fellowship but is not itself a substitute for fellowship. But without justice, the relationship based on love can become demonic and a perversion of genuine mutuality. For example, if I owe you money and refuse to pay it back, intending to substitute for justice a benevolence which gives you double what I owe you, I may seem to be more loving but in fact I have actually destroyed any basis of trust between us because not only did I not fulfill my obligation to be fair to you, but I have now established our relationship on the basis of my freedom, not yours, to decide arbitrarily how we shall relate to each other. I have, in effect, made you an unequal partner in the relationship. The function of justice is to ensure that the relations between people are at least equal with respect to their freedom vis-à-vis each other, even if it cannot ensure that they are more than that.

"To maintain equality of persons in relation is justice; and without it generosity becomes purely sentimental and wholly egocentric. My care for you is only moral if it includes the intention to preserve your freedom as an agent, which is your independence of me ... In the relation of two agents, ... each remains himself and differentiated from the other; there must be no self-identification of one with the other, or the reciprocity will be lost and the heterocentricity of the relation will be only apparent."[74] When love presumes to override or destroy justice, then it runs the very real risk of destroying the independence and freedom of the other as a personal agent equal to me with respect to his freedom and independence. Therefore, justice is an indispensable part of the infrastructure of the mutual/personal community, even though it is ultimately for the sake of mutuality and not a substitute for it.

Justice is the bond which holds any social form of cooperation together. "Wherever there is a *de facto* relation between myself and another person; wherever my activity and his activity are functionally related in the nexus of human co-operation, I am under a moral obligation to act in a way that is just and fair to him. For my freedom of action then depends on his, and I must not exercise my freedom at the expense of his."[75] The securing of justice will occur through such pragmatic devices as the contract which, in effect, "determines reciprocal rights and obligations which we engage ourselves to respect"[76] in our dealings with others. As long as the social order has a sufficient level of trust among its members, (which is normally established over time through the experience of cooperation), then justice can be maintained.

Because of the habit of social cooperation, the various activities which work to establish and maintain justice become possible. These are the activities of politics; and what they seek to enact are laws. Politics is the negotiation for the creation of laws which determine how justice is to be expressed in particular situations within the social order. It depends upon cooperation and indirect relations between large numbers of persons. The law which politics creates is "a mechanism which will automatically adjust the relations between the individuals concerned in such a fashion that the activities of each do not injure the others."[77] The law is, in effect, justice in practice: it is "the means to justice in the indirect relations of the members of an association of persons co-operating for the production and distribution of the means of personal life."[78]

The state is itself ultimately in the service of justice, the law, and therefore of the community as a whole. It is a mistake to identify the state with the community. The state is the legal organization of the community, the pragmatic infrastructure for ensuring obedience to the law and the maintenance of justice. Like any pragmatic device, therefore, it is to be judged internally by the standard of efficiency and externally by how well it serves the overarching intention for mutuality. "Its only value lies in its efficiency: it is a means, not an end, and has no intrinsic value in itself."[79] "Law ... is a technological device, and the State is a set of technical devices for the development and maintenance of law."[80] This understanding of the state has the extremely important implication that the state is not self-justifying and must not be treated as a Whole (as it often is in the organic model) to which all other elements, including the mutual relations of persons, are to be subordinated. "The State is a public utility, and should be treated and judged as such. It is a dangerous error to personalize the State and to attribute to it characters or qualities which belong only to human beings ... To worship the State is to indulge in idolatry. To personify the State is to pervert it, so that it tends to the destruction of [community], not to its preservation."[81]

Nevertheless, within their own spheres of action, the state, the law, and the justice which depends on cooperation have a right to employ power and to require obedience, provided only that power and obedience are in the service of freedom and mutuality. This is not far from the claims Hegel made on behalf of the state and its role in the realization of true freedom, but unlike Hegel, Macmurray insists that the relations between persons be governed by personal mutuality, not by organic functionality. Power wielded by the state is an important part of the community and cannot be denied until the problematic of persons in relation is abolished. The state is "a necessary device which cannot be dispensed with or exchanged for any other, so soon at least as the necessary co-operation in society requires an adjustment of indirect human relations ... Without justice, social co-operation is impossible, without law, justice is impossible and without power law is futile and ineffective, a mere ideal."[82]

The problem is to remember that the devices of power and the state are to be employed intentionally in the service of a higher end. If power becomes an end in itself, the state, which governs the just use of power, becomes an end in itself as well. When that happens, persons and their relations become a means to the end of serving the state. And that is the complete reversal and perversion of what a mutual/personal community intends to be. If the state determines our value, then when the state determines that we have no value (as happened in Nazi Germany, or in the Ukraine, or in the American treatment of black persons and native Americans), the state can exterminate us. Hobbes' Leviathan then reigns supreme and love between persons becomes at best an irrelevance to the state and at worst a fundamental threat to it which must be eliminated.

This brings us, finally, to the delicate balance which must exist in any mutual community between the realism of power and the hope for love and grace. This delicate balance, or dialectic, between love and power, grace and realism, has been traditionally the concern of religion, in particular of the Christianity which has influenced so much of our Western understanding of persons in relation. With its doctrines of sin and grace, Christianity has tried to speak both to the need for relationships based on power and functional subordination, and the hope for relationships based on what it has called agape, or love. It has described the sinful condition of humankind in the terms of power politics and prophesied an eschatological condition in the language of the kingdom of God. When it has dwelt too much on the description of sin, it has been accused of undue pessimism and of justifying the injustice and oppression of the status quo. When it has dwelt too much on the hope for the kingdom, it has been accused of utopianism, unrealism, and escapism into a fantasy world. I believe that the model of the mutual/personal community can provide the dialectic which holds together in delicate synthesis both the concessions to "realism" demanded by those who focus upon the need for power relations in the world as it is, and the hopes of a future community demanded by those who focus upon the promise of loving relations in the world as God intends it to be.

NOTES TO CHAPTER 6

1. Macmurray, *Persons in Relation*, 157–58.
2. Ibid., 158.
3. Ibid.
4. Ibid.
5. Ibid., 211.
6. Ibid.
7. Macmurray, *Conditions of Freedom*, 82.
8. Ibid., 82–83.
9. John Macmurray, *Freedom in the Modern World*. Broadcast talks on modern problems, with a preface by C.A. Siepmann (London: Faber and Faber, 1932), 179.
10. Ibid., 178–80.
11. Macmurray, *Interpreting the Universe*, 134.
12. Ibid, 136.
13. Ibid, 137.
14. Macmurray, *Persons in Relation*, 158.
15. Macmurray, *Interpreting the Universe*, 140.
16. Macmurray, *Persons in Relation*, 158.
17. Ibid.
18. Macmurray, *Freedom in the Modern World*, 177.
19. Ibid., 180.
20. Macmurray, *Persons in Relation*, 156.
21. Ibid., 157.
22. John Macmurray, *The Structure of Religious Experience* (London: Faber and Faber, 1936), 30–31.
23. Macmurray, *Persons in Relation*, 159.
24. Ibid.
25. Macmurray, *Conditions of Freedom*, 83–84.
26. Ibid., 85.

27. Ibid., 161.
28. Ibid., 163.
29. Ibid.
30. John Macmurray, *Religion, Art, and Science: A Study of the Reflective Activities in Man*. The Forwood Lectures 1960 (Liverpool: Liverpool University Press, 1961), 60–61.
31. Macmurray, *Persons in Relation*, 164.
32. Macmurray, *Religion, Art, and Science*, 73.
33. Macmurray, *Persons in Relation*, 222.
34. John Macmurray, *The Clue to History* (London: Student Christian Movement Press, 1938), 95.
35. Ibid., 96.
36. John Macmurray, "Religion in the Modern World," notes taken by Harriet and Eugene Forsey of a lecture by John Macmurray in Belleville, Ontario, Canada, June 1936 (Montreal: Associated Literature Service, 1936), 23.
37. Macmurray, *The Clue to History*, 94.
38. Ibid., 100.
39. Ibid.
40. Ibid., 101.
41. Ibid., 54.
42. Macmurray, *Creative Society*, 20–21.
43. Ibid., 115–16.
44. Ibid., 113–14.
45. John Macmurray, "The Nature of Religion," notes taken from a Report of the St. Asaph Conference, August 1938 (London: SCM Auxiliary), 9.
46. Ibid.
47. Macmurray, *The Clue to History*, 30–31.
48. Ibid., 85.
49. Macmurray, *The Self as Agent*, 221.
50. Ibid.
51. Ibid., 22.
52. Macmurray, *Persons in Relation*, 165.
53. Ibid., 192.
54. Ibid., 137.
55. Ibid., 142.
56. Ibid., 198.
57. Ibid., 186.
58. Macmurray, *Creative Society*, 78.
59. John Macmurray, "The Challenge of Communism." in H.G. Wood and John Macmurray, *Christianity and Communism* (London: Industrial Christian Fellowship, 1934), 23.
60. John Macmurray, "The Nature and Function of Ideologies," in *Marxism*, by J.M. Murry et al. (New York: John Wiley and Sons, 1935), 63.

61. John Macmurray, "The Provisional Basis of the Christian Left," with Irene Grant, no. 10, February 1938 (London: The Christian Left, 1938), 6.
62. Macmurray, *Persons in Relation*, 186.
63. Ibid., 186–87.
64. Ibid., 187.
65. Ibid.
66. Ibid., 188.
67. Ibid., 187.
68. Ibid., 191.
69. Ibid., 188.
70. Ibid., 201.
71. Ibid., 197.
72. Ibid.
73. Ibid., 189.
74. Ibid., 190, 189.
75. Ibid., 190.
76. Ibid., 191.
77. Ibid., 194.
78. Ibid.
79. Ibid., 197.
80. Ibid., 198.
81. Ibid., 197–98.
82. Ibid., 199–200.

7. Conclusion: Koinonia as a Community among Communities

THE NATURE OF AGAPE

The delicate balance between love and power, grace and realism, is required by any theory of community which both recognizes that persons are not always heterocentrically motivated and believes that there is something inherent in the nature of persons which can be realized only in and through a genuine love for others. The delicate balance is often upset when the belief has no metaphysical ground to stand upon or when it has no place for the actions of a divine agent who alone has the power to override the conditions which fuel the egocentric impulses which work against heterocentric love. In Macmurray's metaphysically grounded and religiously informed vision of the mutual/personal community, there is the possibility of both recognizing sin and believing for good reasons that it is not the final word about persons in relation because it cannot ultimately override or undermine the intentions of God the Creator.

At the heart of the Christian vision of human life, in its redeemed and reconciled state, is the notion of agape, or love. In its basic form, agape is understood to be love of the neighbor for the neighbor's sake. It has been expressed with consummate style and succinctness by H. Richard Niebuhr in a way that fully captures what I believe Macmurray means by heterocentric love and mutuality:

> Love is rejoicing over the existence of the beloved one; it is the desire that he be rather than not be; it is longing for his presence when he is absent; it is happiness in the thought of him; it is profound satisfaction over everything that makes

him great and glorious. Love is gratitude: it is thankfulness for the existence of the beloved; it is the happy acceptance of everything that he gives without the jealous feeling that the self ought to be able to do as much; . . . it is wonder over the other's gift of himself in companionship. Love is reverence: it keeps its distance even as it draws near; it does not seek to absorb the other in the self or want to be absorbed by it; it rejoices in the otherness of the other; it desires the beloved to be what he is and does not seek to refashion him into a replica of the self or to make him a means to the self's advancement. As reverence love is and seeks knowledge of the other, not by way of curiosity nor for the sake of gaining power but in rejoicing and in wonder. In all such love there is an element of that 'holy fear' which is not a form of flight but rather deep respect for the otherness of the beloved and the profound unwillingness to violate his integrity. Love is loyalty; it is the willingness to let the self be destroyed rather than that the other cease to be; it is the commitment of the self by self-binding will to make the other great.[1]

H. Richard Niebuhr's description of Christian agape reflects well Macmurray's understanding of love as the heterocentric intention to live for the sake of the other as other. As Gene Outka, in his important study of agape, puts it, "the other is held to be irreducibly valuable."[2]

The problem, of course, is how to assess the possibilities of living in this world in accord with the ideal of agape. Can the person actually love others in the way Niebuhr and Macmurray envision in their descriptions of love? It is not uncommon to find some writers suggesting that such love might exist, under extraordinary circumstances, between two persons or perhaps even within a small family. But virtually no writers who are taken seriously by social philosophers have claimed that such agape can be realized in large communities, let alone societies.

Love and Social Realism. There is no writer who has done more to persuade contemporary religious and social thinkers that the possibilities for love between two or at most a few individual persons cannot be made the basis for relations between persons in society than H. Richard Niebuhr's brother, Reinhold. In the words of his most famous work, there might be moral man, but only an immoral society, or, as he is reported to have said later, immoral man and even more immoral society. The Christian faith, he contends, "holds that human nature contains both self-regarding and social impulses and that the former is stronger than the latter. This assumption is the basis of Christian realism."[3] The human being, as finite and as sinful, is both "as individual and also in relationship with his fellows and his community, always . . . contradicting and defying the law of love."[4]

The problem for Christianity, and for the Judaism out of which it was born, is to hold onto the truth of the realistic picture of man in his sinful, self-regarding, and prideful state while at the same time keeping alive the messianic hope of a renewed, reconciled, and redeemed kingdom to come in which love will be the dominant form of relationship, a kingdom which, in Niebuhr's words, would be where "man would live with man in a universal and peaceful community, and all the frustrations and contradictions of history would be eliminated."[5] Balancing the truth and the hope about human relations has meant, in practice, that "the religious traditions of the West, both Jewish and Christian, are potential generators of an idealistic utopian vision, creative in projecting ultimate and ideal goals for human communities, but confusing whenever they obscure the perennial force of the factors in human nature which prevent the fulfillment of these ideal goals."[6]

Niebuhr was well known not only for not abandoning the need to balance realism with idealism, but also for his penetrating and realistic analysis of the way in which "the perennial forces of the factors in human nature" do, in the political and economic structures of social life, actually impede the vision of the kingdom. In one of his last books, the one from which the previous quotations have been taken, Niebuhr reflected on the success of his realistic analysis of men and nations, and was led to say that while "the consistent tendencies of nations to seek their own interests is so marked that the realistic interpretation of international relations would seem to be the only valid description of their behavior," nevertheless it is important to raise the question of "whether a realistic interpretation may or may not err in obscuring the residual capacity for justice and devotion to the larger good, even when it is dealing with a dimension of collective behavior in which the realistic assumptions about human nature are most justified."[7]

One of the reasons why Niebuhr leaves the door somewhat open to "the residual capacity for . . . devotion to the larger good" is because there do exist small communities in which love and regard for others, approximating the kind of agape described in his brother's eloquent description, seem to be present. While refusing to deny his life-long belief that man's concern for others is generally to be found "only in limited communities, and in those defined by the unique marks of racial and tribal distinction, which clearly violate and obscure the common humanity of man,"[8] Niebuhr acknowledges that the unique power of human freedom (which distinguishes persons from animals) "is truly the basis of a common humanity and of a potential sense of kinship with all men."[9]

Niebuhr also is willing to recognize that it is only some kind of community, perhaps as small as the family, that is "the primary source of the self's security [and thus its ability] to love and relate its life to others."[10] What gives the members of the family that essential sense of security is what Niebuhr calls the "gift" of "common grace," that is, the ability to care for others without succumbing completely to self-regard. As a result of this gift of grace, the self is able to recognize, in however minimal a way, the fact that consistent self-regard is self-frustrating and that regard for others can be the means to self-realization.[11]

Niebuhr did not pursue some of the most important implications of his recognition of the capacity of grace to empower persons to experience genuine love for others. The most relevant of these implications is that which has to do with the intentions and actions of a divine agent who has created the conditions of history and the nature of human beings such that, no matter how much "realism" is appropriate in the description of their present state, it does not completely or ultimately exhaust their possibilities.

I am not suggesting that Niebuhr paid no attention to God: in fact, his realistic analysis is always set within the context of a profoundly Christian theology. But the intention of God for humanity is relegated by Niebuhr, by and large, to the end of history, and the action of God seems to be restricted to the teaching and resurrection of Jesus. And Jesus is so identified by Niebuhr with the "impossible" claims of love that his "event" seems to become more of an ideal for the eschaton than a decisive act by which the structures of reality are fundamentally altered here and now, prior to the end of history. The resources Jesus provided appear to be confined primarily to the individual in his relation to God, and only in a secondary and not very clear way to his relation to other persons. The "new life in Christ represents the perfection of complete and heedless self-giving which obscures the contrary impulse of self-regard. It is a moral ideal scarcely possible for the individual and certainly not relevant to the morality of self-regarding nations."[12]

Although Jesus taught that self-regard is ultimately self-defeating and that "self-giving is bound to contribute ultimately to self-realization,"[13] this truth could not be made an effective part of human intentions in the world as it is. To live by the ethic of Jesus is to live a life out of touch with reality. "The perfect disinterestedness of the divine love can have a counterpart in history only in a life which ends tragically, because it refuses to participate in the claims and counterclaims of historical existence."[14]

The question one needs to raise about Niebuhr's analysis is not its accuracy with respect to the behavior of much of what we know of social and national institutions and collectivities, but its adequacy as a description of all forms of social relations now and in the future. What Niebuhr seems consistently to disregard is the possibility of change in the "spirit and the forms of love." Part of his disregard can be traced to his disillusionment with the continual betrayals of idealism in the behavior of groups and nations. But the other part of his disregard can be traced, I believe, to his failure to see the hand of God in the actions of "common grace," and in the course of history this side of the kingdom.

Gene Outka has said of Niebuhr's realism, "One should consider not only what interests men have possessed but also what interests they might acquire."[15] Conflict, for example, "is not as much of a fixed datum as Niebuhr appears to believe."[16] Vernard Eller has said of Niebuhr's understanding of God that he "has failed to reckon with the fact that God is actively present and available, forwarding his kingly rule and bringing it to consummation, and that this has the effect of opening possibilities which simply are not calculable by sinful man as being options under history's conditions of sin."[17]

As long as one has no notion of a God who acts, both as creator of the conditions of human fulfillment and as redeemer and reconciler who involves himself in history to rectify and renew failing and frustrated human actions, then it is impossible to hope for new possibilities for love which are not now present. If "idealism" or "utopia" is to become realistic in a sinful world, then they have to be grounded in the power of God as the giver of the gift of common grace. By grounding his metaphysics in the primacy of the agent, Macmurray has made it possible for us to conceive of God as an agent whose action need not be restricted to the original creative act but can be manifest throughout the course of history. Jesus may be seen (as Macmurray seems to do) as both a decisive act of God through which he reveals his intention most clearly and as one of many divine acts linked to each other by the overarching divine intention to bring into being a universal community of persons.

If that community is to be more than a pious hope or an illusory escape from the "real" problems of a sinful, recalcitrant world, then realism must be challenged at appropriate and effective points by a vision of a better, more loving world. This vision must be able to engender what Outka describes as "a radical hope in and striving for God's promised reign [which] anticipates transformation and newness uncalculable by present experience."[18] Without that hope nurtured by the vision of "the beloved community," we are likely to bewail our present frustrations and failures and make no move to challenge them. If Christians take seriously the eschatological dimension of their faith, then they have a beacon by which the way ahead is always lit for them, even when that light fades and dims from time to time. But no matter how dim, the light of God's promise does at least show in outline what the perfect community will be like and it illuminates what Buber has called the "active path [which] leads from the present."[19] And Buber has forthrightly claimed that when that path is made visible it energizes the intention to work for what lies at its end. "What may seem impossible as a concept arouses, as an image, the whole might of faith, ordains purpose and plan."[20] The eschatological vision, ultimately, has the power to do this because, and only because, "it is in league with powers latent in the depths of reality."[21] In this sense, Buber concludes, "eschatology, in so far as it is prophetic," has "the character of realism."[22]

This claim is precisely what Macmurray has tried to establish in his metaphysics of community. The "powers latent in the depths of reality" are the powers placed there by God in his original creative act. The eschatological vision is God's intention for his creation. And "the whole might of faith" is the human person's decision to "ordain purpose and plan" so as to conform his intentions to God's and, through so doing, to bring his own nature to fulfillment. Because of his freedom, he has made and will continue to make wrong choices, to fall short of his intention, to even lose sight of it, to suppress and deny it. And when that happens, Niebuhr's realism is the only accurate way of describing his condition. But the Christian claim is that finally "human existence in general 'cannot ultimately defy its own norm'," that "a life of love somehow goes with the grain of the universe and will not be unsupported".[23]

In her study of viable utopian communities, sociologist Rosabeth Moss Kanter has said that "underlying the vision of utopia is the assumption that harmony, cooperation, and mutuality of interests are natural to human existence, rather than conflict, competition, and exploitation."[24] Utopian communities would not have survived at all unless they were supported in large part by each member's conviction that at some deep level community is "expressive of his own inner being."[25] In his metaphysics of community, Macmurray has, I believe, provided the principles and the arguments by which this conviction can be grounded, and has done so in a way which coheres with the essence of the Jewish and Christian visions of community in relation to the intention of God.

But if the vision of the loving community is not to be dismissed simply because it transcends the realities of the human condition in its present state, how is the vision to be experienced or manifested short of the kingdom?

THE CHURCH AS A COMMUNITY AMONG COMMUNITIES

It has always been an implicit claim of Christianity that the life within the community of the church is, as Stanley Hauerwas has put it, "the truest possible for human community,"[26] because ultimately Christian convictions about reality are true. While often falling far short of its own ideal for community, the church has its ultimate justification only to the degree that it tries to be faithful to God's grace and empowerment for "koinonia" or fellowship. This common life or sharing is God's down payment on, or the first fruits of, the universal community of love which it is God's intention to bring into being.

The Christian claim is that it is within these gathered bodies of believers, in these communities of love, that persons can begin to experience, can get a foretaste of, the kind of fully loving, mutual community which God intends for the whole human creation. Throughout its history, the Christian church has given rise to, and often nurtured, the development of smaller, intentional communities of persons struggling to recapture what they believe was the experience of the earliest Christians living in koinonia. This experience was continuous with the experience of the Hebrew people, who also had tried to live out a sense of common life under the lordship of the Creator.

The sharing of the common life among Christians has always been predicated upon the power and grace of God. What lifts the experience of Christians from time to time above the limits of Niebuhrian "realism" is the gift of common grace by which God empowers the life of koinonia. The earliest koinonia, as described in the book of Acts, was, in the words of L. S. Thornton, "something altogether new, originated by an act of God ... through the descent of the Holy Spirit."[27] It presupposed a transformed and renewed heart in each of its members and it led to a transformed and radically new way of living, summarized by the holding of all things in common by those who were of one heart and soul. "From the first," Thornton claims, "the new spiritual unity of the community began to have a transforming power over the outward order of its life."[28] This earliest Christian community demonstrated by the form of its common life the unity of thought and practice so essential to the unity of the self as agent and of persons in relation.

There are today, especially in Latin America and in alternative communities in European and American cultures, Christians who are trying to live out, through the power of God's grace, the intention of love. Sometimes called "base communities" because of their attempt to return to the basic values of Christian living, these groups "are already living the new communion between God and human beings, and between human beings themselves, that constitutes the most essential content of the kingdom. They are living it imperfectly in the chiaroscuro of faith and with sinful defects, but they are living it in a real way. This is the deepest underlying secret of the church's life. It is the very life of the risen Jesus Christ communicated to us through the Spirit." It is a gift, lived in and through divine grace.[29]

And because of their conviction that the life of community must ultimately include not only all others but the whole life of each, these basic Christian communities are uniting theory and practice ("by deeds we must turn this grace into truth *in the concrete life* of the church and every single Christian community ... ").[30] The church is "not an island or refuge in the world ... [It must be] a sign and instrument fostering the transformation of human society."[31] This means, at least in part, that the church must own its idealistic or utopian dimension. As an historical anticipation of the kingdom, the church must be "an alluring model and hope-giving 'utopia' for the transformation of human society, to the extent that the church itself, embodied in its representative groups and its institutional structures, can concretely exemplify" the values of the loving community which it intends.[32]

In practice, of course, the "representative groups" of the church will be small. They will be, in Buber's words, which should apply both to the communities of Jews as well as Christians, "the moment's answer to the moment's question."[33] There can be no realization of the inclusive community once and for all time, as long as some persons and some parts of all persons remain unredeemed. (And this will be the case, at least in part, because God will not override our freedom to refuse his intention and to deny our own nature.) "The primary aspiration of all history" may well remain, as Buber has also said, "a genuine community of human beings—genuine because it is *community all through*,"[34] but until the aspiration has been fully realized, we must remain content with the experience of love within communities that necessarily interact with and depend upon associations, in which we are all involved, which are essentially contractual and organic.

I have tried to suggest some of the ways in which a mutual/personal community can employ the infrastructures and instrumentalities of contractual and organic association in the service of loving relationships. The intentionally inclusive community of mutuality will, again in the words of Buber, know and embrace "in itself hard 'calculation', adverse 'chance', the sudden access of 'anxiety'."[35] It will need to use careful, discriminating thought in order to determine when and how to utilize impersonal, contractual relations in order to enhance personal, loving ones. It will have to find a place for cooperation for functional purposes even when it does not lead to mutuality in and for its own sake.

The result will probably be something like Buber's community of communities,[36] or in Munoz's words, "a web of Christian communities that are woven institutionally into a church that is truly communitarian."[37] That is, the larger human or church society will be a community in the sense that it is a commonwealth of smaller communities, perhaps even an "organic commonwealth" in which each smaller community will be functionally supportive of all the others even though it is not in direct mutual relation with them. Within the commonwealth as a whole and probably to some degree within each smaller community, there will be a need for functional and contractual relations with persons and groups able to provide in the most efficient possible way the economic and social services which are the material foundation on which love must be built.

In practice this may mean that the smaller, intentional, more fully mutual communities will exist within and under the authority of an organically constituted state. In the context of current economic and political "reality," the state will serve as the limit and judge of what kind of behavior will be permitted within and between the smaller, intermediate communities that exist under its sovereignty. But this fact should not lead us to abandon our belief in the metaphysical priority which the mutual community has over the organic and atomistic forms of association which are the hallmark of the state. If the human person can find ultimate fulfillment only in mutuality, then any form of association which is not fully mutual must, of necessity, either obstruct mutuality or be an instrument designed to create the conditions for mutuality. Ideally, the state will serve the latter function and should do so in an international context. That is, the state should provide the conditions for mutuality (such as justice and material support) both within its own boundaries and with reference to the unity of all nations, because ultimately the mutual community which it serves cannot be restricted to a single nation or to any group of nations less inclusive than the whole human race. One task of the church as mutual/personal is to remind the nation state that it is not, in Stanley Hauerwas's words, "an ontological necessity for human living. The church, as an international society, is a sign that God, not nations, rule this world."[38]

The church as mutual/personal community in microcosm can serve both as the concrete model of what a fully inclusive community might look like and as catalyst, within the conditions of current political and economic realities, for action intended to bring such a community into existence. We cannot in this study fill in the outline of how a mutual community can define and carry out its task of model and catalyst. Nevertheless, if the vision of the mutual/personal community as developed by Macmurray has its source in a metaphysically true understanding of persons, then such a community should be able to marshal the resources, including the power and grace of God, to begin to make good on the promise of God for community as that promise has been embedded in the potential of human nature.

Within the mutual/personal community, heterocentric love of others for their own sakes—the love which insists on the unique, individual dignity of the other—will be the dominant and controlling intention. Mutual love will ensure that the value of the individual is sustained and enhanced without degenerating into individualism, in which the self concerns itself primarily and almost exclusively with itself as a precondition for any association with others. The hidden, almost forgotten truth in the atomistic individualism of the liberal tradition, the truth that individuals are unique and valuable for their own sakes, will be rescued from the egocentrism, isolationism, and atomism which have buried it for centuries. It will be rescued by the recognition that unless we begin by valuing the individuality of the other, there will be no basis for the mutuality and reciprocity which gives value to our individuality in the I-Thou of personal relationship.

Macmurray's principle of objectivity is significant here. It means being able to live in terms of the other as he or she really is, *objectively*. Objectivity is a prerequisite for mutuality. Through objectivity the individuality of each person is protected. One person cannot use the other simply as a means of self-fulfillment without violating the objectivity, the value in and of itself, of the other's unique individuality. Nor can the person be subsumed as an organic function within a larger whole, because to do so the objectivity of the whole would have to have priority over the objectivity of the part. But persons are irreducibly valuable. The Whole is an abstraction. Even persons-in-relation is an abstraction if the individual persons are subordinated to something called "the relationship." But because persons are able to intend the welfare of the other for the sake of the other, and because each person in a mutual relationship lives primarily by that intention, what we might call (in a somewhat revised sense of Niebuhr's language) common grace—that is, the grace of mutual love—gives to each one the affirmation by which his individuality is recognized and sustained.

In the mutual/personal community there will also be a never-ceasing struggle to maintain social, political, and economic equality and sharing. While it believes that neither material equality nor inequality is an end in itself, the mutual understanding of community insists that persons be valued for their whole selves, not simply for their "spiritual" dimension. It also insists that relationships which are sustained by means of imposed inequalities are fundamentally destructive of genuine mutuality. For these reasons, in a mutual/personal community the infrastructures of economics and politics must be made as egalitarian as possible and be subject to the will of the community as a whole, not just to those parts of the community with the greatest amount of material power. These communities will have to engage in a radical restructuring of the dominant forms of economic relationship in the larger society. The task of that transformation and restructuring is enormous but it has begun in a number of Christian communities in various parts of the world today.

If, as James Gustafson says, "friendship ... is not just the enjoyment of each other, taking delight in the presence of each other; [if] it is also the acceptance of responsibilty for the needs of each other,"[39] then that responsibility will take political and economic form. It will insist that there be institutions which are contractual and organic whose primary purpose, within the larger intention toward mutuality, is to ensure the provision of material needs on the most just and equitable basis possible. While personal life is ultimately fulfilled only in mutual love, it is sustained "by the ordering of economic and political power."[40] In this sense, "community can be interpreted functionally.... Its particular form or order is to be judged by its effectiveness in fulfilling its morally purposive functions."[41] These functions, however, must necessarily be the functions of some higher, controlling intention. In the hierarchical model of the inclusive mutual community, that intention is the one for mutuality.

Without the consciousness of the controlling intention, the devices of economic production and distribution, of political power, and of the machinery of justice can become ends in themselves, to be served by persons rather than serving persons. In a sense the two other models of community, the atomistic and the organic, recognize at least implicitly the need for controlling intentions, but the ones they have raised up are not oriented toward mutuality. Most of us live today in communities controlled by atomism and contract. We live for ourselves and with others only because we find that establishing some kind of agreement with them is the best way of advancing our own interests. As individualists, we control our actions by considering what is best for us. As individualists with a conscience, we try to believe that what is best for us is ultimately best for everyone else, provided they too follow their own self-interests. Genuine public policy in such a society cannot exist, as Stanley Hauerwas

Koinonia as a Community among Communities   233

has pointed out, because "society is nothing more than an aggregate of self-interested individuals."[42] The result is that a "social order that is designed to work on the presumption that people are self-interested tends to produce that kind of society."[43] Ironically, our initial individualism often leads to a kind of totalitarianism because in an atomistic community it is forbidden to raise the question of whether there is such a thing as the "common" good, or expect a social response to a social need. In this kind of atomistic totalitarianism, the needs of persons who are crushed between the colliding atoms simply cannot be met by the social order as a whole.

From time to time, in reaction against the failures of the atomistic community to meet the social needs of its members, the organic model of association proposes that we create a community which is greater than the sum of its parts. The totalistic, whole community finds a place for each of its members as indispensable organs contributing to its life. Totalitarianism has also found fertile ground within this understanding of persons in relation. The "State" or the "Community" writ large can easily become the only thing of value for which the contributing organs must either provide a function deemed worthwhile by the state or else be eliminated as worthless. The experience of Nazi Germany, Mussolini's Italy, or Stalin's Russia bears sad witness to the dangerous potential within the organic model. And yet, in each of these totalitarian states, there was a controlling intention determining the form and content of each of its subordinate parts.

In the end, we return to the metaphysical basis on which the mutual/personal community rests. Its controlling intention is grounded in the nature of reality and, religiously, in the intention of God for his creation. It is this metaphysical conviction, sustained by faith and hope, that gives the various, small, scattered intentional communities of mutuality the courage to go on being and doing what they believe to be the way to ultimate fulfillment and correspondence to reality. These communities will have the task of challenging the dominance of the atomistic and organic forms of community and transforming them into instruments or infrastructures to be utilized in the creation and maintenance of the conditions for, but not the content of, the mutuality which God intends. The powers of the liberal and organic views of social relations are not to be underestimated: they are so strong that anyone questioning their metaphysical dominance may be accused of being unrealistic and utopian.

Nevertheless, the mutual/personal community lives in and through the trust that in the end, truth "will out." It trusts that trust itself and the mutual love which enfolds it is "finally a deeper reality in our lives than distrust."[44] Such a view, Hauerwas concludes, in words that bring together the metaphysical and religious vision of the beloved community, "is not an unrealistic, idealistic, or utopian strategy; it is built on the profoundly realistic hope that God, not man, rules the world."[45]

Notes to Chapter 7

1. H. Richard Niebuhr, *The Purpose of the Church and Its Ministry* (New York: Harper, 1956), 35.
2. Gene Outka, *Agape: An Ethical Analysis* (New Haven: Yale University Press, 1972), 12.
3. Reinhold Niebuhr, *Man's Nature and His Communities,* essays on the dynamics and enigmas of man's personal and social existence (New York: Charles Scribner's Sons, 1965), 39.
4. Ibid., 41.
5. Ibid., 39–40.
6. Ibid., 40.
7. Ibid., 71.
8. Ibid., 94.
9. Ibid., 93.
10. Ibid., 107.
11. Ibid., 109.
12. Ibid., 42.
13. Ibid., 107.
14. Outka, *Agape,* 171.
15. Ibid., 43.
16. Ibid., 44.
17. Vernard Eller, *The Promise: Ethics in the Kingdom of God* (Garden City, N.Y.: Doubleday, 1970), 87.
18. Outka, *Agape,* 180.
19. Buber, *Paths in Utopia,* 8.
20. Ibid.
21. Ibid.
22. Ibid.
23. Outka, *Agape,* 184, 191.
24. Rosabeth Moss Kanter, *Commitment and Community: Communes and Utopias in Sociological Perspective* (Cambridge: Harvard University Press, 1973), 1.
25. Ibid., 73.

26. Hauerwas, *A Community of Character*, 2.
27. L.S. Thornton, *The Common Life in the Body of Christ* (London: Dacre Press, 1942), 6.
28. Ibid., 7.
29. Ronaldo Muñoz, "Ecclesiology in Latin America," in *The Challenge of Basic Christian Communities*, papers from the International Ecumenical Congress of Theology, February 20-March 2, 1980. São Paulo, Brazil, ed. Sergio Torres and John Eagleson, trans. John Drury (Maryknoll, N.Y.: Orbis Books, 1981), 156.
30. Ibid.
31. Ibid., 157.
32. Ibid.
33. Buber, *Paths in Utopia*, 134.
34. Ibid., 133.
35. Ibid., 134.
36. Ibid., 136.
37. Muñoz, "Ecclesiology in Latin America," 158.
38. Hauerwas, *A Community of Character*, 109–10.
39. James Gustafson, "A Theology of Christian Community," in *Man in Community: Christian Concern for the Human in Changing Society*, ed. Egbert De Vries (New York: Association Press, 1966), 186.
40. Ibid., 180.
41. Ibid., 182.
42. Hauerwas, *A Community of Character*, 79.
43. Ibid., 79.
44. Ibid., 110.
45. Ibid.

The Eberly Library
Waynesburg College

Waynesburg, Pennsylvania

Class 822.33   Book GS5272